HBJ MATHEMATICS

LOLA J. MAY
Mathematics Consultant
Winnetka Public Schools
Winnetka, Illinois

SHIRLEY M. FRYE
Mathematics Coordinator
Scottsdale Unified School District
Scottsdale, Arizona

DONNA CYRIER JACOBS
Director of Publications
Winnetka Public Schools
Winnetka, Illinois

HBJ MATHEMATICS

CONSULTING EDUCATORS

MARJORIE H. COLEMAN
Amherst Elementary School
Amherst, Virginia

VIRGINIA T. GILBERT
Secondary Mathematics
  Resource Teacher
Clark County School District
Las Vegas, Nevada

ANN HOLMAN
Lu Sutton School
Novato, California

KAREN LIEBERMAN
Harry L. Bain School
West New York, New Jersey

OTHERIE WINFIELD LOVE
Junior Administrative Assistant —
  Math Consultant
Detroit Public Schools
Detroit, Michigan

MERLE SMITH
Coordinator of Elementary
  Mathematics
Weld County Schools District Six
Colorado

ELSIE YOSHII
Eagle Rock Elementary School
Los Angeles, California

HBJ **HARCOURT BRACE JOVANOVICH**
New York Chicago San Francisco Atlanta Dallas *and* London

PHOTOGRAPH ACKNOWLEDGMENTS

Key: T, Top; B, Bottom; L, Left; C, Center; R, Right.

HBJ Photo: 136B.

HBJ Photo by Erik Arnesen: 328TL.

HBJ Photos by Rick Der: 10, 11, 24, 33, 47, 58T, 58B, 59, 68, 77, 80T, 81T, 99T, 99B, 106, 108, 113, 121, 123, 131T, 132, 136T, 137, 145, 150, 172T, 182TR, 187, 191, 192, 220T, 229, 231, 243C, 243B, 244T, 245, 246B, 248, 252TR, 267, 274, 277, 288, 291, 295, 298, 312T, 312B, 313T, 315T, 316, 317T, 327.

HBJ Photo by William Hubbell: 49TR.

HBJ Photo by Regina Kane: 161.

HBJ Photo by P.C. and Connie Peri: 313B.

HBJ Photos by Elliot Varner Smith: 20, 112, 120, 170, 228, 286, 296.

RESEARCH CREDITS: © The Image Bank: 1. Roy King: 2. © Bruce Coleman Inc., Jane Burton: 18T. Roy King: 19T. © Time/Life, Sports Illustrated Inc., Manny Miller: 29. Black Star, Eiji Miyazawa: 30. Jim and Cathy Church: 31CR. Peter Arnold, Inc., Richard Choy: 44. Black Star, Launois-Covello: 45B. Time/Life, Sports Illustrated Inc., Neil Leifer: 46B. Black Star, John Launois: 48TR. Woodfin-Camp, Marvin E. Newman: 53. Roy King: 54. Black Star, Edward Pieratt: 56T. © Karen Fiori 1979: 87. Taurus Photo, Reggie Tucker: 88. The Bettman Archive: 91. Taurus Photo, G. R. Richardson: 98. Woodfin-Camp, Craig Aurness: 119. Black Star, Brian Seed: 128. Peter Arnold, Inc., Werner Müller: 149. Bruce Coleman, Inc., Phil Degginger: 151. Black Star, Ted Spiegal–Rapho Quillumette: 157. © Sygma, Alain Keler: 165B. Frank Wing: 169. John Henshew: 186BR. Stock Boston, Johnathan Rawle: 222B. Roy King: 227. Tom Tracy: 247TL. Time/Life, Sports Illustrated, Inc., Kathy McMillan: 249TR. Roy King: 253TR. Roy King: 253B. Roy King: 254TR. © The Image Bank, Alvis Upitis: 255TL. Alec Duncan: 256TR. Courtesy of NASA: 256B. Roy King: 257T. © The Image Bank, J. Carmichael: 263. Courtesy of Southern Pacific Co.: 264. Peter Arnold, Inc., Richard Choy: 269. Peter Arnold, Inc., J. DiMaggio–J. Kalish: 285. Uniphoto, Fletcher Drake: 306. S. E. Monteith: 321. © Icon, Peter Gerba: 322. Tom Tracy: 329TR.

COVER CREDITS

HBJ Photo by Rick Der. Background © Shelley Grossman, Woodfin-Camp Associates. Numbers by Walter Gasper.

ART ACKNOWLEDGMENTS

Robert Bausch: 35, 36TR, 40, 66, 67B, 78, 79, 100, 164B, 174TR, 232, 233T, 258–259. Larry Baumgardner: 16, 17, 34B, 39B, 64–65, 105, 111B, 141B, 156, 160, 214, 220B, 230, 308, 309B, 317B. Boardworks: 3, 5, 7C, 9B, 15, 19BL, 21, 31T, 31CL, 32, 34T, 36TL, 37, 38, 39T, 45T, 46T, 48TL, 49TL, 61, 73TL, 90, 93TL, 107, 110TL, 122, 141TL, 163, 164T, 165T, 171, 172, 173, 174, 175, 176, 177, 178, 179, 180, 181, 182, 183, 184, 186, 188C, 189C, 193, 195, 196, 197, 202, 203, 204, 205, 206, 215, 216, 217, 218, 219, 221, 222T, 223, 229C, 231T, 233B, 234, 235, 236, 237, 238, 239, 240, 241, 242, 243TL, 244B, 247R, 248T, 249TL, 250T, 251, 252TL, 253TL, 254TL, 255R, 256TL, 257C, 260C, 261C, 271TL, 287T, 292, 294CL, 297, 300, 302, 304, 307TL, 323TL, 324, 325, 326, 327, 328TR, 329, 330C, 331T, 331B, 332T, 332BL, 333T, 333BL, 334. Elizabeth Callen: 41, 42, 43, 74. Carol Etow: 8, 12, 22, 23B, 25. Walter Gasper, (constructions): 20, 59, 123, 145, 187. Barbara Hack: 344, 347, 352, 354, 355, 361, 365, 366, 367, 368, 369, 370. Sharon Harker: 9, 10T, 97. Francis Livingston: 14, 18B, 93TR, 127, 129, 130, 138, 139, 198T, 198B, 279, 290B, 293, 309T, 311. Pat Marshall: 4, 6, 56B, 57B, 63, 70B, 71, 73B. Tony Naganuma: all Challenge, Review, and Calculate graphics, and Chapter Review, Chapter Test, and Brush-Up borders. Susan Nelson: 114–115, 124, 142, 154, 155T, 155B, 208, 211, 314, 315B. Bill Oetinger: 19BR, 96, 110TR, 111T, 290T, 299, 310, 324TR, 330, 331C, 332BR, 333BR. Sharron O'Neil: 69, 82–83, 90TR, 134–135. Don Peterson: 7T, 73TR, 94, 102, 109, 141TR, 152–153, 250, 271TR, 280T, 281, 294CR, 323TR, 325TR. Sandy Popovich: 194, 195TR, 195C, 200, 210, 212, 213, 252B, 254B. Stephanie Reed: 9T, 23T, 55, 57T, 67T, 70T, 72, 162, 185, 201, 265, 275, 280B, 303. Sue Rother: 80B, 81B, 131B, 144, 158, 159, 207, 268, 270, 272, 276, 287B, 307TR, 307B. Karen Scott: 140, 246T.

ISBN 0-15-352052-3

Contents

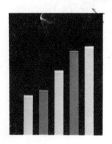

CHAPTER 1

Warm Up

Using Division at Work

Frances Manzano manages a dance school. 92 students are enrolled for classes. Frances has 4 teachers. She works the problem 92 ÷ 4 to find how many students will be in each teacher's class. There will be 23 students in each class.

Adding on a Nomograph

To add on this nomograph, put the edge of a piece of paper along the dashed line. Make sure that you can see the addends 5 and 8, and the sum 13.

addition facts

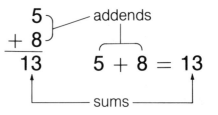

Addend	0	1	2	3	4	5	6	7	8	9
Sum	0 1	2 3	4 5	6 7	8 9	10 11	12 13	14 15	16 17	18
Addend	0	1	2	3	4	5	6	7	8	9

Use the nomograph. Touch the addends. Write the sums.

1. 8
   +6
   14

2. 7
   +4

3. 9
   +4

4. 5
   +6

5. 6
   +7

6. 7
   +6

7. 2
   +9

8. 3
   +9

9. 2
   +7

10. 8
    +8

11. 7
    +5

12. 6
    +5

13. 5
    +5

14. 6
    +6

15. 6
    +4

16. 9
    +7

17. 9
    +3

18. 7
    +8

19. 4
    +5

20. 8
    +7

21. 9
    +9

22. 8
    +9

23. 5
    +9

24. 4
    +8

25. 9
    +5

26. 3
    +8

27. 9
    +6

28. 5
    +3

Adding One-Digit Numbers

Add.

1. $6+7$ 13
2. $8+6$
3. $9+4$
4. $5+8$
5. $6+6$

6. $0+7$
7. $9+5$
8. $9+3$
9. $8+7$
10. $4+1$

11. $7+5$
12. $9+6$
13. $8+8$
14. $9+7$
15. $3+6$

16. $9+8$
17. $4+3$
18. $0+9$
19. $9+2$
20. $7+7$

21. $4+6$
22. $1+8$
23. $2+5$
24. $5+6$
25. $9+9$

26. $8+0$
27. $9+9$
28. $6+5$
29. $6+7$
30. $5+4$

Solve the problems.

31. Cindy had 9 records. She bought 4 more. How many records did she have then?

32. Lucy had 8 records. A friend gave her 7 records. How many records did she have then?

33. Mario had 2 records. He got 5 records for his birthday. How many records did he have then?

Subtracting One-Digit Numbers

$9 - 3 = 6$ is a **subtraction fact**.
6 is the difference.

Subtract 3 from each number.

Number	6	10	11	8	12	7	5	9
Think	6−3	10−3	11−3	8−3	12−3	7−3	5−3	9−3
Difference	3	7	8	5	9	4	2	6

Write the differences.

1. Subtract 1 from each number.
   13, 10, 8, 5, 9, 14
   12

2. Subtract 2 from each number.
   19, 16, 11, 15, 9, 14

3. Subtract 4 from each number.
   8, 10, 11, 7, 12, 13

4. Subtract 5 from each number.
   11, 14, 9, 12, 10, 13

5. Subtract 6 from each number.
   11, 13, 10, 12, 14, 15

6. Subtract 7 from each number.
   13, 16, 11, 14, 15, 12

7. Subtract 8 from each number.
   14, 11, 15, 12, 17, 13

8. Subtract 9 from each number.
   15, 13, 17, 14, 16, 12

⭐ Challenge

Write two addition facts and two subtraction facts using these numbers.

9. 6, 8, 14

10. 9, 8, 17

11. 5, 6, 11

12. 7, 8, 15

13. 9, 3, 12

14. 4, 9, 13

15. 7, 4, 11

16. 6, 4, 10

Subtraction Facts

Subtract.

1. $13 - 6$ 7   2. $11 - 5$ 3. $14 - 6$ 4. $15 - 8$ 5. $12 - 6$

6. $12 - 7$ 7. $16 - 7$ 8. $12 - 8$ 9. $13 - 9$ 10. $14 - 5$

11. $11 - 3$ 12. $14 - 9$ 13. $15 - 6$ 14. $17 - 8$ 15. $14 - 7$

16. $11 - 4$ 17. $14 - 8$ 18. $13 - 5$ 19. $15 - 7$ 20. $16 - 9$

21. $15 - 9$ 22. $12 - 4$ 23. $11 - 6$ 24. $16 - 8$ 25. $10 - 3$

26. $18 - 9$ 27. $9 - 5$ 28. $17 - 9$ 29. $13 - 8$ 30. $12 - 5$

Solve the problems.

31. Anna planted 14 rose bushes. 9 bushes have red roses and the rest have yellow roses. How many bushes have yellow roses?

32. Ray planted 12 flower bulbs. 3 bulbs were tulip bulbs and the rest were daffodil bulbs. How many were daffodil bulbs?

33. Tony weeded for 9 hours in all on Saturday and Sunday. If he weeded for 4 hours on Saturday, how long did he weed on Sunday?

Finding Sums and Differences

Crack the code to answer the riddle.

What did the floor say to the wall?

Code	e	y	u	t	a	h	c	m	o	r	n
	10	14	2	8	3	7	4	1	16	6	11

Add or subtract.

1. $\begin{array}{r} 4 \\ -3 \\ \hline \end{array}$
1, m

2. $\begin{array}{r} 7 \\ +3 \\ \hline \end{array}$

3. $\begin{array}{r} 6 \\ +4 \\ \hline \end{array}$

4. $\begin{array}{r} 16 \\ -\ 8 \\ \hline \end{array}$

5. $\begin{array}{r} 7 \\ +7 \\ \hline \end{array}$

6. $\begin{array}{r} 9 \\ +7 \\ \hline \end{array}$

7. $\begin{array}{r} 4 \\ -2 \\ \hline \end{array}$

8. $\begin{array}{r} 10 \\ -\ 7 \\ \hline \end{array}$

9. $\begin{array}{r} 5 \\ +3 \\ \hline \end{array}$

10. $\begin{array}{r} 4 \\ +4 \\ \hline \end{array}$

11. $\begin{array}{r} 10 \\ -\ 3 \\ \hline \end{array}$

12. $\begin{array}{r} 5 \\ +5 \\ \hline \end{array}$

13. $\begin{array}{r} 10 \\ -\ 6 \\ \hline \end{array}$

14. $\begin{array}{r} 9 \\ +7 \\ \hline \end{array}$

15. $\begin{array}{r} 10 \\ -\ 4 \\ \hline \end{array}$

16. $\begin{array}{r} 6 \\ +5 \\ \hline \end{array}$

17. $\begin{array}{r} 11 \\ -\ 1 \\ \hline \end{array}$

18. $\begin{array}{r} 3 \\ +3 \\ \hline \end{array}$

19. The answer is: __ __ __ __   __ __ __   __ __   __ __ __   __ __ __ __ __ __
  1. 2. 3. 4.   5. 6. 7.   8. 9.   10. 11. 12.   13. 14. 15. 16. 17. 18.

⭐ **Challenge**
Add.

20. $\begin{array}{r} 4 \\ +0 \\ \hline \end{array}$

21. $\begin{array}{r} 6 \\ +1 \\ \hline \end{array}$

22. $\begin{array}{r} 1 \\ +0 \\ \hline \end{array}$

23. $\begin{array}{r} 7 \\ +0 \\ \hline \end{array}$

24. $\begin{array}{r} 9 \\ +1 \\ \hline \end{array}$

25. $\begin{array}{r} 0 \\ +0 \\ \hline \end{array}$

26. $\begin{array}{r} 1 \\ +1 \\ \hline \end{array}$

27. When 0 is an addend, what do you know about the sum?

28. When 1 is an addend, what do you know about the sum?

Service Station Problems

Pablo and Angie run a service station. Solve each problem.
First decide whether to add or subtract.

1. Angie washed 9 windshields in the morning and 8 in the afternoon. How many was that in all?   17

2. Angie patched 12 flat tires. Pablo patched 9. How many fewer did Pablo patch?

3. Pablo sold 3 cans of oil on Monday, 4 cans on Tuesday, and 8 cans on Wednesday. How many cans of oil did he sell?

4. On a winter day, Pablo started 7 cars in the morning and 15 in the afternoon. How many more did he start in the afternoon?

5. One week Angie tuned-up 8 cars and 6 trucks. How many tune-ups did she do in all?

6. In one week, Angie sold 2 U.S. maps, 7 state maps, and 6 county maps. How many maps did she sell?

7. One week Pablo fixed 7 broken taillights and 13 broken headlights. How many more headlights did he fix?

8. Angie had 12 tires to sell. She sold 7 of them. How many were left?

NEW TIRES
4 FOR $200

PARTS AND ACCESSORIES

Ring the Addends Game

A game for one player.

Get ready:
Copy the sums and addends boards below.

To play:
Make a ring around a pair of addends for each sum. The addends must be next to each other like this ⊟ , this ⊏⊐ , or this ⬚⬚ . Cross out each sum as you ring its addends. You may ring an addend more than once.

Sums:	9 = 6 + 3		
9̶	Addends		
14	5	2	5
10	5	6	3
7	8	1	2

Sums:			
15	Addends		
6	3	3	5
11	6	2	8
4	5	7	2

Sums:			
8	Addends		
12	5	3	0
3	2	7	9
18	1	5	9

Sums:			
13	Addends		
5	8	2	8
16	5	3	9
17	9	7	1

Adding More Than Two Numbers

You can add numbers in any order.
The sum is the same.

$8+6=6+8$ and $(8+6)+7=8+(6+7)$

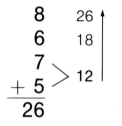

```
 8     26 ↑
 6     18 |
 7        |
+5  > 12  |
───
26
```

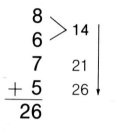

```
 8
 6  > 14 |
 7     21 |
+5     26 ↓
───
26
```

You can add up.   You can add down.

Find the sums.

1.	2.	3.	4.	5.	6.	7.
8	9	8	7	5	9	3
7	4	6	5	9	8	8
+6	+8	+7	+8	+8	+7	+5
21						

8.	9.	10.	11.	12.	13.	14.
5	7	6	4	7	9	6
8	9	5	8	8	9	5
8	5	9	7	9	5	4
+1	+6	+4	+3	+2	+3	+6

15.	16.	17.	18.	19.	20.	21.
3	1	2	7	9	6	4
2	4	4	9	9	4	5
6	9	2	5	1	4	6
+5	+0	+8	+3	+1	+6	+2

22. $4+3+8+5+2$ 23. $9+5+6+3+3$ 24. $8+7+3+4+8$

25. $4+8+5+6+7$ 26. $5+1+9+8+4+2$ 27. $6+3+9+8+2+1$

Addition Patterns

If you know this fact $6 + 7 = 13$, you know all of these.

$16 + 7 = 23$ $6+7$ and 1 more ten

$26 + 7 = 33$ $6+7$ and 2 more tens

$36 + 7 = 43$ $6+7$ and 3 more tens

$46 + 7 = 53$ $6+7$ and 4 more tens

Write the sums.

1.		2.	3.	4.	5.
$9+3$	12	$8+7$	$6+8$	$9+4$	$5+5$
$19+3$	22	$28+7$	$36+8$	$29+4$	$15+5$
$39+3$	42	$48+7$	$76+8$	$59+4$	$35+5$

6.	7.	8.	9.	10.
$6+6$	$7+9$	$3+8$	$6+9$	$3+5$
$46+6$	$17+9$	$23+8$	$16+9$	$23+5$
$86+6$	$57+9$	$43+8$	$36+9$	$53+5$

11.	12.	13.	14.	15.
$5+8$	$5+9$	$7+7$	$7+5$	$9+9$
$25+8$	$35+9$	$37+7$	$27+5$	$19+9$
$65+8$	$65+9$	$47+7$	$47+5$	$49+9$
$75+8$	$75+9$	$87+7$	$67+5$	$59+9$

Review (pp. 3–11)

1.	2.	3.	4.	5.	6.	7.
7	12	3	17	7	6	16
+5	− 9	+8	− 8	−0	+9	− 9

Adding Larger Numbers

Step 1
Add ones.

$$6234$$
$$+\ 2745$$
$$\overline{\qquad 9}$$

Step 2
Add tens.

$$6234$$
$$+\ 2745$$
$$\overline{\qquad 79}$$

Step 3
Add hundreds.

$$6234$$
$$+\ 2745$$
$$\overline{\qquad 979}$$

Step 4
Add thousands.

$$6234$$
$$+\ 2745$$
$$\overline{8979}$$

Add.

1. $\begin{array}{r} 63 \\ +24 \\ \hline 87 \end{array}$

2. $\begin{array}{r} 81 \\ +12 \\ \hline \end{array}$

3. $\begin{array}{r} 704 \\ +173 \\ \hline \end{array}$

4. $\begin{array}{r} 413 \\ +362 \\ \hline \end{array}$

5. $\begin{array}{r} 621 \\ +\ 32 \\ \hline \end{array}$

6. $\begin{array}{r} 4596 \\ +2301 \\ \hline \end{array}$

7. $\begin{array}{r} 2574 \\ +3123 \\ \hline \end{array}$

8. $\begin{array}{r} 5634 \\ +2261 \\ \hline \end{array}$

9. $\begin{array}{r} 8623 \\ +1254 \\ \hline \end{array}$

10. $\begin{array}{r} 2652 \\ +3136 \\ \hline \end{array}$

11. $\begin{array}{r} 6042 \\ +2911 \\ \hline \end{array}$

12. $\begin{array}{r} 1133 \\ +3455 \\ \hline \end{array}$

13. $\begin{array}{r} 1328 \\ +5641 \\ \hline \end{array}$

14. $\begin{array}{r} 8134 \\ +1763 \\ \hline \end{array}$

15. $\begin{array}{r} 3642 \\ +1237 \\ \hline \end{array}$

16. $\begin{array}{r} 23 \\ 141 \\ +423 \\ \hline \end{array}$

17. $\begin{array}{r} 32 \\ 24 \\ +33 \\ \hline \end{array}$

18. $\begin{array}{r} 9 \\ 450 \\ +130 \\ \hline \end{array}$

19. $\begin{array}{r} 20 \\ 8 \\ +671 \\ \hline \end{array}$

20. $\begin{array}{r} 683 \\ 16 \\ +200 \\ \hline \end{array}$

21. Miriam and George Cunningham bought living room furniture for $1630 and bedroom furniture for $1025. How much did they spend?

22. Steve Sanchez spent $23 at the supermarket, $6 at the butcher, and $10 at the florist. How much did he spend in all?

Subtracting Larger Numbers

Step 1
Subtract ones.

$$8975 - 2443$$
$$2$$

Step 2
Subtract tens.

$$8975 - 2443$$
$$32$$

Step 3
Subtract hundreds.

$$8975 - 2443$$
$$532$$

Step 4
Subtract thousands.

$$8975 - 2443$$
$$6532$$

Subtract.

1. $\begin{array}{r}79\\-35\\\hline 44\end{array}$	2. $\begin{array}{r}94\\-54\\\hline\end{array}$	3. $\begin{array}{r}86\\-20\\\hline\end{array}$	4. $\begin{array}{r}87\\-23\\\hline\end{array}$	5. $\begin{array}{r}976\\-505\\\hline\end{array}$
6. $\begin{array}{r}789\\-\ 52\\\hline\end{array}$	7. $\begin{array}{r}285\\-\ 35\\\hline\end{array}$	8. $\begin{array}{r}309\\-108\\\hline\end{array}$	9. $\begin{array}{r}3889\\-2418\\\hline\end{array}$	10. $\begin{array}{r}643\\-530\\\hline\end{array}$
11. $\begin{array}{r}799\\-324\\\hline\end{array}$	12. $\begin{array}{r}9879\\-6523\\\hline\end{array}$	13. $\begin{array}{r}374\\-200\\\hline\end{array}$	14. $\begin{array}{r}6732\\-2510\\\hline\end{array}$	15. $\begin{array}{r}9625\\-\ 521\\\hline\end{array}$
16. $\begin{array}{r}7879\\-4322\\\hline\end{array}$	17. $\begin{array}{r}8888\\-4856\\\hline\end{array}$	18. $\begin{array}{r}9658\\-\ \ 43\\\hline\end{array}$	19. $\begin{array}{r}659\\-\ 49\\\hline\end{array}$	20. $\begin{array}{r}9754\\-4343\\\hline\end{array}$

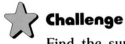 **Challenge**

Find the sum and difference for each pair of numbers.

21. 559 and 240

22. 332 and 666

23. 658 and 331

24. 874 and 122

25. 363 and 212

26. 664 and 322

27. 3043 and 5255

28. 7662 and 2331

29. 8565 and 1234

30. 1401 and 5532

31. 5234 and 1113

32. 7468 and 2331

Circus Problems

Solve each problem.

1. Pickalilly Circus travels 3895 kilometers each year. So far this year, it has traveled 2784 kilometers. How many more kilometers will the circus travel this year? 1111

2. One night Kelly the peanut vender sold 839 bags of peanuts. The next night she sold 899 bags. How many more bags of peanuts did she sell the second night?

3. The circus spent $11,600 to repair a big tent and $1385 to repair a small tent. How much was spent on repairing the two tents?

4. Pickalilly Circus puts on shows 311 days out of the year. How many days does the circus not put on shows? (There are 365 days in a year.)

5. Each month the circus spends $406 to feed the elephants, $351 to feed the horses, and $132 to feed the dogs. How much does the circus spend each month on food for these animals?

6. The circus played in Grand Falls for 3 nights. 1221 people came the first night, 735 came the next night, and 1012 came the last night. How many people saw the circus in those three nights?

Adding and Multiplying

This drawing shows 4 rows of shapes, 3 in each row. To find the total number of shapes, you can add. Since the addends are equal, you can also multiply.

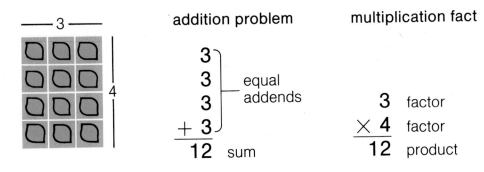

addition problem

$$\left.\begin{array}{r} 3 \\ 3 \\ 3 \\ +\,3 \end{array}\right\} \text{equal addends}$$

12   sum

multiplication fact

$$\begin{array}{r} 3 \\ \times\,4 \\ \hline 12 \end{array}$$ factor
factor
product

Find the sum. Then write a multiplication fact.

1. $\begin{array}{r} 6 \\ 6 \\ +6 \\ \hline 18 \end{array}$ $\begin{array}{r} 6 \\ \times 3 \\ \hline 18 \end{array}$

2. $\begin{array}{r} 7 \\ +7 \\ \hline \end{array}$

3. $\begin{array}{r} 5 \\ 5 \\ +5 \\ \hline \end{array}$

4. $\begin{array}{r} 3 \\ 3 \\ 3 \\ +3 \\ \hline \end{array}$

5. $\begin{array}{r} 4 \\ 4 \\ 4 \\ +4 \\ \hline \end{array}$

6. $\begin{array}{r} 1 \\ 1 \\ +1 \\ \hline \end{array}$

7. $\begin{array}{r} 2 \\ 2 \\ 2 \\ 2 \\ +2 \\ \hline \end{array}$

8. $\begin{array}{r} 7 \\ 7 \\ +7 \\ \hline \end{array}$

9. $\begin{array}{r} 9 \\ +9 \\ \hline \end{array}$

10. $\begin{array}{r} 10 \\ 10 \\ 10 \\ 10 \\ +10 \\ \hline \end{array}$

11. $\begin{array}{r} 8 \\ 8 \\ +8 \\ \hline \end{array}$

12. $\begin{array}{r} 2 \\ 2 \\ +2 \\ \hline \end{array}$

13. $\begin{array}{r} 9 \\ 9 \\ 9 \\ +9 \\ \hline \end{array}$

Find each product.

14. $\begin{array}{r} 5 \\ \times 4 \\ \hline \end{array}$

15. $\begin{array}{r} 7 \\ \times 6 \\ \hline \end{array}$

16. $\begin{array}{r} 8 \\ \times 4 \\ \hline \end{array}$

17. $\begin{array}{r} 6 \\ \times 4 \\ \hline \end{array}$

18. $\begin{array}{r} 5 \\ \times 6 \\ \hline \end{array}$

19. $\begin{array}{r} 9 \\ \times 2 \\ \hline \end{array}$

20. $\begin{array}{r} 8 \\ \times 9 \\ \hline \end{array}$

21. $\begin{array}{r} 8 \\ \times 3 \\ \hline \end{array}$

22. $\begin{array}{r} 7 \\ \times 3 \\ \hline \end{array}$

23. $\begin{array}{r} 9 \\ \times 3 \\ \hline \end{array}$

24. $\begin{array}{r} 4 \\ \times 8 \\ \hline \end{array}$

25. $\begin{array}{r} 5 \\ \times 3 \\ \hline \end{array}$

26. $\begin{array}{r} 7 \\ \times 4 \\ \hline \end{array}$

27. $\begin{array}{r} 5 \\ \times 7 \\ \hline \end{array}$

Multiplying by One-Digit Numbers

You can count by fives to find nine times five:
5, 10, 15, 20, 25, 30, 35, 40, 45.

$$\begin{array}{r} 5 \\ \times\,9 \\ \hline 45 \end{array}$$

Find the products.

1. $\begin{array}{r}5\\\times2\\\hline 10\end{array}$	2. $\begin{array}{r}5\\\times3\\\hline\end{array}$	3. $\begin{array}{r}5\\\times7\\\hline\end{array}$	4. $\begin{array}{r}5\\\times6\\\hline\end{array}$	5. $\begin{array}{r}5\\\times8\\\hline\end{array}$	6. $\begin{array}{r}5\\\times4\\\hline\end{array}$	7. $\begin{array}{r}5\\\times1\\\hline\end{array}$

Multiply.

8. $\begin{array}{r}10\\\times\,9\\\hline\end{array}$	9. $\begin{array}{r}3\\\times4\\\hline\end{array}$	10. $\begin{array}{r}5\\\times3\\\hline\end{array}$	11. $\begin{array}{r}3\\\times3\\\hline\end{array}$	12. $\begin{array}{r}5\\\times2\\\hline\end{array}$	13. $\begin{array}{r}6\\\times4\\\hline\end{array}$	14. $\begin{array}{r}10\\\times\,8\\\hline\end{array}$
15. $\begin{array}{r}3\\\times7\\\hline\end{array}$	16. $\begin{array}{r}2\\\times4\\\hline\end{array}$	17. $\begin{array}{r}5\\\times4\\\hline\end{array}$	18. $\begin{array}{r}3\\\times6\\\hline\end{array}$	19. $\begin{array}{r}10\\\times\,4\\\hline\end{array}$	20. $\begin{array}{r}2\\\times8\\\hline\end{array}$	21. $\begin{array}{r}7\\\times2\\\hline\end{array}$
22. $\begin{array}{r}5\\\times5\\\hline\end{array}$	23. $\begin{array}{r}9\\\times6\\\hline\end{array}$	24. $\begin{array}{r}5\\\times9\\\hline\end{array}$	25. $\begin{array}{r}10\\\times\,5\\\hline\end{array}$	26. $\begin{array}{r}4\\\times4\\\hline\end{array}$	27. $\begin{array}{r}5\\\times10\\\hline\end{array}$	28. $\begin{array}{r}8\\\times3\\\hline\end{array}$

 **Challenge**

29. When 0 is a factor, what do you know about the product?

30. When a number is multiplied by 1, what do you know about the product?

Multiplication Practice

Find the products.

1. 3×2 6
2. 2×2
3. 4×3
4. 4×6
5. 4×4

6. 3×8
7. 8×8
8. 3×9
9. 4×9
10. 3×6

11. 7×7
12. 3×5
13. 3×3
14. 9×6
15. 3×4

16. 3×0
17. 4×1
18. 4×5
19. 2×7
20. 5×6

21. $\begin{array}{r} 6 \\ \times 2 \\ \hline \end{array}$
22. $\begin{array}{r} 5 \\ \times 7 \\ \hline \end{array}$
23. $\begin{array}{r} 10 \\ \times 6 \\ \hline \end{array}$
24. $\begin{array}{r} 4 \\ \times 7 \\ \hline \end{array}$
25. $\begin{array}{r} 4 \\ \times 0 \\ \hline \end{array}$
26. $\begin{array}{r} 5 \\ \times 9 \\ \hline \end{array}$
27. $\begin{array}{r} 2 \\ \times 4 \\ \hline \end{array}$

28. $\begin{array}{r} 2 \\ \times 0 \\ \hline \end{array}$
29. $\begin{array}{r} 2 \\ \times 8 \\ \hline \end{array}$
30. $\begin{array}{r} 9 \\ \times 9 \\ \hline \end{array}$
31. $\begin{array}{r} 5 \\ \times 5 \\ \hline \end{array}$
32. $\begin{array}{r} 10 \\ \times 3 \\ \hline \end{array}$
33. $\begin{array}{r} 8 \\ \times 7 \\ \hline \end{array}$
34. $\begin{array}{r} 10 \\ \times 9 \\ \hline \end{array}$

Write the answers.

35. Sally plays ball 8 times a week. She plays for 4 hours each time. How many hours a week does she play ball?

36. Jason runs 5 kilometers every day. How many kilometers does he run in a week?

37. Susan goes swimming 4 times a week. She swims for 2 hours each time. How many hours a week does she swim?

38. Jerome plays tennis 3 times a week. He plays for 3 hours each time. How many hours a week does he play tennis?

Writing Multiplication Facts

Here are three ways to write two times five equals ten.

$$\begin{array}{r} 5 \\ \times 2 \\ \hline 10 \end{array}$$
$2 \times 5 = 10$
$2 \text{ fives} = 10$

Complete each sentence. Write the fact three ways.

1. Eight times three equals ▯.   24 $\begin{array}{r} 3 \\ \times 8 \\ \hline 24 \end{array}$ $8 \times 3 = 24$ 8 threes = 24

2. Seven times ten equals ▯.

3. Seven times five equals ▯.

4. Eight times four equals ▯.

5. Nine times four equals ▯.

6. Eight times five equals ▯.

7. Seven times four equals ▯.

8. Nine times three equals ▯.

9. Nine times five equals ▯.

10. Three times five equals ▯.

11. Five times three equals ▯.

12. Six times four equals ▯.

13. Seven times eight equals ▯.

14. Captain Katt went on 9 trips to search for treasure. On each trip he found 6 treasure chests. How many treasure chests did he find in all?

Switching Factors

Switch the factors. Write another fact.

$6 \times 2 = 12$

$2 \times 6 = 12$

The order of factors does not change the product.

Multiply. Then switch the factors and multiply again.

1. 4×5 20, $5 \times 4 = 20$ 2. 3×4 3. 3×5 4. 2×4

5. 3×2 6. 5×2 7. 4×1 8. 1×2

9. 9×4 10. 9×3 11. 6×7 12. 6×3

Write two facts for each pair.

13. 6, 2   14. 6, 3   15. 6, 4   16. 6, 5

17. 7, 2   18. 7, 3   19. 7, 4   20. 7, 5

21. 8, 2   22. 8, 3   23. 8, 4   24. 8, 5

 Calculate

Find the missing numbers. Use multiplication and look for the patterns.

25.

2	3	?	5	6	7	8	9
9	?	7	?	?	4	3	?
18	24	28	30	30	?	?	?

Juice Problems

Heidi and Henry are selling juice. Solve each problem.

1. Heidi uses 9 oranges to make a pitcher of orange juice. How many oranges does she need for 6 pitchers?   54

2. Henry uses 6 bunches of grapes to make a pitcher of grape juice. How many bunches of grapes does he need for 8 pitchers?

3. Heidi and Henry sold apricot juice for 8¢ a cup. How much for 5 cups?

4. Heidi and Henry sold orange juice for 7¢ a cup. How much for 7 cups?

5. Henry uses 5 carrots to make one glass of carrot juice. How many carrots does he need for 7 glasses?

6. Heidi sold 8 cups of grape juice. If grape juice costs 9¢ a cup, what was the cost?

Writing Division Facts

This drawing shows 27 shapes in 3 rows. To find out how many shapes in each row, you divide.

division fact

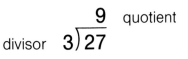

Find the quotients.

1. 7)28

2. 3)15

3. 2)14

4. 6)18

5. 8)32

6. 5)45

7. 3)21

8. 4)36

9. 7)56

10. 8)72

11. 6)54

12. 9)63

13. 6)42

14. 6)48

15. 4)28

16. 4)20

17. 8)48

18. 9)54

19. 6)36

20. 5)25

21. 2)18

22. 6)30

23. 4)16

24. 8)56

25. 9)81

⭐ Challenge

Write four division facts for each number.

26. Number: 24
Use 3, 4, 6, and 8 as divisors.

27. Number: 12
Use 2, 3, 4, and 6 as divisors.

28. Number: 36
Use 2, 3, 6, and 9 as divisors.

29. Number: 20
Use 2, 4, 5, and 10 as divisors.

Division Practice

Divide.

1. $18 \div 2$ 9
2. $24 \div 3$
3. $27 \div 9$
4. $42 \div 6$

5. $48 \div 6$
6. $54 \div 9$
7. $56 \div 7$
8. $72 \div 8$

9. $63 \div 7$
10. $42 \div 7$
11. $48 \div 8$
12. $56 \div 8$

13. $72 \div 9$
14. $63 \div 9$
15. $54 \div 6$
16. $32 \div 8$

17. $36 \div 4$
18. $24 \div 6$
19. $36 \div 9$
20. $30 \div 6$

21. $40 \div 5$
22. $15 \div 3$
23. $36 \div 6$
24. $45 \div 9$

25. $30 \div 5$
26. $24 \div 4$
27. $21 \div 3$
28. $35 \div 5$

29. Tina puts 4 photos on each page of her photo album. How many pages does she need for 32 photos?

30. Film costs $6 a roll. How many rolls can Tina buy for $18?

Review (pp. 3–22)

1. $6 + 7$
2. $15 - 8$
3. 6×3
4. $35 \div 5$
5. 8×4

6. $17 - 9$
7. 4×6
8. $9 + 8$
9. $49 \div 7$
10. 9×9

Writing Facts

Write two multiplication facts and two division facts. Use the numbers 3, 4, and 12.

$3 \times 4 = 12$
$4 \times 3 = 12$

$12 \div 4 = 3$
$12 \div 3 = 4$

Write two multiplication and two division facts for each.

1. 2, 18, 9 $2 \times 9 = 18$ $9 \times 2 = 18$ $18 \div 9 = 2$ $18 \div 2 = 9$

2. 5, 3, 15
3. 4, 6, 24
4. 3, 8, 24
5. 7, 10, 70

6. 4, 9, 36
7. 6, 9, 54
8. 7, 6, 42
9. 72, 8, 9

10. 56, 7, 8
11. 9, 63, 7
12. 8, 48, 6
13. 4, 28, 7

14. 5, 45, 9
15. 2, 6, 3
16. 8, 40, 5
17. 7, 35, 5

18. 4, 12, 3
19. 7, 3, 21
20. 6, 30, 5
21. 4, 5, 20

22. Herbert buys 9 paintbrushes. Each one costs $3. How much does he spend for paintbrushes?

23. Linda spends $27 for 9 paintbrushes. How much does each paintbrush cost?

Two-Step Problems

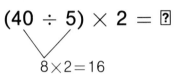

(   ) mean **Do me first.**

Step 1
Divide.

$$(40 \div 5) \times 2 = \boxed{?}$$

8

Step 2
Multiply.

$$(40 \div 5) \times 2 = \boxed{?}$$

$8 \times 2 = 16$

Solve each problem. Watch for $+$, $-$, $\times$, and $\div$.

1. $(4+2) \times 3$ 18

2. $(3 \times 4) - 2$

3. $(49 \div 7) \times 5$

4. $(12-4) \times 8$

5. $(25 \div 5) \times 3$

6. $(56 \div 7) \times 3$

7. $7 \times (2+3)$

8. $(81 \div 9) \times 4$

9. $(28 \div 7) - 2$

10. $(12 \div 4) \times 9$

11. $(3+6) \times 7$

12. $4 \times (5+3)$

13. $(72 \div 9) \times 5$

14. $4 \times (13-5)$

15. $(45 \div 5) \times 6$

16. $(2 \times 2) \times 8$

17. $(36 \div 6) \times 3$

18. $(6 \times 3) - 7$

19. $4 \times (16-9)$

20. $6 \times (3 \times 4)$

21. $(2 \times 5) - 4$

 **Calculate**

Copy and complete. Continue these patterns.

22a. $2 \div 2 = \boxed{?}$
 b. $6 \div 3 = \boxed{?}$
 c. $12 \div 4 = \boxed{?}$
 d. $\boxed{?} \div \boxed{?} = \boxed{?}$
 e. $\boxed{?} \div \boxed{?} = \boxed{?}$

23a. $242 \div 22 = \boxed{?}$
 b. $276 \div 23 = \boxed{?}$
 c. $312 \div 24 = \boxed{?}$
 d. $\boxed{?} \div \boxed{?} = \boxed{?}$
 e. $\boxed{?} \div \boxed{?} = \boxed{?}$

24a. $672 \div 32 = \boxed{?}$
 b. $726 \div 33 = \boxed{?}$
 c. $782 \div 34 = \boxed{?}$
 d. $\boxed{?} \div \boxed{?} = \boxed{?}$
 e. $\boxed{?} \div \boxed{?} = \boxed{?}$

Map Problems

Some children in Mr. Yamaguchi's class are making maps of the United States. Solve each problem.

1. It takes 4 sheets of colored paper to make one map. How many sheets of colored paper for 7 maps? 28

2. 8 children work at one table. If there are 32 children in the class, how many tables do they need?

3. 3 children can share one pair of scissors. If 27 children use scissors, how many pairs do they need?

4. Mr. Yamaguchi uses 8 tacks to pin up each map. How many tacks will he use to pin up 10 maps?

5. 6 children can share one box of colored pens. If 24 children use colored pens, how many boxes do they need?

6. 24 maps will be pinned up on 8 bulletin boards. If Mr. Yamaguchi puts the same number of maps on each bulletin board, how many maps will go on each board?

Chapter Review

Add or subtract. (ex. 1-7: p. 3), (ex. 8-14: p. 5), (ex. 15-21: p. 10)

1. 8 +2	2. 5 +9	3. 3 +4	4. 2 +7	5. 5 +5	6. 8 +6	7. 9 +8

8. 10 − 4	9. 15 − 8	10. 13 − 9	11. 12 − 6	12. 9 −5	13. 14 − 5	14. 18 − 9

15. 5 8 +7	16. 8 8 +2	17. 6 4 2 +6	18. 2 3 5 +5	19. 7 1 7 +8	20. 4 4 6 +9	21. 1 9 5 +9

Add or subtract. (ex. 22-24: p. 12), (ex. 25-26: p. 13)

22. 48 +31	23. 581 +317	24. 7802 +2165	25. 737 −426	26. 6798 −2643

Multiply or divide. (ex. 27-43: p. 15), (ex. 44-58: p. 21)

27. 8 ×4	28. 3 ×7	29. 9 ×2	30. 5 ×5	31. 8 ×9	32. 6 ×0	33. 4 ×3

34. 8×2	35. 4×4	36. 8×6	37. 9×9	38. 7×5
39. 6×5	40. 7×7	41. 3×9	42. 9×4	43. 4×6

44. $3\overline{)21}$	45. $5\overline{)20}$	46. $7\overline{)49}$	47. $9\overline{)81}$	48. $8\overline{)32}$
49. $16 \div 4$	50. $28 \div 4$	51. $36 \div 6$	52. $56 \div 7$	53. $15 \div 3$
54. $12 \div 4$	55. $56 \div 8$	56. $40 \div 5$	57. $42 \div 6$	58. $21 \div 7$

Chapter Test

Add or subtract.

1.	2.	3.	4.	5.	6.	7.
6 +5	10 − 6	9 +8	15 − 8	6 +3	13 − 4	7 +4

8.	9.	10.	11.	12.	13.	14.
10 − 7	4 +5	17 − 8	6 8 +5	7 6 2 +4	8 1 5 +6	2 9 4 +3

Add or subtract.

15.	16.	17.	18.	19.
98 −76	4202 +1695	191 +408	7457 − 234	6584 −5572

Multiply or divide.

20.	21.	22.	23.	24.	25.	26.
7 ×6	9 ×5	8 ×7	6 ×3	5 ×0	3 ×3	9 ×8

27. 6)‾36‾ 28. 5)‾40‾ 29. 7)‾42‾ 30. 3)‾27‾ 31. 9)‾81‾

32. 5×5 33. 8×6 34. $12 \div 4$ 35. $63 \div 7$ 36. 9×0

37. $72 \div 8$ 38. 7×1 39. $35 \div 7$ 40. $21 \div 7$ 41. 5×4

Brush Up

Add or subtract.

1. $6+7$ 2. $8-5$ 3. $9+2$ 4. $5+7$ 5. $12-4$

6. $8+9$ 7. $9+7$ 8. $15-8$ 9. $14-6$ 10. $11-5$

11. $3+9$ 12. $17-8$ 13. $13-2$ 14. $6+6$ 15. $16-7$

16.
$$\begin{array}{r} 5 \\ 6 \\ 9 \\ +8 \\ \hline \end{array}$$

17.
$$\begin{array}{r} 3 \\ 5 \\ 4 \\ +6 \\ \hline \end{array}$$

18.
$$\begin{array}{r} 5 \\ 5 \\ 4 \\ +3 \\ \hline \end{array}$$

19.
$$\begin{array}{r} 81 \\ 11 \\ +\ 6 \\ \hline \end{array}$$

20.
$$\begin{array}{r} 601 \\ 43 \\ +\ \ 4 \\ \hline \end{array}$$

21.
$$\begin{array}{r} 82 \\ +12 \\ \hline \end{array}$$

22.
$$\begin{array}{r} 44 \\ +15 \\ \hline \end{array}$$

23.
$$\begin{array}{r} 93 \\ -81 \\ \hline \end{array}$$

24.
$$\begin{array}{r} 945 \\ +\ 52 \\ \hline \end{array}$$

25.
$$\begin{array}{r} 87 \\ -46 \\ \hline \end{array}$$

26.
$$\begin{array}{r} 421 \\ -301 \\ \hline \end{array}$$

27.
$$\begin{array}{r} 3669 \\ -2435 \\ \hline \end{array}$$

28.
$$\begin{array}{r} 4873 \\ +2124 \\ \hline \end{array}$$

29.
$$\begin{array}{r} 6341 \\ +3456 \\ \hline \end{array}$$

30.
$$\begin{array}{r} 8599 \\ -4345 \\ \hline \end{array}$$

Multiply or divide.

31. 6×8 32. 7×10 33. $24\div8$ 34. $21\div7$ 35. 8×4

36. 4×9 37. 8×0 38. $9\div9$ 39. $35\div5$ 40. 5×5

41. 9×6 42. $63\div7$ 43. $27\div3$ 44. $72\div8$ 45. 6×5

46.
$$\begin{array}{r} 6 \\ \times4 \\ \hline \end{array}$$

47.
$$\begin{array}{r} 4 \\ \times4 \\ \hline \end{array}$$

48.
$$\begin{array}{r} 7 \\ \times6 \\ \hline \end{array}$$

49.
$$\begin{array}{r} 3 \\ \times5 \\ \hline \end{array}$$

50.
$$\begin{array}{r} 9 \\ \times8 \\ \hline \end{array}$$

51. $7\overline{)56}$ 52. $4\overline{)32}$ 53. $3\overline{)18}$ 54. $4\overline{)12}$ 55. $5\overline{)20}$

56. 9×6 57. $21\div3$ 58. $49\div7$ 59. 8×2 60. $16\div8$

61. 6×6 62. $56\div8$ 63. 7×9 64. $21\div7$ 65. 8×8

CHAPTER 2

Numbers

Using Numbers at Work

Sherman Lum is a marine biologist. He found 32 different kinds of sea urchins near one island and 17 different kinds near another. In his report, he rounds the numbers to the nearest ten. 32 rounds to 30; 17 rounds to 20. His report says about 30 different kinds of sea urchins live near one island and about 20 different kinds live near the other.

Place Value

This place-value chart shows the place value for each digit in the number 786,532.

Hundred Thousands	Ten Thousands	Thousands	Hundreds	Tens	Ones
100,000	10,000	1000	100	10	1
7	8	6	5	3	2

You can write an addition problem to show the total value of each digit in a number.

Hundred Thousands	7	700,000
Ten Thousands	8	80,000
Thousands	6	6 000
Hundreds	5	500
Tens	3	30
Ones	2	+ 2

786,532

Use the number 943,267.

1. In which place is the 6?   tens

2. In which place is the 4?

3. In which place is the 9?

4. In which place is the 7?

5. In which place is the 3?

6. In which place is the 2?

Write an addition problem that shows the total value of each digit.

7. 1811

8. 12,980

9. 3459

10. 18,956

11. 604,010

12. 106,320

13. 87,094

14. 400,001

Reading and Writing Numbers

On this chart, the places are grouped into periods.

Thousands Period			Ones Period		
Hundreds	Tens	Ones	Hundreds	Tens	Ones
4	7	3	6	2	5

Commas are used to separate periods. 473,625 is read
four hundred seventy-three thousand, six hundred twenty-five.

Copy these numbers. Put in the commas.

1. 624179   624,179
2. 80123
3. 700090
4. 80903

5. 741386
6. 45231
7. 900773
8. 214435

Write the numbers.

9. three hundred eighty-two thousand, three hundred eighty-two

10. six hundred thousand, two hundred seventy-five

11. eighty-four thousand, seventeen

12. seven hundred fifty thousand, four hundred six

13. sixty-eight thousand, nine hundred fifty-six

14. nine hundred thirty-nine thousand, seven hundred fifty-six

Write the words.

15. 84,200
16. 485,485
17. 600,108
18. 56,982

Ordering Numbers

Compare digits to put numbers in order.

Compare the digits in the thousands period.

138,000 and 114,400

138 thousand **is greater than** 114 thousand, so **138,000 > 114,400**.

If thousands digits are the same, compare the digits in the ones period.

12,160 and 12,660

160 **is less than** 660, so **12,160 < 12,660**.

Write **> or < to order the numbers.**

1. 3900 ⬤< 3999

2. 20,000 ◯ 30,000

3. 23,000 ◯ 22,900

4. 35,670 ◯ 35,500

5. 13,124 ◯ 13,400

6. 89,417 ◯ 87,699

7. 123,678 ◯ 123,900

8. 406,817 ◯ 406,718

9. 4,817 ◯ 4,765

10. 40,000 ◯ 70,000

11. 92,617 ◯ 92,817

12. 87,540 ◯ 87,140

13. 25,619 ◯ 25,691

14. 617,813 ◯ 617,892

15. 15,981 ◯ 15,891

 **Challenge**
Write the answers.

16. Count by 1000 from 158,716 to 162,716.

17. Count by 10,000 from 656,300 to 706,300.

Millions

This place-value chart shows the place value and period for each digit in the number 823,465,109.

Millions Period			Thousands Period			Ones Period		
Hundreds	Tens	Ones	Hundreds	Tens	Ones	Hundreds	Tens	Ones
8	2	3	4	6	5	1	0	9

Use the number 823,465,109. Write the digit that is in each place.

1. hundred millions place   8

2. one millions place

3. ten millions place

4. hundred thousands place

5. one thousands place

6. ten thousands place

Use the number 206,539,187. Write the place value and period for each digit.

7. 6

8. 0

9. 2

10. 9

11. 3

12. 5

13. 8

14. 1

15. The planet Venus is 108,000,000 kilometers from the sun. Earth is 150,000,000 kilometers from the sun. Which planet is closer to the sun?

16. The planet Jupiter is 780,000,000 kilometers from the sun. Mars is 228,000,000 kilometers from the sun. Which planet is farther away from the sun?

Reading and Writing Millions

Commas make large numbers easier to read.

823,465,109 is read *eight hundred twenty-three million,*
four hundred sixty-five thousand, one hundred nine.

Copy these numbers. Put in the commas.

1. 72680 72,680
2. 6178004
3. 85341024
4. 924176503

Write the numbers.

5. eight hundred thousand, four hundred sixty-five

6. six hundred sixty-one million, two hundred fifty thousand, six hundred forty-one

7. nine million, nine hundred ninety-nine thousand, nine hundred nine

8. one hundred million
9. eight million
10. forty million

Write the words.

11. 10,000,000
12. 21,869
13. 370,000
14. 491,000,000

15. 381,560,030
16. 6,603,366
17. 785,430
18. 11,800,500

Population Problems

Estimated State Populations

	1990	2000
Texas	13,808,000	15,217,000
Virginia	5,696,000	6,272,000
Florida	10,110,000	11,830,000
Arizona	2,652,000	3,102,000
Oklahoma	2,839,000	3,009,000
Tennessee	4,382,000	4,654,000
Illinois	12,771,000	13,668,000

Use the chart to answer the questions.

1. Which state will have more people in 1990, Texas or Florida?   Texas

2. Which state will have more people in 2000, Virginia or Illinois?

3. Which state will have more people in 1990, Arizona or Oklahoma?

4. Which state will have more people in 2000, Florida or Tennessee?

5. Which state will have the most people in 1990? the least?

6. Which state will have the most people in 2000? the least?

7. List the states in order of estimated population from greatest to least for 1990.

8. List the states in order of estimated population from least to greatest for 2000.

Review   (pp. 31–36)

Write > or < to order the numbers.

1. 138,000 ◯ 183,500

2. 56,174 ◯ 56,714

3. 567,090 ◯ 565,900

4. 945,459 ◯ 954,945

5. 79,364 ◯ 77,643

6. 875,211 ◯ 857,121

Rounding to the Nearest Ten

To round to the nearest ten, look at the ones digit.

| 70 | 71 | 72 | 73 | 74 | 75 | 76 | 77 | 78 | 79 | 80 |

75 is in the middle.
It rounds to 80.

If the ones digit is 0, 1, 2, 3, or 4, the tens digit stays the same.

If the ones digit is 5, 6, 7, 8, or 9, the tens digit increases by 1.

Think about the nearest ten. Write the answers.

1a. 43 is between 40 and ▨.   50
 b. 43 rounds to ▨.   40

2a. 57 is between ▨ and 60.
 b. 57 rounds to ▨.

3a. 39 is between 30 and ▨.
 b. 39 rounds to ▨.

4a. 64 is between ▨ and ▨.
 b. 64 rounds to ▨.

5. Write the numbers between 30 and 40 that round to 30.

6. Write the numbers between 30 and 40 that round to 40.

Round to the nearest ten.

| 7. 92 | 8. 65 | 9. 28 | 10. 98 | 11. 37 | 12. 16 |
| 13. 32 | 14. 49 | 15. 55 | 16. 11 | 17. 74 | 18. 88 |

Now round these to the nearest ten.

| 19. 468   470 | 20. 389 | 21. 1659 | 22. 2832 | 23. 791 |
| 24. 4063 | 25. 9871 | 26. 444 | 27. 6192 | 28. 758 |

Rounding to the Nearest Hundred

To round to the nearest hundred, look at the tens digit.

200   210   220   230   240   250   260   270   280   290   300

If the tens digit is 0, 1, 2, 3, or 4, the hundreds digit stays the same.

If the tens digit is 5, 6, 7, 8, or 9, the hundreds digit increases by 1.

Think about the nearest hundred. Write the answers.

1a. 210 is between 200 and ⍰.   300
  b. 210 rounds to ⍰.   200

2a. 380 is between ⍰ and 400.
  b. 380 rounds to ⍰.

3a. 531 is between 500 and ⍰.
  b. 531 rounds to ⍰.

4a. 789 is between ⍰ and 800.
  b. 789 rounds to ⍰.

5a. 349 is between ⍰ and ⍰.
  b. 349 rounds to ⍰.

6a. The middle number between 200 and 300 is ⍰.
  b. The middle number rounds to ⍰.

Round to the nearest hundred.

7. 851

8. 609

9. 435

10. 763

11. 913

12. 650

13. 349

14. 702

15. 888

16. 921

17. 1350

18. 1985

19. 1243

20. 2094

21. 8888

Calculate

Add or subtract from left to right. Round the answer to the nearest hundred.

22. $199 + 201 - 98 - 52 + 49 + 104 + 99 = ⍰$

Rounding to the Nearest Thousand

To round to the nearest thousand, look at the hundreds digit.

| 4000 | 4100 | 4200 | 4300 | 4400 | 4500 | 4600 | 4700 | 4800 | 4900 | 5000 |

If the hundreds digit is 0, 1, 2, 3, or 4, the thousands digit stays the same.

If the hundreds digit is 5, 6, 7, 8, or 9, the thousands digit increases by 1.

Think about the nearest thousand. Write the answers.

1a. 4200 is between 4000 and ☐.   5000
 b. 4200 rounds to ☐.   4000

2a. 5700 is between 5000 and ☐.
 b. 5700 rounds to ☐.

3a. 7625 is between 7000 and ☐.
 b. 7625 rounds to ☐.

4a. 3217 is between ☐ and 4000.
 b. 3217 rounds to ☐.

5a. 3840 is between ☐ and ☐.
 b. 3840 rounds to ☐.

6a. The middle number between 4000 and 5000 is ☐.
 b. The middle number rounds to ☐.

Round to the nearest thousand.

7. 9840   8. 6599   9. 8760   10. 5500   11. 7512

12. 4892   13. 3077   14. 5882   15. 7900   16. 8311

17. The diameter of the planet Saturn is about 120,900 kilometers. Round the diameter of Saturn to the nearest thousand kilometers.

Rounding Problems

Round each of these numbers.

1. Charles Garcia's company makes 23,768 boxes a day. Round to the nearest thousand. **24,000**

2. Joseph Dunne's odometer reads 9278 kilometers. Round to the nearest hundred.

3. Jane Yanahero drove 2742 kilometers. Round to the nearest hundred.

4. A factory makes 5138 cars a day. Round to the nearest ten.

5. Patti Loyd's math book has 384 pages. Round to the nearest ten.

6. The population of Silverville is 2384. Round to the nearest ten.

7. The population of Jefferson is 14,768. Round to the nearest hundred.

8. Oak School has 623 students. Round to the nearest hundred.

⭐ Challenge

Round each number to the nearest hundred. Then add.

9.	10.	11.	12.	13.
233	1679	8990	777	6785
+389	+ 251	+3010	+491	+ 542

Addition Patterns

406, 408, 410, ⬚
To find the next number, look for clues.

First clue: The numbers become greater.

Second clue: **408** is **2** more than **406.**

410 is **2** more than **408.**

The pattern is: Add 2.
The next number is: **410 + 2 = 412**

Find the pattern. Write the next number.

1. 64, 68, 72, ⬚   Add 4, 76

2. 70, 80, 90, ⬚

3. 10, 15, 20, ⬚

4. 33, 36, 39, ⬚

5. 335, 340, 345, ⬚

6. 903, 906, 909, ⬚

7. 221, 226, 231, ⬚

8. 408, 410, 412, ⬚

9. 761, 767, 773, ⬚

10. 2424, 2428, 2432, ⬚

11. 1804, 1808, 1812, ⬚

12. 7905, 7910, 7915, ⬚

13. 9010, 9020, 9030, ⬚

14. 8600, 8606, 8612, ⬚

Write the next three numbers.

15. Start with 914. Add 2.

16. Start with 15. Add 3.

17. Start with 77. Add 5.

18. Start with 549. Add 6.

19. Start with 7840. Add 10.

20. Start with 4333. Add 3.

Subtraction Patterns

748, 746, 744, 🔲
To find the next number, look for clues.

First clue:	The numbers become less.
Second clue:	**746** is **2** less than **748**.
	744 is **2** less than **746**.
The pattern is:	Subtract 2.
The next number is:	**744 − 2 = 742**

Find the pattern. Write the next number.

1. 66, 64, 62, 🔲   Subtract 2, 60

2. 50, 45, 40, 🔲

3. 33, 30, 27, 🔲

4. 82, 80, 78, 🔲

5. 690, 680, 670, 🔲

6. 530, 527, 524, 🔲

7. 866, 860, 854, 🔲

8. 901, 899, 897, 🔲

9. 3940, 3936, 3932, 🔲

10. 9431, 9429, 9427, 🔲

11. 8555, 8550, 8545, 🔲

12. 2024, 2020, 2016, 🔲

13. 4460, 4450, 4440, 🔲

14. 3179, 3177, 3175, 🔲

Write the next three numbers.

15. Start with 619. Subtract 4.

16. Start with 1255. Subtract 5.

17. Start with 89. Subtract 9.

18. Start with 786. Subtract 6.

19. Start with 3333. Subtract 3.

20. Start with 6577. Subtract 7.

More Patterns

9820, 9825, 9830, 9835
Patterns like these are called **sequences**.

Write the next number.

1. 634, 636, 638, ⬚ 640

2. 870, 865, 860, ⬚

3. 926, 928, 930, ⬚

4. 475, 470, 465, ⬚

5. 9702, 9705, 9708, ⬚

6. 1680, 1690, 1700, ⬚

7. 9426, 9423, 9420, ⬚

8. 8840, 8836, 8832, ⬚

Write the next three numbers.

9. Start with 782. Add 6.

10. Start with 561. Subtract 2.

11. Start with 3540. Add 3.

12. Start with 3540. Subtract 3.

Calculate
Find the missing numbers.

13. 4297, 4956, 5615, 6274, ⬚, ⬚

14. 9040, 8338, 7636, 6934, ⬚, ⬚

Pattern Practice

Look for the pattern. Write the next three numbers.

1. 612, 614, 616, ▢, ▢, ▢ *618, 620, 622*

2. 6720, 6730, 6740, ▢, ▢, ▢

3. 8300, 8400, 8500, ▢, ▢, ▢

4. 9936, 9932, 9928, ▢, ▢, ▢

5. 870, 860, 850, ▢, ▢, ▢

6. 117, 114, 111, ▢, ▢, ▢

7. 4624, 4620, 4616, ▢, ▢, ▢

8. 11,565, 11,570, 11,575, ▢, ▢, ▢

9. 7635, 7640, 7645, ▢, ▢, ▢

10. 257, 263, 269, ▢, ▢, ▢

11. 75,439, 75,436, 75,433, ▢, ▢, ▢

12. 59,707, 59,700, 59,693, ▢, ▢, ▢

Write the next five numbers.

13. Start with 817. Add 3.

14. Start with 990. Subtract 10.

15. Start with 3440. Add 3.

16. Start with 37,800. Subtract 100.

17. Start with 119,768. Subtract 2.

18. Start with 436,840. Add 5.

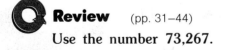

Review (pp. 31–44)

Use the number 73,267.

1. Write the number in words.

2. Round to the nearest hundred.

3. Which digit is in the tens place?

4. Add 2. Write the next three numbers.

Decimals and Place Value

The number 7984.52 is a **decimal**. This chart shows the place values of its digits.

Thousands	Hundreds	Tens	Ones	Tenths	Hundredths
1000	100	10	1	0.1	0.01
7	9	8	4	5	2

5 is in the tenths place. Its total value is 5 tenths.
2 is in the hundredths place. Its total value is 2 hundredths.

Use the number 4851.63. Write the values.

1a. 8 is in the ⬚ place.   hundreds
 b. It has a total value of ⬚.   8 hundreds

2a. 5 is in the ⬚ place.
 b. It has a total value of ⬚.

3a. 4 is in the ⬚ place.
 b. It has a total value of ⬚.

4a. 3 is in the ⬚ place.
 b. It has a total value of ⬚.

5a. 1 is in the ⬚ place.
 b. It has a total value of ⬚.

6a. 6 is in the ⬚ place.
 b. It has a total value of ⬚.

Challenge

Use the number 555.55. Answer these questions. (Hint: 5 in the hundreds place is 10 times greater than 5 in the tens place.)

7. 5 in the tens place is how many times greater than 5 in the ones place?

8. 5 in the ones place is how many times greater than 5 in the tenths place?

Thousandths

This place-value chart shows thousandths.

Hundreds	Tens	Ones	Tenths	Hundredths	Thousandths
100	10	1	0.1	0.01	0.001
3	4	7	1	5	8

8 is in the thousandths place. Its total value is 8 thousandths.

Use the number **891.542.** Write the place value and the total value of each digit.

1. 2
   thousandths
   2 thousandths

2. 1

3. 9

4. 4

5. 8

6. 5

Use the number **245,671.089.** Write the place value and the total value of each digit.

7. 0

8. 4

9. 2

10. 5

11. 7

12. 8

13. 1

14. 9

15. 6

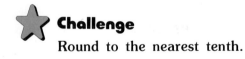 **Challenge**

Round to the nearest tenth.

16. 43.36

17. 0.632

18. 7.09

19. 5.93

20. 76.341

21. 9.77

22. 0.32

23. 6.68

24. 82.82

Reading and Writing Decimals

When you read decimals, say **and** for the decimal point.

326.749 is read *three hundred twenty-six and seven hundred forty-nine thousandths.*

Write the numbers.

1. nine and two hundred fifty-five thousandths   9.255

2. one hundred seventeen and six-thousandths

3. forty and thirty-six hundredths

4. six hundred seven and five-tenths

5. eighty-eight and eighty-eight hundredths

6. two hundred fourteen and five hundred two-thousandths

7. three hundred and one-thousandth

8. fifty and three-tenths

Write the words.

9. 11.5   10. 96.9   11. 32.2   12. 908.8   13. 213.65

14. 73.06   15. 5.97   16. 30.002   17. 40.19   18. 34.987

Egyptian Numerals

Egyptian numerals were invented over 5000 years ago.

Thousand	Hundred	Ten	One
1000	100	10	1

Egyptian numerals may be written from left to right or from right to left. When reading the number, always start with the numeral that has the greatest value.

2431 may be written: or

Either way it is read *two thousand, four hundred thirty-one.*

Look for the numeral that has the greatest value. Write these numbers.

1.   2134

2.

3.

4.

5.

6.

Write an Egyptian numeral for each.

7. 14   8. 46   9. 436   10. 3187   11. 1052

Roman Numerals

The Romans used these symbols to name numbers.

I	V	X	L	C	D	M
1	5	10	50	100	500	1000

To find the value of a Roman numeral, you use addition and subtraction.

Add if the symbols that follow each other are alike or if they decrease in value from left to right.

$XV = 10 + 5$, or 15

$MCXVII = 1000 + 100 + 10 + 5 + 1 + 1$, or 1117

Subtract if the value of the first symbol is less than the value of the second symbol.

In IV, I is less than V.
$IV = 5 - 1$, or 4

In XL, X is less than L.
$XL = 50 - 10$, or 40

Find the value of each.

1. XXX 30
2. CM
3. VII
4. XC
5. VIII

6. IX
7. XI
8. XXV
9. IV
10. XII

11. XXII
12. XVI
13. CD
14. LXX
15. XX

16. III
17. XV
18. CL
19. DC
20. CC

Challenge

Find the value of each.

21. DLXX
22. MCDLVI
23. MMCCXXIV
24. MCLX
25. MCLXIV

Chapter Review

Write the numbers. (ex. 1: p. 32), (ex. 2: p. 35), (ex. 3-4: p. 47)

1. six hundred twenty-one thousand, one hundred ninety-three

2. one hundred forty-nine million, two hundred thirty
    thousand, nine hundred ten

3. two hundred eighty-nine and six-tenths

4. sixty and four-thousandths

Write the words. (ex. 5-7: p. 32), (ex. 8-9: p. 35), (ex. 10-12: p. 47)

5. 38,601   6. 934,098   7. 10,947   8. 12,600,521

9. 575,242,865   10. 15.7   11. 49.49   12. 95.002

Write > or < to order these numbers. (ex. 13-16: p. 33)

13. 189,417 ◯ 198,714   14. 713,358 ◯ 713,318

15. 11,312 ◯ 11,213   16. 200,001 ◯ 200,010

**Round each number twice—once to the nearest hundred and once
to the nearest ten.** (ex. 17-21: pp. 37–38)

17. 178   18. 426   19. 1231   20. 8459   21. 23,656

Round to the nearest thousand. (ex. 22-26: p. 39)

22. 6980   23. 7105   24. 3954   25. 2638   26. 1499

Chapter Test

Write the numbers.

1. three hundred thirty-two thousand, eight hundred forty-one

2. four hundred sixty-three million, one hundred eighty thousand, seven hundred six

3. seventy-five and six-tenths

4. twenty and two-thousandths

Write the words.

5. 130,309

6. 12,471

7. 7.33

8. 59.142

Write > or < to order these numbers.

9. 64,466 ◯ 46,664

10. 100,059 ◯ 100,095

11. 300,090 ◯ 300,900

12. 776,677 ◯ 676,776

Round each number twice—once to the nearest hundred and once to the nearest ten.

13. 349

14. 2652

15. 865

16. 5818

17. 961

Round to the nearest thousand.

18. 8888

19. 1065

20. 4551

21. 1326

22. 5001

Brush Up

Add or subtract.

1. 44
    +35

2. 87
    −66

3. 81
    +18

4. 59
    −46

5. 37
    −25

6. 258
    +141

7. 4996
    −1872

8. 869
    −448

9. 2603
    +7245

10. 8751
    + 243

11. 1999
    − 843

12. 6587
    −4244

13. 3200
    + 589

14. 4536
    +4243

15. 7398
    − 252

16. 21
    35
    +100

17. 304
    4
    + 81

18. 65
    11
    +612

19. 1041
    314
    232
    + 12

20. 2541
    222
    20
    + 6

Multiply or divide.

21. 3×3

22. 4×7

23. 5×8

24. 6×6

25. 9×5

26. $21 \div 7$

27. $30 \div 6$

28. $20 \div 4$

29. $7 \div 7$

30. $36 \div 4$

31. 3×5

32. 2×6

33. 6×9

34. 5×5

35. 3×0

36. $6 \overline{)18}$

37. $9 \overline{)27}$

38. $7 \overline{)42}$

39. $4 \overline{)24}$

40. $5 \overline{)45}$

Copy and complete.

41. 486 = ⬚ hundreds ⬚ tens ⬚ ones

42. 38 = ⬚ tens ⬚ ones

43. 5691 = ⬚ thousands ⬚ hundreds ⬚ tens ⬚ ones

44. 83,984 = ⬚ ten thousands ⬚ thousands ⬚ hundreds ⬚ tens ⬚ ones

CHAPTER 3

Addition and Subtraction

Using Addition at Work

Lucy Ramirez works in a bicycle repair shop. When she replaces a broken brake cable, she charges $1.25 for the cable and $3.50 for her labor. She adds $1.25 + $3.50 to find the total charge. Lucy charges a total of $4.75 to replace a broken brake cable.

Trading Ones in Addition

10 ones equal 1 ten.

Step 1
Add ones.
Trade 10 ones for 1 ten.

$$
\begin{array}{r}
{}^{2} \\
38 \\
27 \\
+\ 16 \\
\hline
1
\end{array}
$$

Step 2
Add tens.

$$
\begin{array}{r}
{}^{2} \\
38 \\
27 \\
+\ 16 \\
\hline
81
\end{array}
$$

Add.

1. $\begin{array}{r} 58 \\ +\ 9 \\ \hline 67 \end{array}$
2. $\begin{array}{r} 67 \\ +\ 6 \\ \hline \end{array}$
3. $\begin{array}{r} 79 \\ +\ 5 \\ \hline \end{array}$
4. $\begin{array}{r} 37 \\ +\ 8 \\ \hline \end{array}$
5. $\begin{array}{r} 46 \\ +\ 9 \\ \hline \end{array}$
6. $\begin{array}{r} 29 \\ +\ 5 \\ \hline \end{array}$

7. $\begin{array}{r} 37 \\ +25 \\ \hline \end{array}$
8. $\begin{array}{r} 58 \\ +16 \\ \hline \end{array}$
9. $\begin{array}{r} 29 \\ +48 \\ \hline \end{array}$
10. $\begin{array}{r} 37 \\ +55 \\ \hline \end{array}$
11. $\begin{array}{r} 74 \\ +16 \\ \hline \end{array}$
12. $\begin{array}{r} 86 \\ +14 \\ \hline \end{array}$

13. $\begin{array}{r} 28 \\ +36 \\ \hline \end{array}$
14. $\begin{array}{r} 17 \\ +49 \\ \hline \end{array}$
15. $\begin{array}{r} 23 \\ +57 \\ \hline \end{array}$
16. $\begin{array}{r} 12 \\ +38 \\ \hline \end{array}$
17. $\begin{array}{r} 28 \\ +17 \\ \hline \end{array}$
18. $\begin{array}{r} 37 \\ +59 \\ \hline \end{array}$

19. $\begin{array}{r} 24 \\ 18 \\ +16 \\ \hline \end{array}$
20. $\begin{array}{r} 32 \\ 8 \\ +29 \\ \hline \end{array}$
21. $\begin{array}{r} 7 \\ 48 \\ +26 \\ \hline \end{array}$
22. $\begin{array}{r} 37 \\ 29 \\ +14 \\ \hline \end{array}$
23. $\begin{array}{r} 18 \\ 5 \\ +56 \\ \hline \end{array}$
24. $\begin{array}{r} 10 \\ 78 \\ +\ 9 \\ \hline \end{array}$

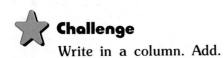 **Challenge**

Write in a column. Add.

25. $15+27+52$
26. $36+18+19$
27. $20+49+15$
28. $14+59+13$

More Trading Ones

Add four, five, or more numbers the same way you add two numbers.

```
  2              3
 34             24
 62             73
 17             67
+38             28
───          + 39
151            ───
               231
```

Add.

1. 16
    8
  40
+19
  83
	2. 95
	  12
	  76
	+43
		3. 25
		  35
		   9
		+17
			4. 29
			  65
			  41
			+32
				5. 37
				  85
				  14
				+42

6. 47
  92
  15
  26
+31
	7. 33
	  86
	  47
	  90
	+ 6
		8. 12
		  22
		  32
		  42
		+99
			9. 65
			  71
			  30
			  26
			+73
				10. 82
				  18
				  46
				  57
				+63

11. There are 16 red bicycles, 9 green bicycles, 22 blue bicycles, and 12 brown bicycles in the schoolyard. How many bicycles in all?

12. There are 19 white cars, 9 yellow cars, 3 orange cars, 11 silver cars, and 5 purple cars in the parking lot. How many cars in all?

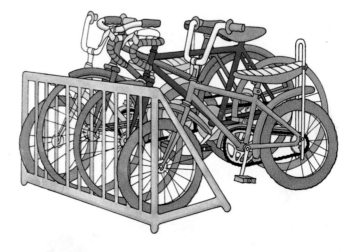

Trading Tens in Addition

10 tens equal 1 hundred.

Step 1
Add ones.

Step 2
Add tens. Trade 10 tens for 1 hundred.

Step 3
Add hundreds.

$$\begin{array}{r} 264 \\ 594 \\ +\ 131 \\ \hline 9 \end{array}$$

$$\begin{array}{r} ^{1} \\ 264 \\ 594 \\ +\ 131 \\ \hline 89 \end{array}$$

$$\begin{array}{r} ^{1} \\ 264 \\ 594 \\ +\ 131 \\ \hline 989 \end{array}$$

Add.

1. $\begin{array}{r} 481 \\ +293 \\ \hline 774 \end{array}$

2. $\begin{array}{r} 276 \\ +392 \\ \hline \end{array}$

3. $\begin{array}{r} 354 \\ +490 \\ \hline \end{array}$

4. $\begin{array}{r} 581 \\ +248 \\ \hline \end{array}$

5. $\begin{array}{r} 280 \\ +128 \\ \hline \end{array}$

6. $\begin{array}{r} 596 \\ +\ 23 \\ \hline \end{array}$

7. $\begin{array}{r} 653 \\ +\ 91 \\ \hline \end{array}$

8. $\begin{array}{r} 793 \\ +\ 52 \\ \hline \end{array}$

9. $\begin{array}{r} 891 \\ +\ 24 \\ \hline \end{array}$

10. $\begin{array}{r} 479 \\ +\ 50 \\ \hline \end{array}$

11. $\begin{array}{r} 72 \\ 183 \\ +\ 94 \\ \hline \end{array}$

12. $\begin{array}{r} 242 \\ 383 \\ +\ 91 \\ \hline \end{array}$

13. $\begin{array}{r} 43 \\ 382 \\ +\ 71 \\ \hline \end{array}$

14. $\begin{array}{r} 61 \\ 482 \\ +\ 23 \\ \hline \end{array}$

15. $\begin{array}{r} 91 \\ 34 \\ +422 \\ \hline \end{array}$

16. Angie has 224 books. Her brother William has 91 books. How many books do they have together?

17. There are 670 books in one room of a library and 242 books in another room. How many books are there in both rooms?

Practicing Addition

Review the kinds of addition you have learned.

No trading.	Trading ones.	Trading tens.
	¹	¹
246	356	483
+ 43	+ 238	+ 346
289	594	829

Add.

1. 428
    +357
    785

2. 611
    +237

3. 564
    +291

4. 816
    +127

5. 463
    +331

6.   39
    126
    +417

7. 481
    234
    + 52

8. 807
     80
    + 91

9. 326
    249
    + 17

10. 381
    264
    + 73

11. 47
    + 6

12. 381
    +490

13. 137
    +604

14. 253
    +372

15. 430
    +118

16. 453
     14
     19
    + 6

17. 809
    120
    231
    + 17

18. 121
     13
    303
    + 32

19. 781
    234
    362
    +492

20.   14
    801
    731
    + 63

21. Suki delivered 237 newspapers on Friday, 128 on Saturday, and 209 on Sunday. How many newspapers did she deliver in all?

22. Suki earned $12.75 one week, $14.80 the next week, and $16.50 the week after that. How much did she earn in all?

Collection Problems

1. Marc collects rocks. He found 137 rocks at the seashore and 49 rocks on a beach at a lake. How many rocks did he find in all?   186

2. Nina collects sports cards. She has 151 baseball cards and 98 basketball cards. How many cards does Nina have in all?

3. Marge collects stamps. She has 285 stamps from the United States, 193 stamps from Asia, and 115 stamps from Europe. How many stamps does Marge have in all?

4. Stephen collects post cards. He has 109 post cards that show country scenes and 187 post cards that show city scenes. How many post cards does Stephen have in all?

5. Alberto collects coins. He has 326 pennies, 55 dimes, and 117 nickels. How many coins does Alberto have in all?

6. Helena collects shells. She had 55 shells and found 135 more shells. How many shells did she have then?

Trading Ones and Tens

Step 1
Add ones. Trade.

¹
286
179
+ 342
———
7

Step 2
Add tens. Trade.

^{2 1}
286
179
+ 342
———
07

Step 3
Add hundreds.

^{2 1}
286
179
+ 342
———
807

Add.

1. 237	2. 349	3. 568	4. 699	5. 768
+ 86	+ 75	+ 74	+ 37	+ 93
323				

6. 486	7. 375	8. 783	9. 567	10. 298
+195	+466	+197	+289	+246

11. 27	12. 137	13. 286	14. 347	15. 946
186	49	347	68	64
+294	+375	+ 29	+195	+136

16. 489	17. 653	18. 34	19. 897	20. 99
62	47	562	465	989
+ 34	+102	+ 98	+382	+475

 **Challenge**
Write in a column. Add.

21. 416 + 39 + 287 + 14

22. 9 + 289 + 36 + 7

23. 307 + 17 + 248 + 26

24. 27 + 386 + 6 + 33

25. 100 + 16 + 343 + 5

26. 99 + 37 + 465 + 8

Block-Out Addends

Use this box to find the numbers for the block-out problem.

387	23	94
392	278	77
504	716	189

Step 1
Think: The numbers under the shaded squares are 23, 94, and 504.

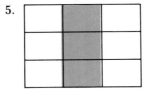

Step 2
Use these numbers to write and solve an addition problem.

$$\begin{array}{r} \overset{1}{2}3 \\ 94 \\ +\ 504 \\ \hline 621 \end{array}$$

Use the box above. Write an addition problem for each block-out. Then solve the problem.

1.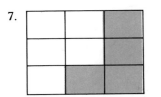

$$\begin{array}{r} 387 \\ 23 \\ +\ 392 \\ \hline 802 \end{array}$$

2.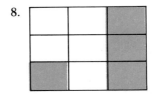

3.

4.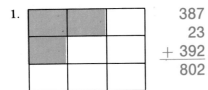

5.

6.

7.

8.

9.

Adding Thousands

Watch for these kinds of addition.

Trade ones.	Trade tens.	Trade ones and tens.	Trade ones, tens, and hundreds.
$\begin{array}{r} 1 \\ 1867 \\ +\ 2129 \\ \hline 3996 \end{array}$	$\begin{array}{r} 1 \\ 2094 \\ +\ 3333 \\ \hline 5427 \end{array}$	$\begin{array}{r} 1\ 1 \\ 6549 \\ +\ 2283 \\ \hline 8832 \end{array}$	$\begin{array}{r} 1\ 1\ 1 \\ 5767 \\ +\ 1456 \\ \hline 7223 \end{array}$

Find the sums.

1. $\begin{array}{r} 1462 \\ +5189 \\ \hline 6651 \end{array}$
2. $\begin{array}{r} 6528 \\ +1379 \\ \hline \end{array}$
3. $\begin{array}{r} 4234 \\ +2675 \\ \hline \end{array}$
4. $\begin{array}{r} 7896 \\ +1285 \\ \hline \end{array}$
5. $\begin{array}{r} 2643 \\ +3239 \\ \hline \end{array}$

6. $\begin{array}{r} 3461 \\ +2526 \\ \hline \end{array}$
7. $\begin{array}{r} 2732 \\ +5332 \\ \hline \end{array}$
8. $\begin{array}{r} 3631 \\ +4116 \\ \hline \end{array}$
9. $\begin{array}{r} 6321 \\ +2212 \\ \hline \end{array}$
10. $\begin{array}{r} 4412 \\ +3131 \\ \hline \end{array}$

11. $\begin{array}{r} 1542 \\ 2181 \\ +3364 \\ \hline \end{array}$
12. $\begin{array}{r} 462 \\ 3017 \\ +5517 \\ \hline \end{array}$
13. $\begin{array}{r} 6341 \\ 1219 \\ +2027 \\ \hline \end{array}$
14. $\begin{array}{r} 6320 \\ 1540 \\ +\ 929 \\ \hline \end{array}$
15. $\begin{array}{r} 339 \\ 2328 \\ +5234 \\ \hline \end{array}$

16. $\begin{array}{r} 347 \\ 1181 \\ 32 \\ +4651 \\ \hline \end{array}$
17. $\begin{array}{r} 4503 \\ 108 \\ 369 \\ +\ 25 \\ \hline \end{array}$
18. $\begin{array}{r} 21 \\ 1496 \\ 145 \\ +\ 368 \\ \hline \end{array}$
19. $\begin{array}{r} 947 \\ 2280 \\ 6539 \\ +\ 195 \\ \hline \end{array}$
20. $\begin{array}{r} 3939 \\ 1206 \\ 486 \\ +\ 36 \\ \hline \end{array}$

⭐ **Challenge**

Add.

21. $\begin{array}{r} 41{,}000 \\ 3698 \\ +82{,}465 \\ \hline \end{array}$
22. $\begin{array}{r} 7650 \\ 32{,}347 \\ +23{,}122 \\ \hline \end{array}$
23. $\begin{array}{r} 2386 \\ 56{,}432 \\ +13{,}421 \\ \hline \end{array}$
24. $\begin{array}{r} 650{,}387 \\ 763{,}491 \\ +204{,}705 \\ \hline \end{array}$

Estimating Sums

You can use rounding to estimate a sum.

Step 1
Round each number to the nearest thousand.

3987	4000
+ 2123	+ 2000

Step 2
Add the rounded numbers mentally.

$$\begin{array}{r} 4000 \\ + 2000 \\ \hline 6000 \end{array}$$ The sum is about 6000.

Round to the nearest thousand. Then add to estimate the sum.

1. $\begin{array}{r} 5045 \\ +4082 \end{array}$ $\begin{array}{r} 5000 \\ + 4000 \\ \hline 9000 \end{array}$

2. $\begin{array}{r} 5982 \\ +6841 \end{array}$

3. $\begin{array}{r} 1220 \\ +6842 \end{array}$

4. $\begin{array}{r} 3461 \\ +3990 \end{array}$

5. $\begin{array}{r} 4795 \\ +2047 \end{array}$

Estimate the sum by rounding to the nearest thousand. Then find the exact sum.

6. $\begin{array}{r} 6079 \\ +8524 \end{array}$

7. $\begin{array}{r} 8759 \\ +4115 \end{array}$

8. $\begin{array}{r} 7669 \\ +9465 \end{array}$

9. $\begin{array}{r} 2891 \\ +2163 \end{array}$

10. $\begin{array}{r} 3340 \\ +6887 \end{array}$

11. $\begin{array}{r} 7093 \\ +3498 \end{array}$

12. $\begin{array}{r} 4065 \\ +5273 \end{array}$

13. $\begin{array}{r} 5866 \\ +1989 \end{array}$

14. $\begin{array}{r} 9598 \\ +8429 \end{array}$

15. $\begin{array}{r} 6779 \\ +2862 \end{array}$

16. Carol Collins bought a tennis racket for $20.95, tennis shoes for $28.99, and tennis balls for $2.35. Round each amount to the nearest dollar. Then add to estimate how much Carol spent.

Vacation Problems

Wayne, Charlotte, Jennifer, and Adam Seymour went camping for two weeks. Solve these problems.

1. For supper one night the Seymours had hamburgers for $4.95 and milk for $1.25. How much did both cost?
$6.20

2. The Seymours traveled 138 kilometers Monday morning and 179 kilometers Monday afternoon. How far did they travel that Monday?

3. The Seymours took 48 photographs on Monday and 64 photographs on Tuesday. How many photographs did they take on those two days?

4. The Seymours bought one roll of film for $2.49 and one for $3.75. How much did they spend for the two rolls of film?

5. Pinetree Waterfall is 340 meters high. Roaring Rock Waterfall is 254 meters higher. How high is Roaring Rock Waterfall?

6. The Snake River is 846 kilometers long. Twisting River is 246 kilometers longer. How long is Twisting River?

7. Skytop Mountain is 2097 meters above sea level. Mount Brook is 2100 meters higher. How high is Mount Brook?

8. One night the Seymours spent $2.50 to camp, $0.95 for firewood, and $0.49 for matches. How much did they spend in all?

9. The Seymours drove 214 kilometers on Friday and 185 kilometers on Saturday. How many kilometers did they drive on those two days?

10. The Seymours sent 39 post cards the first week and 47 post cards the second week. How many post cards did they send in those two weeks?

11. Wayne and Charlotte spent $15 each for a river rafting trip. Adam and Jennifer spent $9 each. How much did they all spend?

12. Two trains passed the Seymours' car. One train had 128 cars. The other had 76 cars. How many cars were there on both trains?

Palindromes

Palindromes are numbers that read the same left to right or right to left.

747   4334   5225

You can make a palindrome by adding.

1964	Write the number.
+ 4691	Reverse the digits and add.
6655	This sum is not a palindrome.
+ 5566	Reverse the digits and add again.
12,221	This sum is a palindrome.

Reverse the digits. Then add. Repeat until you get a palindrome.

1. 2346
      2346
    + 6432
      8778

2. 4561

3. 2384

4. 6915

5. 3232

6. 7286

7. 5328

8. 1960

9. 8627

10. 5214

11. Find the palindrome for the year you were born.

12. Find the palindrome for the year 1860.

Review (pp. 55–66)
Add.

1.   173
   + 426

2.   614
   + 39

3.   272
   + 352

4.   365
   + 488

5. 1746
   + 3924

Trading Tens in Subtraction

In 43−28, you need more ones to subtract.

Step 1
Trade 1 ten
for 10 ones.

Step 2
Subtract ones.
Subtract tens.

$$
\begin{array}{r}
{\scriptstyle 3\ 13} \\
\cancel{4}\cancel{3} \\
-\ 28 \\
\hline
\end{array}
$$

$$
\begin{array}{r}
{\scriptstyle 3\ 13} \\
\cancel{4}\cancel{3} \\
-\ 28 \\
\hline
15
\end{array}
$$

Are there enough ones to subtract?
Write **yes** or **no**. Do not subtract.

1. 36 −18 no	2. 47 −19	3. 35 −20	4. 94 −48	5. 78 −21	6. 82 −54

Subtract.

7. 47 − 9	8. 52 − 8	9. 90 − 6	10. 34 −18	11. 51 −27	12. 83 −46
13. 70 −34	14. 91 −29	15. 84 −36	16. 62 −56	17. 60 −37	18. 65 −47

19. 35 people were on a bus. 17 people got off at the shopping center. How many people were left?

20. 31 people were on a streetcar. 19 people got off at the zoo. How many people were left?

Checking Subtraction

You can check subtraction by adding.

Subtract.   Check.

$$\begin{array}{r} 73 \\ -\,38 \\ \hline 35 \end{array}$$ — These numbers should be the same. — $$\begin{array}{r} 38 \\ +\,35 \\ \hline 73 \end{array}$$

Subtract. Write the check.

1. $\begin{array}{r} 47 \\ -29 \\ \hline 18 \end{array}$ $\begin{array}{r} 29 \\ +18 \\ \hline 47 \end{array}$
2. $\begin{array}{r} 60 \\ -38 \\ \hline 22 \end{array}$
3. $\begin{array}{r} 82 \\ -37 \\ \hline 45 \end{array}$
4. $\begin{array}{r} 92 \\ -58 \\ \hline 34 \end{array}$
5. $\begin{array}{r} 78 \\ -23 \\ \hline 55 \end{array}$

Subtract. Add to check.

6. $\begin{array}{r} 78 \\ -29 \end{array}$
7. $\begin{array}{r} 94 \\ -58 \end{array}$
8. $\begin{array}{r} 50 \\ -23 \end{array}$
9. $\begin{array}{r} 83 \\ -49 \end{array}$
10. $\begin{array}{r} 68 \\ -39 \end{array}$
11. $\begin{array}{r} 78 \\ -23 \end{array}$

12. $\begin{array}{r} 52 \\ -23 \end{array}$
13. $\begin{array}{r} 94 \\ -28 \end{array}$
14. $\begin{array}{r} 61 \\ -47 \end{array}$
15. $\begin{array}{r} 93 \\ -29 \end{array}$
16. $\begin{array}{r} 40 \\ -13 \end{array}$
17. $\begin{array}{r} 92 \\ -67 \end{array}$

18. $\begin{array}{r} 86 \\ -39 \end{array}$
19. $\begin{array}{r} 70 \\ -23 \end{array}$
20. $\begin{array}{r} 89 \\ -37 \end{array}$
21. $\begin{array}{r} 30 \\ -17 \end{array}$
22. $\begin{array}{r} 66 \\ -49 \end{array}$
23. $\begin{array}{r} 80 \\ -26 \end{array}$

24. $\begin{array}{r} 38 \\ -19 \end{array}$
25. $\begin{array}{r} 95 \\ -79 \end{array}$
26. $\begin{array}{r} 86 \\ -47 \end{array}$
27. $\begin{array}{r} 73 \\ -24 \end{array}$
28. $\begin{array}{r} 82 \\ -19 \end{array}$
29. $\begin{array}{r} 43 \\ -37 \end{array}$

30. $70-44$
31. $87-58$
32. $24-18$
33. $63-47$
34. $91-75$

35. $89-33$
36. $75-46$
37. $32-16$
38. $59-37$
39. $25-18$

Trading Hundreds to Subtract

Step 1
Subtract ones.
Trade 1 hundred for 10 tens.

$$\begin{array}{r} {\scriptstyle 7\ 13} \\ \cancel{8}\cancel{3}7 \\ -\ 261 \\ \hline 6 \end{array}$$

Step 2
Subtract tens.
Subtract hundreds.

$$\begin{array}{r} {\scriptstyle 7\ 13} \\ \cancel{8}\cancel{3}7 \\ -\ 261 \\ \hline 576 \end{array}$$

Check

$$\begin{array}{r} 576 \\ +\ 261 \\ \hline 837 \end{array}$$

The ones are done for you. Are there enough tens to subtract?
Write **yes** or **no**.

1. $\begin{array}{r} 423 \\ -331 \\ \hline 2 \end{array}$ no

2. $\begin{array}{r} 876 \\ -243 \\ \hline 3 \end{array}$

3. $\begin{array}{r} 584 \\ -291 \\ \hline 3 \end{array}$

4. $\begin{array}{r} 487 \\ -212 \\ \hline 5 \end{array}$

5. $\begin{array}{r} 523 \\ -290 \\ \hline 3 \end{array}$

Subtract. Check.

6. $\begin{array}{r} 428 \\ -\ 63 \\ \hline \end{array}$

7. $\begin{array}{r} 617 \\ -\ 42 \\ \hline \end{array}$

8. $\begin{array}{r} 703 \\ -\ 51 \\ \hline \end{array}$

9. $\begin{array}{r} 829 \\ -\ 44 \\ \hline \end{array}$

10. $\begin{array}{r} 314 \\ -\ 80 \\ \hline \end{array}$

11. $\begin{array}{r} 647 \\ -282 \\ \hline \end{array}$

12. $\begin{array}{r} 726 \\ -253 \\ \hline \end{array}$

13. $\begin{array}{r} 839 \\ -574 \\ \hline \end{array}$

14. $\begin{array}{r} 967 \\ -583 \\ \hline \end{array}$

15. $\begin{array}{r} 407 \\ -192 \\ \hline \end{array}$

 **Challenge**

16. 129 actors tried out for the school play. 17 of them got important parts. 49 of them got smaller parts. How many actors did not get parts in the play?

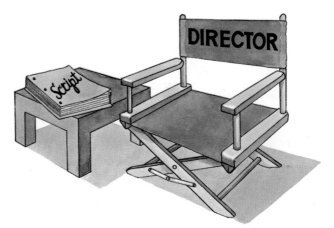

Trading Tens and Hundreds

When you need more ones and tens, you trade two times.

Step 1
Trade a ten.
Subtract ones.

$$\begin{array}{r} \overset{1\ 13}{8\cancel{2}\cancel{3}} \\ -\ 267 \\ \hline 6 \end{array}$$

Step 2
Trade a hundred.
Subtract tens.
Subtract hundreds.

$$\begin{array}{r} \overset{11}{\underset{}{7\ \cancel{8}\ \overset{1\ 13}{\cancel{2}\cancel{3}}}} \\ -\ 267 \\ \hline 556 \end{array}$$

Subtract. Check the first row.

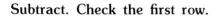

1.	2.	3.	4.	5.
723	611	544	837	936
− 68	− 34	− 69	− 59	− 78
655				

6.	7.	8.	9.	10.
814	423	652	913	734
−279	−165	−278	−278	−569

11. 930 − 278   12. 714 − 289   13. 826 − 578   14. 564 − 189

15. 637 − 289   16. 817 − 358   17. 545 − 386   18. 713 − 435

19. Paul and Margaret Hawkins are putting together a puzzle that has 353 pieces. They have put together 64 pieces. How many pieces are left?

20. Elizabeth and Frank Dodson are putting together a puzzle that has 624 pieces. They have put together 186 pieces. How many pieces are left?

Practicing Subtraction

Review the kinds of subtraction you have learned.

No trading.   Trading tens.   Trading hundreds.   Trading twice.

```
                          6 12                    8 12                          12
                                                                            7 2 14
       598               372                    926                          834
     − 326             − 144                  − 274                        − 568
     ─────             ─────                  ─────                        ─────
       272               228                    652                          266
```

Subtract. Check the first row.

1.	489 −236 253	2.	684 −237	3.	712 −285	4.	870 −236	5.	911 −567
6.	678 −234	7.	547 −283	8.	643 −368	9.	760 −289	10.	913 −479
11.	746 − 37	12.	826 − 58	13.	979 − 23	14.	746 − 29	15.	423 − 68
16.	689 −123	17.	670 −248	18.	713 −467	19.	890 −236	20.	375 −192

21. Neil is reading a book that has 364 pages. He has read 128 pages. How many pages does he have left to read?

22. Geneva's book has 424 pages. She has read 215 pages. How many pages does she have left to read?

Subtracting with Zeros

When you need more ones and tens, begin by trading 1 hundred for 10 tens.

Step 1
Trade 1 hundred
for 10 tens.

$$\begin{array}{r} \overset{5\ 10}{\cancel{6}\cancel{0}0} \\ -\ 239 \\ \hline \end{array}$$

Step 2
Trade 1 ten
for 10 ones.

$$\begin{array}{r} \overset{\quad 9}{\overset{5\ \cancel{10}\ 10}{\cancel{6}\cancel{0}\cancel{0}}} \\ -\ 239 \\ \hline \end{array}$$

Step 3
Subtract.

$$\begin{array}{r} \overset{\quad 9}{\overset{5\ \cancel{10}\ 10}{\cancel{6}\cancel{0}\cancel{0}}} \\ -\ 239 \\ \hline 361 \end{array}$$

Will Trade! 1 hundred for 10 tens

Subtract. Check the first row.

1. $\begin{array}{r}400\\-189\\\hline 211\end{array}$	2. $\begin{array}{r}800\\-374\\\hline\end{array}$	3. $\begin{array}{r}900\\-618\\\hline\end{array}$	4. $\begin{array}{r}700\\-234\\\hline\end{array}$	5. $\begin{array}{r}200\\-\ \ 34\\\hline\end{array}$
6. $\begin{array}{r}500\\-\ \ 63\\\hline\end{array}$	7. $\begin{array}{r}700\\-\ \ 89\\\hline\end{array}$	8. $\begin{array}{r}900\\-\ \ 54\\\hline\end{array}$	9. $\begin{array}{r}600\\-198\\\hline\end{array}$	10. $\begin{array}{r}700\\-249\\\hline\end{array}$
11. $\begin{array}{r}800\\-436\\\hline\end{array}$	12. $\begin{array}{r}500\\-134\\\hline\end{array}$	13. $\begin{array}{r}700\\-399\\\hline\end{array}$	14. $\begin{array}{r}600\\-\ \ 87\\\hline\end{array}$	15. $\begin{array}{r}300\\-184\\\hline\end{array}$

Subtract.

16. $\begin{array}{r}708\\-249\\\hline\end{array}$	17. $\begin{array}{r}780\\-299\\\hline\end{array}$	18. $\begin{array}{r}610\\-234\\\hline\end{array}$	19. $\begin{array}{r}904\\-666\\\hline\end{array}$	20. $\begin{array}{r}505\\-278\\\hline\end{array}$
21. $\begin{array}{r}303\\-260\\\hline\end{array}$	22. $\begin{array}{r}480\\-195\\\hline\end{array}$	23. $\begin{array}{r}605\\-394\\\hline\end{array}$	24. $\begin{array}{r}707\\-658\\\hline\end{array}$	25. $\begin{array}{r}903\\-444\\\hline\end{array}$
26. $\begin{array}{r}604\\-352\\\hline\end{array}$	27. $\begin{array}{r}760\\-273\\\hline\end{array}$	28. $\begin{array}{r}404\\-125\\\hline\end{array}$	29. $\begin{array}{r}960\\-774\\\hline\end{array}$	30. $\begin{array}{r}805\\-216\\\hline\end{array}$

Subtraction Code

Crack the code to answer the riddle.

What begins with *p* and ends with *e* and has more than a thousand letters?

Code	o	s	f	e	c	p	t	i
	194	17	101	531	148	176	164	157

Subtract.

1. 600
   − 424
   176, p

2. 303
   − 109

3. 200
   − 183

4. 400
   − 236

5. 600
   − 406

6. 707
   − 606

7. 500
   − 399

8. 470
   − 313

9. 800
   − 652

10. 800
    − 269

11. The answer is: ___ ___ ___ ___   ___ ___ ___ ___ ___ ___

       1.   2.   3.   4.   5.   6.   7.   8.   9.   10.

T-shirt Problems

Jungle Trading Post

T-shirt Inventory

	Lion	Gorilla	Alligator	Elephant	Tiger
Red	90	302	400	120	140
Yellow	608	140	350	500	880
Blue	120	900	90	302	200
Green	370	200	700	300	606

Use the chart to solve each problem.

1. How many fewer green lion T-shirts than yellow lion T-shirts? 238

2. How many more yellow elephant T-shirts than red elephant T-shirts?

3. How many fewer red gorilla T-shirts than blue gorilla T-shirts?

4. How many more green alligator T-shirts than yellow alligator T-shirts?

5. How many more green tiger T-shirts than blue tiger T-shirts?

6. How many fewer green elephant T-shirts than yellow elephant T-shirts?

7. How many more yellow lion T-shirts than red lion T-shirts?

8. How many fewer yellow alligator T-shirts than green alligator T-shirts?

Subtracting Thousands

Watch for these kinds of subtraction.

Trade tens.	Trade hundreds.	Trade tens and hundreds.	Trade tens, hundreds, and thousands.

$$\begin{array}{r} \scriptstyle 5\ 12 \\ 48\cancel{6}\cancel{2} \\ -\ 3628 \\ \hline 1234 \end{array}$$

$$\begin{array}{r} \scriptstyle 6\ 12 \\ 8\cancel{7}26 \\ -\ 7473 \\ \hline 1253 \end{array}$$

$$\begin{array}{r} \scriptstyle 11 \\ \scriptstyle 4\ \cancel{1}\ 13 \\ 6\cancel{5}2\cancel{3} \\ -\ 2168 \\ \hline 4355 \end{array}$$

$$\begin{array}{r} \scriptstyle 14\ 17 \\ \scriptstyle 3\ \cancel{4}\ \cancel{7}\ 16 \\ \cancel{4}\cancel{5}\cancel{8}\cancel{6} \\ -\ 1798 \\ \hline 2788 \end{array}$$

Subtract.

1. $\begin{array}{r} 6237 \\ -1899 \\ \hline 4338 \end{array}$
   2. $\begin{array}{r} 7915 \\ -2586 \\ \hline \end{array}$
   3. $\begin{array}{r} 5688 \\ -2397 \\ \hline \end{array}$
   4. $\begin{array}{r} 2634 \\ -1518 \\ \hline \end{array}$
   5. $\begin{array}{r} 8285 \\ -3768 \\ \hline \end{array}$

6. $\begin{array}{r} 7143 \\ -2382 \\ \hline \end{array}$
   7. $\begin{array}{r} 9346 \\ -2228 \\ \hline \end{array}$
   8. $\begin{array}{r} 5312 \\ -1897 \\ \hline \end{array}$
   9. $\begin{array}{r} 8293 \\ -2148 \\ \hline \end{array}$
   10. $\begin{array}{r} 9143 \\ -4867 \\ \hline \end{array}$

11. $\begin{array}{r} 7817 \\ -2382 \\ \hline \end{array}$
   12. $\begin{array}{r} 3565 \\ -1446 \\ \hline \end{array}$
   13. $\begin{array}{r} 6877 \\ -4495 \\ \hline \end{array}$
   14. $\begin{array}{r} 5463 \\ -2574 \\ \hline \end{array}$
   15. $\begin{array}{r} 4763 \\ -3644 \\ \hline \end{array}$

16. $\begin{array}{r} 9436 \\ -7218 \\ \hline \end{array}$
   17. $\begin{array}{r} 5356 \\ -3168 \\ \hline \end{array}$
   18. $\begin{array}{r} 8547 \\ -6669 \\ \hline \end{array}$
   19. $\begin{array}{r} 7879 \\ -4585 \\ \hline \end{array}$
   20. $\begin{array}{r} 3625 \\ -1776 \\ \hline \end{array}$

Challenge
Subtract.

21. $\begin{array}{r} 85,753 \\ -\ \ 1489 \\ \hline \end{array}$
   22. $\begin{array}{r} 73,264 \\ -\ \ 8927 \\ \hline \end{array}$
   23. $\begin{array}{r} 74,539 \\ -21,268 \\ \hline \end{array}$
   24. $\begin{array}{r} 646,743 \\ -425,852 \\ \hline \end{array}$

Estimating Differences

You can use rounded numbers to estimate a difference. This
will help you check to see that your answers are correct.

8756	9000
− 2939	− 3000
5817 exact difference	**6000** estimated difference

Since the exact difference and the estimated difference are close,
5817 is a sensible answer.

Round to choose the correct answer.

1. 6424
   −3988
   (1565, 2436, or 4210) 2436

2. 9985
   −5140
   (3045, 5445, or 4845)

3. 7721
   −2122
   (5599, 9955, or 5259)

4. 9229
   −4980
   (4249, 3685, or 1250)

5. 8886
   −7194
   (692, 1692, or 2692)

6. 3780
   −1140
   (2640, 1040, or 3850)

Estimate the difference. Then find the exact difference.

7. 8460
   −7109

8. 9479
   −4465

9. 7263
   −5890

10. 5472
    −1198

11. 6798
    −2657

12. 4694
    −2802

13. 5597
    −1040

14. 3767
    −2059

15. 9639
    −5774

16. 8785
    −7149

17. $24.18
    − 12.81

18. $97.95
    − 23.90

19. $64.65
    − 57.24

20. $39.43
    − 12.75

21. $76.42
    − 47.24

Subtracting with Zeros

Start trading at thousands.

Step 1
Trade.

$$
\begin{array}{r}
{\scriptstyle 9\ \ 9} \\
{\scriptstyle 4\ \cancel{10}\ \cancel{10}\ 10} \\
\cancel{5000} \\
-\ 3281 \\
\end{array}
$$

Step 2
Subtract.

$$
\begin{array}{r}
{\scriptstyle 9\ \ 9} \\
{\scriptstyle 4\ \cancel{10}\ \cancel{10}\ 10} \\
\cancel{5000} \\
-\ 3281 \\
\hline
1719 \\
\end{array}
$$

Subtract. Check the first row of problems.

1. 6000
   −2467
   3533

2. 8000
   −3493

3. 4000
   −1624

4. 9000
   −6782

5. 1000
   − 645

6. 5000
   − 137

7. 7000
   − 498

8. 3000
   − 117

9. 2000
   − 945

10. 8000
    −3789

Subtract.

11. 6004
    −3477

12. 8001
    −2497

13. 4003
    −1176

14. 6009
    −4026

15. 4080
    −2642

16. 1900
    − 91

17. 8006
    −3095

18. 9010
    −3599

19. 6030
    −1736

20. 2800
    −1960

Review (pp. 55-77)
Add or subtract.

1. 426
   +387

2. 417
   − 39

3. 1483
   +6425

4. 400
   −311

5. 825
   +677

Addition and Subtraction Practice

Watch for + and −.

Add or subtract.

1. 478 +206 **684**	2. 67 −49	3. 679 +186	4. 80 −34	5. 986 +264
6. 23 167 + 89	7. 700 −239	8. 423 26 +517	9. 7143 +2829	10. 901 −238
11. 3146 +9239	12. 1179 +2378	13. 5143 −1896	14. 8000 −2496	15. 6179 +1514
16. 7001 −2348	17. 7000 − 814	18. 36,147 1829 + 617	19. 8000 −2713	20. 27 114 +6128

 Calculate

First add or subtract from left to right. Then add or subtract from right to left. Do you get the same answer?

21. $43+26-22+17-38+64$

22. $83-77+69-24-13+20$

Spaceship Problems

1. Spaceship Aries astronauts spend 237 hours getting ready for their trip. Spaceship Sagittarius astronauts spend 375 hours. How much more time do the Sagittarius astronauts spend?   138 hours

2. The astronauts from Spaceship Aries spend 26 hours on the moon. Then the astronauts from Spaceship Sagittarius spend 73 hours on the moon. For how many hours are there astronauts on the moon?

3. Spaceship Aries flies for 147 hours. Spaceship Sagittarius flies for 195 hours. How much longer does Spaceship Sagittarius fly?

4. Spaceship Aries is 109 meters long. After the first stage drops off, the spaceship is 68 meters long. How long is the first stage?

5. After the first stage drops off, the spaceship is 68 meters long. After the second stage drops off, the spaceship is 44 meters long. How long is the second stage?

6. Spaceship Aries brings back 91 kilograms of moon rocks. Spaceship Sagittarius brings back 168 kilograms. How many kilograms do both spaceships bring back?

Adding Money

Add money the same way you add whole numbers.

```
    2              1            1  1
  $4.39         $5.42        $1.18
   2.16       +  2.73         4.73
+  1.28         $8.15      +  3.58
  $7.83                      $9.49
```

Add. Remember to use $ and . in your answers.

1. $2.79 + 3.28 $6.07	2. $4.28 + 3.57	3. $5.70 + 2.98	4. $3.45 + 2.75	5. $4.46 + 2.81
6. $0.85 2.37 + 1.29	7. $2.13 0.24 + 1.52	8. $3.78 1.29 + 1.06	9. $0.09 0.27 + 3.92	10. $0.46 1.11 + 5.22
11. $4.13 2.24 + 0.32	12. $5.67 0.28 + 1.89	13. $4.09 1.26 + 0.18	14. $7.99 1.08 + 0.37	15. $8.62 0.44 + 0.50

16. Kiyo spent $3.40 for wooden beads, $2.76 for clay beads, and $1.47 for glass beads. How much did she spend in all?

17. Juan spent $6.27 for beads, $4.35 for shells, and $2.79 for seeds. How much did he spend in all?

18. Christopher spent $0.70 for string, $3.89 for glass beads, and $2.50 for clay beads. How much did he spend in all?

Subtracting Money

Subtract money the same way you subtract whole numbers.

$$\begin{array}{r} \overset{4\ 11}{\$6.5\cancel{1}} \\ -\ 2.37 \\ \hline \$4.14 \end{array}$$

$$\begin{array}{r} \overset{4\ \ 12}{\$5.\cancel{2}9} \\ -\ 1.87 \\ \hline \$3.42 \end{array}$$

$$\begin{array}{r} \overset{\ \ \ \ 11}{\overset{4\ \ \cancel{12}\ 13}{\$5.\cancel{2}\cancel{3}}} \\ -\ 3.84 \\ \hline \$1.39 \end{array}$$

Subtract. Remember to use $ and . in your answers.

1. $8.31 − 3.57 $4.74	2. $9.81 − 6.39	3. $8.03 − 1.84	4. $7.03 − 1.48	5. $8.74 − 5.26
6. $7.44 − 2.15	7. $7.49 − 4.56	8. $9.11 − 1.84	9. $7.00 − 4.68	10. $6.07 − 4.56
11. $9.01 − 4.67	12. $4.63 − 0.39	13. $8.00 − 2.95	14. $5.74 − 1.89	15. $8.31 − 3.26

16. Michael bought a book for $3.98. He gave the clerk $5.00. How much change did he receive?

 **Calculate**

17. $374,082.65
   269,719.39
+ 80,255.01

18. $9,246.35
− 8,573.98

19. $429,651.63
  107,346.50
+ 992,163.36

20. $7,498.03
− 5,365.99

Sale Problems

Use the prices shown in the pictures. Add or subtract to solve each problem.

1. How much more does the shirt cost than the hat? 50¢

2. Jo Anne buys the vase and the plant. How much does she spend?

3. Jackson has $3.00 to spend. He wants to buy the lamp. How much more money does he need?

4. Rick buys the shirt, the book, and the record. How much money does he spend?

5. How much more does the lamp cost than the jump rope?

6. Jackson buys the umbrella and the kite. How much does he spend?

7. How much more does the wagon cost than the book?

8. How much more does the umbrella cost than the book?

9. How much do the lamp and the ironing board cost together?

10. How much do the wagon and the kite cost together?

11. What two items could be bought for exactly $5.25?

12. What two items could be bought for exactly $10.00?

13. Maria has $5.00 to spend. Which item can she buy and have 25¢ left?

14. What items could be bought for exactly $1.70?

15. Jo Anne pays for the vase and the plant with a $10.00 bill. How much change should she receive?

16. Rick pays for the shirt, the book, and the record with a $20.00 bill. How much change should he receive?

Chapter Review

Add.   (ex. 1-3: p. 55),   (ex. 4-6: p. 57),
  (ex. 7-10: p. 60),   (ex. 11-15: p. 62)

1. 28	2. 12	3. 47	4. 610	5. 723
14	89	23	245	283
+36	+ 5	+15	+192	+ 81

6. 390	7. 37	8. 465	9. 987	10. 446
426	163	579	325	587
+133	+245	+306	+213	+709

11. 2867	12. 1096	13. 5649	14. 8698	15. 7786
+3124	+4342	+3273	+2435	+2375

Subtract.   (ex. 16-18: p. 67),   (ex. 19-20: p. 69),   (ex. 21-23: p. 70),
  (ex. 24-25: p. 72),   (ex. 26-28: p. 75),   (ex. 29-30: p. 77)

16. 52	17. 80	18. 34	19. 867	20. 459
−46	−44	−16	−583	−264

21. 575	22. 733	23. 845	24. 500	25. 300
−386	−569	−459	−328	−165

26. 3821	27. 4513	28. 7432	29. 6000	30. 1000
−1439	−2374	−5556	−4692	− 697

Add or subtract.   (ex. 31-35: pp. 80-81)

31. $1.65	32. $6.00	33. $7.95	34. $2.09	35. $9.99
3.84	− 3.95	− 4.66	3.54	2.39
+ 6.28			+ 7.47	+ 4.65

Chapter Test

Add.

1.	16	2.	75	3.	364	4.	871	5.	697
	25		35		233		654		435
	+14		+15		+142		+329		+779

6.	1549	7.	7688	8.	4376	9.	8989	10.	3768
	+2336		+3378		+4275		+2463		+2345

Subtract.

11.	96	12.	75	13.	423	14.	717	15.	545
	−49		−26		−232		−388		−256

16.	400	17.	4635	18.	6000	19.	203	20.	6732
	−169		−2316		−1479		−185		−4587

Add or subtract.

21.	$7.56	22.	$9.85	23.	$5.00	24.	$9.09	25.	$3.00
	− 4.66		3.62		+ 6.67		+ 7.59		6.08
			+ 5.49						+ 4.75

Brush Up

Multiply or add.

1. 4×6
2. 8×6
3. 8×8
4. 5×7
5. 9×8

6. 9×3
7. 7×5
8. 4×3
9. 6×6
10. 5×8

11. 9×9
12. 2×6
13. 4×9
14. 5×5
15. 6×9

16. $21 + 4$
17. $45 + 4$
18. $27 + 9$
19. $35 + 4$
20. $48 + 6$

21. $42 + 6$
22. $36 + 8$
23. $15 + 5$
24. $27 + 2$
25. $63 + 7$

Add.

26. $\begin{array}{r} 564 \\ +940 \end{array}$
27. $\begin{array}{r} 464 \\ +580 \end{array}$
28. $\begin{array}{r} 76 \\ +380 \end{array}$
29. $\begin{array}{r} 369 \\ +410 \end{array}$
30. $\begin{array}{r} 68 \\ +680 \end{array}$

31. $\begin{array}{r} 879 \\ +14,650 \end{array}$
32. $\begin{array}{r} 250 \\ +2100 \end{array}$
33. $\begin{array}{r} 2849 \\ +24,420 \end{array}$
34. $\begin{array}{r} 318 \\ +650 \end{array}$
35. $\begin{array}{r} 1205 \\ +7230 \end{array}$

Write the numbers.

36. 5 tens
37. 9 hundreds
38. 6 thousands

39. 76 thousands
40. 138 thousands
41. 80 million

Round each number to the nearest hundred.

42. 853
43. 777
44. 928
45. 425
46. 356

47. 9443
48. 3089
49. 8422
50. 6599
51. 2105

52. 381
53. 1659
54. 664
55. 7801
56. 988

CHAPTER 4
Multiplication

Using Multiplication at Work

Jim Brickley is a cattle rancher. His workers can brand 6 cattle in one hour. The workers work 8 hours a day, 5 days a week. Jim multiplies $6 \times 8 \times 5$ to find how many cattle the workers can brand in one week. They can brand 240 cattle in one week.

Multiplying Tens

If you can add, then you can multiply.

Step 1 Add ones.	Step 2 Add tens.	Step 1 Multiply ones.	Step 2 Multiply tens.

$$
\begin{array}{r} 21 \\ 21 \\ 21 \\ + 21 \\ \hline 4 \end{array}
\qquad
\begin{array}{r} 21 \\ 21 \\ 21 \\ + 21 \\ \hline 84 \end{array}
\qquad
\begin{array}{r} 21 \\ \times\ 4 \\ \hline 4 \end{array}
\qquad
\begin{array}{r} 21 \\ \times\ 4 \\ \hline 84 \end{array}
$$

Solve by adding.

1. $\begin{array}{r} 32 \\ \times\ 2 \\ \hline \end{array}$ $\begin{array}{r} 32 \\ +32 \\ \hline 64 \end{array}$

2. $\begin{array}{r} 40 \\ \times\ 4 \\ \hline \end{array}$

3. $\begin{array}{r} 51 \\ \times\ 2 \\ \hline \end{array}$

4. $\begin{array}{r} 24 \\ \times\ 2 \\ \hline \end{array}$

5. $\begin{array}{r} 43 \\ \times\ 3 \\ \hline \end{array}$

Multiply. Check the first row by adding.

6. $\begin{array}{r} 21 \\ \times\ 3 \\ \hline \end{array}$

7. $\begin{array}{r} 42 \\ \times\ 4 \\ \hline \end{array}$

8. $\begin{array}{r} 50 \\ \times\ 5 \\ \hline \end{array}$

9. $\begin{array}{r} 32 \\ \times\ 3 \\ \hline \end{array}$

10. $\begin{array}{r} 44 \\ \times\ 2 \\ \hline \end{array}$

11. $\begin{array}{r} 14 \\ \times\ 2 \\ \hline \end{array}$

12. $\begin{array}{r} 71 \\ \times\ 4 \\ \hline \end{array}$

13. $\begin{array}{r} 60 \\ \times\ 5 \\ \hline \end{array}$

14. $\begin{array}{r} 73 \\ \times\ 3 \\ \hline \end{array}$

15. $\begin{array}{r} 82 \\ \times\ 2 \\ \hline \end{array}$

16. $\begin{array}{r} 80 \\ \times\ 5 \\ \hline \end{array}$

17. $\begin{array}{r} 93 \\ \times\ 3 \\ \hline \end{array}$

18. $\begin{array}{r} 53 \\ \times\ 3 \\ \hline \end{array}$

19. $\begin{array}{r} 70 \\ \times\ 9 \\ \hline \end{array}$

20. $\begin{array}{r} 91 \\ \times\ 8 \\ \hline \end{array}$

21. $\begin{array}{r} 21 \\ \times\ 6 \\ \hline \end{array}$

22. $\begin{array}{r} 63 \\ \times\ 3 \\ \hline \end{array}$

23. $\begin{array}{r} 50 \\ \times\ 3 \\ \hline \end{array}$

24. $\begin{array}{r} 22 \\ \times\ 4 \\ \hline \end{array}$

25. $\begin{array}{r} 20 \\ \times\ 5 \\ \hline \end{array}$

26. $\begin{array}{r} 11 \\ \times\ 7 \\ \hline \end{array}$

27. $\begin{array}{r} 42 \\ \times\ 3 \\ \hline \end{array}$

28. $\begin{array}{r} 70 \\ \times\ 3 \\ \hline \end{array}$

29. $\begin{array}{r} 51 \\ \times\ 5 \\ \hline \end{array}$

30. 62×4

31. 33×2

32. 41×5

33. 41×4

34. 33×3

Multiply and Add

4 times 3, plus 4 = ▢

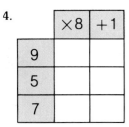

	×3	+4
4	12	16

$4 \times 3 = 12,\ 12 + 4 = 16$

Copy the tables. Fill in the missing numbers.

1.

	×9	+3
4	36	39
6		
8		

2.

	×3	+5
4		
7		
8		

3.

	×5	+6
6		
9		
4		

4.

	×8	+1
9		
5		
7		

5.

	×3	+5
3		
8		
6		

6.

	×4	+6
7		
8		
5		

7.

	×7	+2
8		
2		
4		

8.

	×3	+8
7		
5		
8		

9.

	×2	+9
3		
8		
6		

Trading in Multiplication

Step 1
Multiply ones.
Trade 10 ones for 1 ten.

$$
\begin{array}{r}
^{1}\,15 \\
\times\ \ 3 \\
\hline
5
\end{array}
$$

$3 \times 5 = 15$
$15 = 1$ ten, 5 ones

Step 2
Multiply tens.
Add the traded ten.

$$
\begin{array}{r}
^{1}\,15 \\
\times\ \ 3 \\
\hline
45
\end{array}
$$

3×1 ten $= 3$ tens
3 tens $+ 1$ ten $= 4$ tens

Add to check.

$$
\begin{array}{r}
15 \\
15 \\
+\ 15 \\
\hline
45
\end{array}
$$

Multiply. Check the first row by adding.

1. 23
    × 4
    —
    92

2. 59
    × 2

3. 53
    × 4

4. 64
    × 3

5. 36
    × 3

6. 22
    × 8

7. 34
    × 3

8. 54
    × 6

9. 67
    × 3

10. 83
    × 5

11. 94
    × 3

12. 34
    × 6

13. 92
    × 5

14. 62
    × 8

15. 73
    × 8

16. 52
    × 7

17. 84
    × 7

18. 99
    × 3

19. 49
    × 7

20. 76
    × 8

21. 87
    × 6

22. 93
    × 4

23. 67
    × 5

24. 27
    × 8

25. The Earth goes around the Sun once in 12 months. How many months does it take for the Earth to go around the Sun 9 times?

26. There are 24 hours in a day. How many hours are there in a week? (There are 7 days in a week.)

Multiplying Three Factors

To multiply three factors, first multiply any two of the factors.
Then multiply their product by the third factor. You can
multiply the factors in any order.

$7 \times 5 \times 4$

$35 \times 4 = 140$

$7 \times 5 \times 4$

$7 \times 20 = 140$

$7 \times 5 \times 4$

$5 \times 28 = 140$

Multiply.

1. $2 \times 6 \times 3$ 36
2. $5 \times 7 \times 3$
3. $4 \times 6 \times 5$

4. $4 \times 5 \times 3$
5. $3 \times 4 \times 5$
6. $6 \times 7 \times 1$

7. $7 \times 6 \times 4$
8. $5 \times 3 \times 9$
9. $8 \times 3 \times 4$

10. $9 \times 3 \times 2$
11. $8 \times 2 \times 2$
12. $2 \times 9 \times 4$

13. $5 \times 4 \times 3$
14. $2 \times 9 \times 5$
15. $4 \times 7 \times 6$

16. $7 \times 5 \times 4$
17. $8 \times 2 \times 7$
18. $9 \times 3 \times 4$

19. $15 \times 2 \times 1$
20. $40 \times 3 \times 2$
21. $20 \times 6 \times 3$

22. $8 \times 9 \times 6$
23. $30 \times 4 \times 2$
24. $5 \times 9 \times 7$

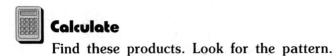 **Calculate**

Find these products. Look for the pattern.

25a. 3×37
  b. 6×37
  c. 9×37
  d. 12×37
  e. 15×37
  f. 18×37
  g. 21×37
  h. 24×37

26a. Can you find 27×37 without
  multiplying?
  b. Write the next product in the
  pattern.

Game Ball Problems

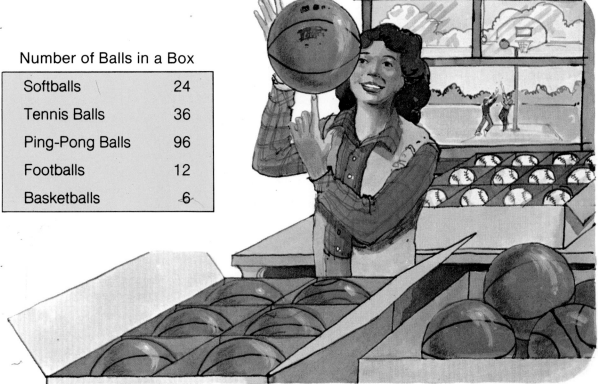

Number of Balls in a Box	
Softballs	24
Tennis Balls	36
Ping-Pong Balls	96
Footballs	12
Basketballs	6

The Game Ball Company makes and sells balls for different sports. Use the chart to solve each problem.

1. How many softballs in 2 boxes?   48

2. How many footballs in 4 boxes?

3. How many tennis balls in 3 boxes?

4. How many footballs in 8 boxes?

5. How many basketballs in 9 boxes?

6. How many softballs in 9 boxes?

7. One day the company shipped 4 boxes of softballs and 6 boxes of footballs. How many balls did they ship that day?

8. On another day they shipped 3 boxes of tennis balls and 5 boxes of ping-pong balls. How many balls did they ship that day?

9. Michaelson's Sports Store ordered 3 boxes of tennis balls and 7 boxes of basketballs. How many balls did they order in all?

10. Downtown Sports ordered 6 boxes of ping-pong balls and 7 boxes of basketballs. How many balls did they order in all?

Multiplying Hundreds

$501 + 501 + 501 + 501 = \boxed{?}$

You can add or multiply to solve this problem.

Add ones.   Multiply ones.
Add tens.   Multiply tens.
Add hundreds.   Multiply hundreds.

```
  501
  501
  501            501
+ 501          ×   4
 2004           2004
```

Solve by adding.

1. 331 331	2. 220	3. 504	4. 723	5. 421
× 2 +331	× 3	× 2	× 3	× 2
662				

Multiply. Check the first row by adding.

6. 224	7. 601	8. 324	9. 722	10. 421
× 2	× 7	× 2	× 3	× 4

11. 103	12. 402	13. 433	14. 811	15. 204
× 3	× 4	× 3	× 5	× 2

16. 412	17. 213	18. 142	19. 423	20. 311
× 3	× 3	× 2	× 3	× 5

21. 601 × 4	22. 132 × 3	23. 512 × 4	24. 731 × 2	25. 633 × 2

Trading Ones and Tens

Step 1
Multiply ones.
Trade ones.

Step 2
Multiply tens.
Add traded tens.
Trade tens.

Step 3
Multiply hundreds.
Add traded hundreds.

$$\begin{array}{r} \overset{1}{576} \\ \times \quad 3 \\ \hline 8 \end{array}$$

$3 \times 6 = 18$

$$\begin{array}{r} \overset{2\ 1}{576} \\ \times \quad 3 \\ \hline 28 \end{array}$$

3×7 tens $= 21$ tens

21 tens $+ 1$ ten $= 22$ tens

$$\begin{array}{r} \overset{2\ 1}{576} \\ \times \quad 3 \\ \hline 1728 \end{array}$$

3×5 hundreds $= 15$ hundreds

15 hundreds $+ 2$ hundreds $= 17$ hundreds

Solve by adding.

1. $\begin{array}{r} 856 \\ \times \quad 2 \\ \hline \end{array}$ $\begin{array}{r} 856 \\ + 856 \\ \hline 1712 \end{array}$

2. $\begin{array}{r} 674 \\ \times \quad 4 \\ \hline \end{array}$

3. $\begin{array}{r} 468 \\ \times \quad 2 \\ \hline \end{array}$

4. $\begin{array}{r} 374 \\ \times \quad 3 \\ \hline \end{array}$

5. $\begin{array}{r} 274 \\ \times \quad 3 \\ \hline \end{array}$

Multiply.

6. $\begin{array}{r} 468 \\ \times \quad 3 \\ \hline \end{array}$

7. $\begin{array}{r} 627 \\ \times \quad 6 \\ \hline \end{array}$

8. $\begin{array}{r} 584 \\ \times \quad 7 \\ \hline \end{array}$

9. $\begin{array}{r} 746 \\ \times \quad 3 \\ \hline \end{array}$

10. $\begin{array}{r} 924 \\ \times \quad 8 \\ \hline \end{array}$

11. $\begin{array}{r} 378 \\ \times \quad 9 \\ \hline \end{array}$

12. $\begin{array}{r} 436 \\ \times \quad 8 \\ \hline \end{array}$

13. $\begin{array}{r} 927 \\ \times \quad 8 \\ \hline \end{array}$

14. $\begin{array}{r} 724 \\ \times \quad 6 \\ \hline \end{array}$

15. $\begin{array}{r} 627 \\ \times \quad 8 \\ \hline \end{array}$

16. $\begin{array}{r} 567 \\ \times \quad 3 \\ \hline \end{array}$

17. $\begin{array}{r} 639 \\ \times \quad 8 \\ \hline \end{array}$

18. $\begin{array}{r} 368 \\ \times \quad 7 \\ \hline \end{array}$

19. $\begin{array}{r} 956 \\ \times \quad 2 \\ \hline \end{array}$

20. $\begin{array}{r} 389 \\ \times \quad 5 \\ \hline \end{array}$

21. 635×6

22. 479×5

23. 863×5

24. 495×7

25. 847×7

26. 619×8

27. 475×3

28. 785×9

29. 654×4

30. 839×4

Invention Problems

Multiply to find the year each was invented.

1. Telephone

$$\begin{array}{r} 268 \\ \times\ 7 \\ \hline 1876 \end{array}$$

2. Bicycle

$$\begin{array}{r} 227 \\ \times\ 8 \\ \hline \end{array}$$

3. Television

$$\begin{array}{r} 321 \\ \times\ 6 \\ \hline \end{array}$$

4. Nylon

$$\begin{array}{r} 215 \\ \times\ 9 \\ \hline \end{array}$$

5. Motorcycle

$$\begin{array}{r} 377 \\ \times\ 5 \\ \hline \end{array}$$

6. Sewing Machine

$$\begin{array}{r} 358 \\ \times\ 5 \\ \hline \end{array}$$

7. Automobile

$$\begin{array}{r} 377 \\ \times\ 5 \\ \hline \end{array}$$

8. Zipper

$$\begin{array}{r} 631 \\ \times\ 3 \\ \hline \end{array}$$

9. Telegraph

$$\begin{array}{r} 469 \\ \times\ 4 \\ \hline \end{array}$$

10. Refrigerator

$$\begin{array}{r} 917 \\ \times\ 2 \\ \hline \end{array}$$

11. Camera

$$\begin{array}{r} 913 \\ \times\ 2 \\ \hline \end{array}$$

12. Safety Pin

$$\begin{array}{r} 365 \\ \times\ 5 \\ \hline \end{array}$$

A game for one player.

Get ready:
Get paper and a pencil.

To play, use digits

2 3 4 5 6 7 8 9

Use each digit only once in each problem. Make ten different multiplication problems like this:

$$
\begin{array}{r}
936 \\
\times\ \ 7 \\
\hline
6552
\end{array}
$$

Each product must be greater than 6000.

Multiplying Thousands

Step 1
Multiply ones.
Trade ones.

$$\begin{array}{r} {\scriptstyle 2} \\ 4638 \\ \times \quad 3 \\ \hline 4 \end{array}$$

Step 2
Multiply tens.
Add traded tens.

$$\begin{array}{r} {\scriptstyle 1\,2} \\ 4638 \\ \times \quad 3 \\ \hline 14 \end{array}$$

Step 3
Multiply hundreds.
Add traded hundreds.

$$\begin{array}{r} {\scriptstyle 1\,1\,2} \\ 4638 \\ \times \quad 3 \\ \hline 914 \end{array}$$

Step 4
Multiply thousands.
Add traded thousands.

$$\begin{array}{r} {\scriptstyle 1\,1\,2} \\ 4638 \\ \times \quad 3 \\ \hline 13{,}914 \end{array}$$

Multiply.

1. $\begin{array}{r} 1568 \\ \times \quad 2 \\ \hline 3136 \end{array}$

2. $\begin{array}{r} 7539 \\ \times \quad 3 \\ \hline \end{array}$

3. $\begin{array}{r} 5674 \\ \times \quad 4 \\ \hline \end{array}$

4. $\begin{array}{r} 4635 \\ \times \quad 2 \\ \hline \end{array}$

5. $\begin{array}{r} 8234 \\ \times \quad 6 \\ \hline \end{array}$

6. $\begin{array}{r} 5256 \\ \times \quad 7 \\ \hline \end{array}$

7. $\begin{array}{r} 3474 \\ \times \quad 5 \\ \hline \end{array}$

8. $\begin{array}{r} 6378 \\ \times \quad 4 \\ \hline \end{array}$

9. $\begin{array}{r} 5139 \\ \times \quad 8 \\ \hline \end{array}$

10. $\begin{array}{r} 6427 \\ \times \quad 6 \\ \hline \end{array}$

Multiply. Watch out for zeros.

11. $\begin{array}{r} 2020 \\ \times \quad 6 \\ \hline \end{array}$

12. $\begin{array}{r} 5070 \\ \times \quad 4 \\ \hline \end{array}$

13. $\begin{array}{r} 4065 \\ \times \quad 7 \\ \hline \end{array}$

14. $\begin{array}{r} 5046 \\ \times \quad 8 \\ \hline \end{array}$

15. $\begin{array}{r} 6001 \\ \times \quad 5 \\ \hline \end{array}$

16. 6050×3

17. 1090×5

18. 2095×4

19. 9030×4

20. It is 5631 kilometers from New York to London, England. If you travel from New York to London and back, how far will you go?

21. It is 8263 kilometers from London to Houston, Texas. If you travel from London to Houston and back, how far will you go?

Multiplying and Money

Multiply money the same way you multiply whole numbers.

$$\begin{array}{r} \overset{2\ 1\ 2}{\$15.37} \\ \times\quad\quad 4 \\ \hline \$61.48 \end{array}$$

Multiply. Remember to use $ and . in your answers.

1. $7.68
   × 4
   $30.72

2. $0.89
   × 5

3. $50.86
   × 3

4. $7.68
   × 4

5. $36.52
   × 5

6. $1.44
   × 7

7. $4.27
   × 6

8. $52.96
   × 3

9. $8.07
   × 4

10. $90.02
    × 6

11. $2.34
    × 5

12. $70.20
    × 9

13. $74.30
    × 2

14. $3.73
    × 3

15. $6.21
    × 8

16. $0.23
    × 9

17. $44.29
    × 2

18. $1.09
    × 5

19. $11.41
    × 8

20. Martha bought 2 pairs of shoes. Each pair cost $34.29. How much did Martha spend?

ANY
PAIR
$34.29

Airline Distance Problems

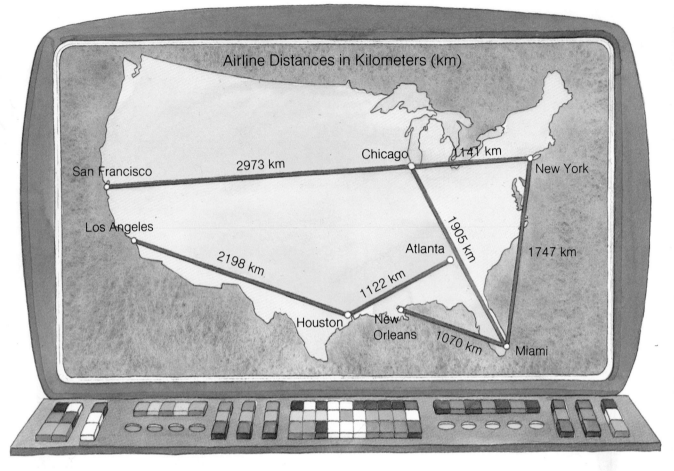

Airline Distances in Kilometers (km)

2973 km — San Francisco to Chicago
1141 km — Chicago to New York
1905 km — Chicago to Miami
1747 km — New York to Miami
2198 km — Los Angeles to Houston
1122 km — Houston to Atlanta
1070 km — New Orleans to Miami

Use the map to solve the problems.

1. Tony Juarez lives in Houston. He flies to Los Angeles and back 4 times a year. How many kilometers does he fly each year? 17,584

2. Patricia Jones lives in San Francisco. She flies to Chicago and back 4 times a year. How many kilometers does she fly each year?

3. Martin Lux lives in New Orleans. Last year he flew to Miami and back 2 times. How many kilometers did he fly?

4. Alice Hosley lives in Atlanta. She flies to Houston and back 3 times a month. How many kilometers does she fly each month?

5. A flight attendant made 5 round trips between Chicago and New York. How many kilometers in the 5 round trips?

6. A pilot made 4 round trips between Chicago and Miami. How many kilometers in the 4 round trips?

Reviewing Multiplication

Review the kinds of multiplication you have learned.

No trading.	Trading ones.	Trading ones and tens.	Trading ones, tens, and hundreds.
$\begin{array}{r} 132 \\ \times\ \ 3 \\ \hline 396 \end{array}$	$\begin{array}{r} ^4 \\ 28 \\ \times\ \ 6 \\ \hline 168 \end{array}$	$\begin{array}{r} ^{4\ 3} \\ 465 \\ \times\ \ \ 7 \\ \hline 3255 \end{array}$	$\begin{array}{r} ^{4\ 2\ 4} \\ 3748 \\ \times\ \ \ \ 6 \\ \hline 22{,}488 \end{array}$

Multiply.

1. $\begin{array}{r} 24 \\ \times\ 2 \\ \hline 48 \end{array}$
2. $\begin{array}{r} 433 \\ \times\ \ \ 2 \\ \hline \end{array}$
3. $\begin{array}{r} 512 \\ \times\ \ \ 4 \\ \hline \end{array}$
4. $\begin{array}{r} 3123 \\ \times\ \ \ \ 3 \\ \hline \end{array}$
5. $\begin{array}{r} 26 \\ \times\ 8 \\ \hline \end{array}$

6. $\begin{array}{r} 427 \\ \times\ \ \ 4 \\ \hline \end{array}$
7. $\begin{array}{r} 608 \\ \times\ \ \ 9 \\ \hline \end{array}$
8. $\begin{array}{r} 7008 \\ \times\ \ \ \ 9 \\ \hline \end{array}$
9. $\begin{array}{r} 37 \\ \times\ 9 \\ \hline \end{array}$
10. $\begin{array}{r} 538 \\ \times\ \ \ 6 \\ \hline \end{array}$

11. $\begin{array}{r} 4712 \\ \times\ \ \ \ 8 \\ \hline \end{array}$
12. $\begin{array}{r} 608 \\ \times\ \ \ 3 \\ \hline \end{array}$
13. $\begin{array}{r} 98 \\ \times\ 7 \\ \hline \end{array}$
14. $\begin{array}{r} 708 \\ \times\ \ \ 9 \\ \hline \end{array}$
15. $\begin{array}{r} 834 \\ \times\ \ \ 6 \\ \hline \end{array}$

16. $\begin{array}{r} 8034 \\ \times\ \ \ \ 8 \\ \hline \end{array}$
17. $\begin{array}{r} 61 \\ \times\ 9 \\ \hline \end{array}$
18. $\begin{array}{r} 402 \\ \times\ \ \ 2 \\ \hline \end{array}$
19. $\begin{array}{r} 7657 \\ \times\ \ \ \ 3 \\ \hline \end{array}$
20. $\begin{array}{r} 96 \\ \times\ 3 \\ \hline \end{array}$

21. $\begin{array}{r} 659 \\ \times\ \ \ 3 \\ \hline \end{array}$
22. $\begin{array}{r} 47 \\ \times\ 7 \\ \hline \end{array}$
23. $\begin{array}{r} 7036 \\ \times\ \ \ \ 5 \\ \hline \end{array}$
24. $\begin{array}{r} 496 \\ \times\ \ \ 8 \\ \hline \end{array}$
25. $\begin{array}{r} 566 \\ \times\ \ \ 8 \\ \hline \end{array}$

Review (pp. 89–101)

Multiply.

1. $\begin{array}{r} 7004 \\ \times\ \ \ \ 9 \\ \hline \end{array}$
2. $\begin{array}{r} 2378 \\ \times\ \ \ \ 3 \\ \hline \end{array}$
3. $\begin{array}{r} 68 \\ \times\ 7 \\ \hline \end{array}$
4. $\begin{array}{r} 80 \\ \times\ 9 \\ \hline \end{array}$
5. $\begin{array}{r} 487 \\ \times\ \ \ 4 \\ \hline \end{array}$

Multiplying Tens, Hundreds, and Thousands

When you multiply tens, hundreds, or thousands by one digit, think of the multiplication fact.

Step 1
Multiply 4 times each zero.

$$\begin{array}{r} 2000 \\ \times\quad 4 \\ \hline 000 \end{array}$$

Step 2
Multiply 4 times 2.

$$\begin{array}{r} 2000 \\ \times\quad 4 \\ \hline 8000 \end{array}$$ 4×2 thousands $= 8$ thousands

Multiply.

1. $\begin{array}{r} 40 \\ \times\ 6 \\ \hline 240 \end{array}$

2. $\begin{array}{r} 700 \\ \times\ 3 \\ \hline \end{array}$

3. $\begin{array}{r} 2000 \\ \times\ 9 \\ \hline \end{array}$

4. $\begin{array}{r} 600 \\ \times\ 5 \\ \hline \end{array}$

5. $\begin{array}{r} 20 \\ \times\ 8 \\ \hline \end{array}$

6. $\begin{array}{r} 8000 \\ \times\ 3 \\ \hline \end{array}$

7. $\begin{array}{r} 90 \\ \times\ 5 \\ \hline \end{array}$

8. $\begin{array}{r} 200 \\ \times\ 7 \\ \hline \end{array}$

9. $\begin{array}{r} 4000 \\ \times\ 5 \\ \hline \end{array}$

10. $\begin{array}{r} 60 \\ \times\ 6 \\ \hline \end{array}$

11. $\begin{array}{r} 3000 \\ \times\ 2 \\ \hline \end{array}$

12. $\begin{array}{r} 200 \\ \times\ 4 \\ \hline \end{array}$

13. $\begin{array}{r} 50 \\ \times\ 8 \\ \hline \end{array}$

14. $\begin{array}{r} 7000 \\ \times\ 6 \\ \hline \end{array}$

15. $\begin{array}{r} 800 \\ \times\ 8 \\ \hline \end{array}$

16. 400×8

17. 70×3

18. 6000×5

19. 3000×9

20. 80×4

Challenge
Find the missing factor.

21. $6 \times \square = 420$

22. $7000 \times \square = 42{,}000$

23. $900 \times \square = 2700$

24. $80 \times \square = 480$

Multiplying Tens and Hundreds by Tens

tens × tens = hundreds

   6 tens   **60**
× **8** tens   × **80**
48 hundreds   **4800**

tens × hundreds = thousands

   5 hundreds   **500**
× **4** tens   × **40**
20 thousands **20,000**

Multiply.

1a. 5 tens
    ×7 tens
    35 hundreds

b.   50
  ×70
 3500

2a. 6 hundreds
    ×4 tens

b.   600
 × 40

3a. 8 hundreds
    ×3 tens

b.   800
 × 30

4a. 4 tens
    ×9 tens

b.   40
 ×90

5a. 7 tens
    ×7 tens

b.   70
 ×70

6a. 9 hundreds
    ×5 tens

b.   900
 × 50

Find the products.

7. 300
 × 20

8. 400
 × 70

9. 200
 × 30

10. 90
  ×80

11. 60
  ×60

12. 40
  ×20

13. 300
 × 40

14. 20
  ×20

15. 90
  ×70

16. 700
 × 50

17. 20
  ×60

18. 60
  ×50

19. 70
  ×50

20. 80
  ×40

21. 50
  ×40

22. 200
 × 90

23. 40
  ×80

24. 600
 × 60

25. 20
  ×30

26. 50
  ×60

27. 300
 × 30

28. 500
 × 90

29. 40
  ×70

30. 70
  ×20

Multiplying by Tens, Hundreds, and Thousands

If you know that $3 \times 29 = 87$, you can do these.

$$\begin{array}{r} 29 \\ \times\ 30 \\ \hline 870 \end{array}$$ 3 tens   87 tens

$$\begin{array}{r} 29 \\ \times\ 300 \\ \hline 8700 \end{array}$$ 3 hundreds   87 hundreds

$$\begin{array}{r} 29 \\ \times\ 3000 \\ \hline 87,000 \end{array}$$ 3 thousands   87 thousands

Multiply.

1. $\begin{array}{r} 46 \\ \times 20 \\ \hline 920 \end{array}$
2. $\begin{array}{r} 47 \\ \times 500 \\ \hline \end{array}$
3. $\begin{array}{r} 29 \\ \times 400 \\ \hline \end{array}$
4. $\begin{array}{r} 74 \\ \times 30 \\ \hline \end{array}$
5. $\begin{array}{r} 24 \\ \times 3000 \\ \hline \end{array}$

6. $\begin{array}{r} 47 \\ \times 5000 \\ \hline \end{array}$
7. $\begin{array}{r} 74 \\ \times 20 \\ \hline \end{array}$
8. $\begin{array}{r} 58 \\ \times 300 \\ \hline \end{array}$
9. $\begin{array}{r} 72 \\ \times 800 \\ \hline \end{array}$
10. $\begin{array}{r} 28 \\ \times 40 \\ \hline \end{array}$

11. $\begin{array}{r} 39 \\ \times 500 \\ \hline \end{array}$
12. $\begin{array}{r} 84 \\ \times 600 \\ \hline \end{array}$
13. $\begin{array}{r} 34 \\ \times 6000 \\ \hline \end{array}$
14. $\begin{array}{r} 72 \\ \times 8000 \\ \hline \end{array}$
15. $\begin{array}{r} 56 \\ \times 30 \\ \hline \end{array}$

16. $\begin{array}{r} 89 \\ \times 5000 \\ \hline \end{array}$
17. $\begin{array}{r} 54 \\ \times 7000 \\ \hline \end{array}$
18. $\begin{array}{r} 71 \\ \times 600 \\ \hline \end{array}$
19. $\begin{array}{r} 25 \\ \times 700 \\ \hline \end{array}$
20. $\begin{array}{r} 91 \\ \times 20 \\ \hline \end{array}$

21. $\begin{array}{r} 63 \\ \times 40 \\ \hline \end{array}$
22. $\begin{array}{r} 18 \\ \times 30 \\ \hline \end{array}$
23. $\begin{array}{r} 48 \\ \times 500 \\ \hline \end{array}$
24. $\begin{array}{r} 92 \\ \times 5000 \\ \hline \end{array}$
25. $\begin{array}{r} 74 \\ \times 3000 \\ \hline \end{array}$

26. $\begin{array}{r} 66 \\ \times 300 \\ \hline \end{array}$
27. $\begin{array}{r} 45 \\ \times 60 \\ \hline \end{array}$
28. $\begin{array}{r} 18 \\ \times 2000 \\ \hline \end{array}$
29. $\begin{array}{r} 79 \\ \times 50 \\ \hline \end{array}$
30. $\begin{array}{r} 43 \\ \times 6000 \\ \hline \end{array}$

 **Challenge**

Find the missing factor.

31. $3 \times \boxed{?} \times 1000 = 15,000$
32. $6 \times 8 \times \boxed{?} = 48,000$
33. $\boxed{?} \times 7 \times 100 = 49,000$

Multiplying by Two Digits

Follow these steps to multiply by two digits.

Step 1
Multiply by
the ones.

$$\begin{array}{r} 18 \\ \times\ 12 \\ \hline 36 \end{array}\ \ {\scriptstyle 2\times 18}$$

Step 2
Multiply by
the tens.

$$\begin{array}{r} 18 \\ \times\ 12 \\ \hline 36 \\ 180 \end{array}\ \ {\scriptstyle 1\ ten\times 18\ =\ 18\ tens}$$

Step 3
Add the
two products.

$$\begin{array}{r} 18 \\ \times\ 12 \\ \hline 36 \\ +\ 180 \\ \hline 216 \end{array}$$

Multiply.

1. $\begin{array}{r} 34 \\ \times 14 \\ \hline 476 \end{array}$
2. $\begin{array}{r} 33 \\ \times 16 \end{array}$
3. $\begin{array}{r} 72 \\ \times 18 \end{array}$
4. $\begin{array}{r} 53 \\ \times 19 \end{array}$
5. $\begin{array}{r} 67 \\ \times 13 \end{array}$
6. $\begin{array}{r} 84 \\ \times 12 \end{array}$

7. $\begin{array}{r} 48 \\ \times 17 \end{array}$
8. $\begin{array}{r} 94 \\ \times 16 \end{array}$
9. $\begin{array}{r} 58 \\ \times 13 \end{array}$
10. $\begin{array}{r} 72 \\ \times 15 \end{array}$
11. $\begin{array}{r} 68 \\ \times 11 \end{array}$
12. $\begin{array}{r} 41 \\ \times 19 \end{array}$

13. $\begin{array}{r} 99 \\ \times 15 \end{array}$
14. $\begin{array}{r} 63 \\ \times 12 \end{array}$
15. $\begin{array}{r} 83 \\ \times 14 \end{array}$
16. $\begin{array}{r} 65 \\ \times 11 \end{array}$
17. $\begin{array}{r} 44 \\ \times 14 \end{array}$
18. $\begin{array}{r} 56 \\ \times 12 \end{array}$

19. 87×13
20. 48×15
21. 50×17
22. 35×16
23. 58×15

24. Erin wants to join the swimming
team. Each day for 13 weeks she
practices 75 minutes. How many
minutes does she practice?

More Multiplying by Two Digits

If you can do these,   you can do this.

$$\begin{array}{r} 37 \\ \times\ 4 \\ \hline 148 \end{array} \qquad \begin{array}{r} 37 \\ \times\ 20 \\ \hline 740 \end{array} \qquad \begin{array}{r} 37 \\ \times\ 24 \\ \hline 148 \\ +\ 740 \\ \hline 888 \end{array}$$

24×37 is the sum of 4×37 and 20×37.

Multiply.

1. $\begin{array}{r}57\\ \times 62\\ \hline 3534\end{array}$	2. $\begin{array}{r}43\\ \times 28\\ \hline\end{array}$	3. $\begin{array}{r}72\\ \times 34\\ \hline\end{array}$	4. $\begin{array}{r}63\\ \times 46\\ \hline\end{array}$	5. $\begin{array}{r}86\\ \times 37\\ \hline\end{array}$	6. $\begin{array}{r}76\\ \times 29\\ \hline\end{array}$
7. $\begin{array}{r}47\\ \times 33\\ \hline\end{array}$	8. $\begin{array}{r}94\\ \times 54\\ \hline\end{array}$	9. $\begin{array}{r}82\\ \times 27\\ \hline\end{array}$	10. $\begin{array}{r}46\\ \times 42\\ \hline\end{array}$	11. $\begin{array}{r}96\\ \times 39\\ \hline\end{array}$	12. $\begin{array}{r}29\\ \times 35\\ \hline\end{array}$
13. $\begin{array}{r}24\\ \times 63\\ \hline\end{array}$	14. $\begin{array}{r}78\\ \times 47\\ \hline\end{array}$	15. $\begin{array}{r}81\\ \times 79\\ \hline\end{array}$	16. $\begin{array}{r}61\\ \times 45\\ \hline\end{array}$	17. $\begin{array}{r}93\\ \times 58\\ \hline\end{array}$	18. $\begin{array}{r}37\\ \times 25\\ \hline\end{array}$

 **Challenge**

19. Is 74×29 nearer to 2100 or 210?

20. Is 56×37 nearer to 150 or 1500?

21. Is 89×37 nearer to 360 or 3600?

22. Is 41×29 nearer to 1200 or 120?

23. Is 52×84 nearer to 4300 or 430?

24. Is 61×39 nearer to 2400 or 240?

25. Is 48×23 nearer to 110 or 1100?

26. Is 32×65 nearer to 250 or 2500?

Multiplying to Find Area

The area of a surface is measured in square units. To find the
area of a surface, multiply its length by its width.

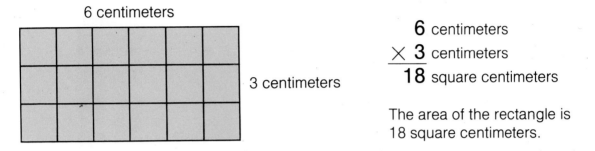

6 centimeters

3 centimeters

6 centimeters
× 3 centimeters
18 square centimeters

The area of the rectangle is
18 square centimeters.

**Find the areas of these surfaces. The shapes are shown smaller
than actual size.**

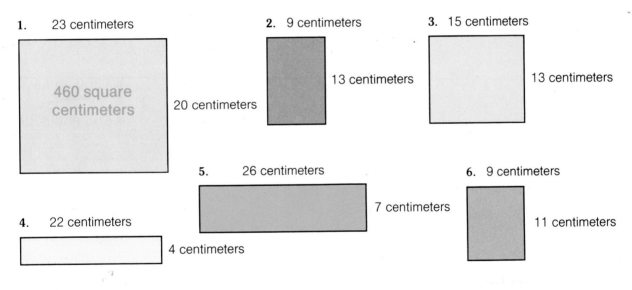

1.   23 centimeters

460 square
centimeters

20 centimeters

2. 9 centimeters

13 centimeters

3. 15 centimeters

13 centimeters

5.   26 centimeters

7 centimeters

6. 9 centimeters

11 centimeters

4.   22 centimeters

4 centimeters

Find these areas.

7. A rectangle that is 67 centimeters
long and 49 centimeters wide.

8. A square with sides that each
measure 4 meters.

9. A square with sides that each
measure 12 centimeters.

10. A rectangle that is 9 meters long
and 4 meters wide.

Switching Factors

It is sometimes easier to multiply by the factor that ends in zero.

Step 1
Notice that the top factor ends in zero.

$$\begin{array}{r} 80 \\ \times\ 37 \\ \hline \end{array}$$

Step 2
Switch factors.

$$\begin{array}{r} 37 \\ \times\ 80 \\ \hline \end{array}$$

Step 3
Multiply.

$$\begin{array}{r} 37 \\ \times\ 80 \\ \hline 2960 \end{array}$$

Multiply.

1. 7 and 600   4200
2. 39 and 80
3. 6 and 40
4. 500 and 4

5. 79 and 60
6. 30 and 54
7. 900 and 8
8. 55 and 8000

Multiply. Switch factors if you want to.

9. $\begin{array}{r} 4000 \\ \times\ \ \ \ 7 \\ \hline \end{array}$
10. $\begin{array}{r} 40 \\ \times 48 \\ \hline \end{array}$
11. $\begin{array}{r} 50 \\ \times 39 \\ \hline \end{array}$
12. $\begin{array}{r} 90 \\ \times\ \ 8 \\ \hline \end{array}$
13. $\begin{array}{r} 600 \\ \times\ \ \ 4 \\ \hline \end{array}$

14. $\begin{array}{r} 50 \\ \times 46 \\ \hline \end{array}$
15. $\begin{array}{r} 80 \\ \times 29 \\ \hline \end{array}$
16. $\begin{array}{r} 60 \\ \times\ \ 7 \\ \hline \end{array}$
17. $\begin{array}{r} 50 \\ \times 38 \\ \hline \end{array}$
18. $\begin{array}{r} 300 \\ \times\ \ \ 8 \\ \hline \end{array}$

19. $\begin{array}{r} 400 \\ \times\ \ \ 7 \\ \hline \end{array}$
20. $\begin{array}{r} 80 \\ \times 67 \\ \hline \end{array}$
21. $\begin{array}{r} 70 \\ \times 19 \\ \hline \end{array}$
22. $\begin{array}{r} 50 \\ \times\ \ 4 \\ \hline \end{array}$
23. $\begin{array}{r} 800 \\ \times\ \ \ 7 \\ \hline \end{array}$

24. $\begin{array}{r} 40 \\ \times 79 \\ \hline \end{array}$
25. $\begin{array}{r} 600 \\ \times\ \ \ 9 \\ \hline \end{array}$
26. $\begin{array}{r} 30 \\ \times\ \ 4 \\ \hline \end{array}$
27. $\begin{array}{r} 72 \\ \times 40 \\ \hline \end{array}$
28. $\begin{array}{r} 86 \\ \times 20 \\ \hline \end{array}$

Practicing Multiplication

Practice the kinds of multiplication you have learned to do.

Multiply.

1. 47
    × 3
    ___
    141

2. 70
    × 8

3. 90
    ×80

4. 417
    ×400

5. 56
    × 3

6. 43
    × 7

7. 424
    ×300

8. 800
    × 9

9. 513
    ×100

10. 29
    ×10

11. 34
    ×50

12. 800
    ×346

13. 6000
    × 9

14. 814
    × 70

15. 5000
    × 39

16. 678
    ×500

17. 465
    × 3

18. 898
    × 8

19. 7846
    × 5

20. 29
    ×30

21. 387
    × 10

22. A small movie theater sold 500
    tickets each night for 28 nights.
    How many tickets were sold in all?

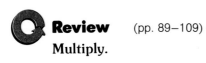

Review   (pp. 89–109)
Multiply.

1. 56
    × 4

2. 69
    × 7

3. 326
    × 2

4. 414
    × 9

5. 147
    × 20

Square Numbers

To square a number, multiply it by itself.

$3 \times 3 = 9$

9 is a square number.
It is the square of 3.

3 squared is written 3^2.
$3^2 = 3 \times 3$, or 9.

Find each square.

1. 5^2 25
2. 10^2
3. 7^2
4. 23^2
5. 8^2
6. 20^2

7. 28^2
8. 4^2
9. 11^2
10. 19^2
11. 9^2
12. 3^2

13. 2^2
14. 18^2
15. 14^2
16. 15^2
17. 12^2
18. 6^2

19. 13^2
20. 16^2
21. 30^2
22. 25^2
23. 17^2
24. 21^2

Copy and complete.

25. $\square \times \square = 25$
26. $\square \times \square = 49$
27. $\square \times \square = 64$
28. $\square \times \square = 81$

29. $\square \times \square = 16$
30. $\square \times \square = 36$
31. $\square \times \square = 144$
32. $\square \times \square = 100$

33. $\square \times \square = 9$
34. $\square \times \square = 121$
35. $\square \times \square = 225$
36. $\square \times \square = 400$

⭐ Challenge
Are these numbers square numbers? Write **yes** or **no**.

37. 13
38. 36
39. 61
40. 9
41. 169
42. 100

Estimating Products

You can estimate products if you do not need an exact answer.

Step 1
Round each factor to the nearest ten.

$$59 \qquad 60$$
$$\times 82 \qquad \times 80$$

Step 2
Multiply the rounded numbers.

$$60$$
$$\times 80$$
$$\overline{4800}$$

Go Swim Team!

Estimate the product by rounding. Then find the exact product.

1. $73 \quad 70 \quad 73$
    $\times 21 \quad \times 20 \quad \times 21$
    $\qquad\quad 1400 \quad 1533$

2. 97
    $\times 52$

3. 32
    $\times 61$

4. 71
    $\times 70$

5. 64
    $\times 39$

6. 88
    $\times 99$

7. 39
    $\times 61$

8. 42
    $\times 79$

9. 22
    $\times 93$

10. 93
    $\times 28$

11. 56
    $\times 41$

Estimate by rounding each factor to the nearest ten.

12. Arlington High School is sending students to a swimming meet. If it costs the school $93 to send each student, about how much will the school spend to send 18 students?

13. The school orders buttons that say *Go, Swim Team!* If there are 75 buttons in each box, about how many buttons in 122 boxes?

Multiplying Hundreds

Follow these steps to multiply three digits by two digits.

Step 1
Multiply by
the ones.

$$
\begin{array}{r}
367 \\
\times \ 24 \\
\hline
1468 \quad {\scriptstyle 4 \times 367}
\end{array}
$$

Step 2
Multiply by
the tens.

$$
\begin{array}{r}
367 \\
\times \ 24 \\
\hline
1468 \\
7340 \quad {\scriptstyle 2\ tens \times 367}
\end{array}
$$

Step 3
Add the two
products.

$$
\begin{array}{r}
367 \\
\times \ 24 \\
\hline
1468 \\
+ \ 7340 \\
\hline
8808
\end{array}
$$

Multiply.

1. 479
    × 27
    12,933

2. 293
    × 53

3. 582
    × 48

4. 241
    × 14

5. 459
    × 65

6. 756
    × 29

7. 225
    × 47

8. 347
    × 51

9. 459
    × 29

10. 407
    × 67

11. 680
    × 32

12. 299
    × 41

13. 385
    × 12

14. 625
    × 55

15. 210
    × 15

16. Katherine Lucas takes the train
    to work. Each week she travels
    146 kilometers. How many
    kilometers does she travel in 1 year
    (52 weeks)?

17. Roger Phelps drives 219 kilometers
    each week. How many kilometers
    does he drive in a year?

More Multiplying Hundreds

If you can do these,   you can do this.

$$
\begin{array}{r} 423 \\ \times\ \ 5 \\ \hline 2115 \end{array}
\qquad
\begin{array}{r} 423 \\ \times\ \ 30 \\ \hline 12{,}690 \end{array}
\qquad
\begin{array}{r} 423 \\ \times\ \ 35 \\ \hline 2115 \\ +\ 12690 \\ \hline 14{,}805 \end{array}
$$

35×423 is the sum of 5×423
and 30×423.

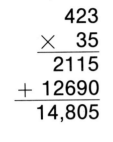

Multiply.

1. 674 × 34 22,916	2. 182 × 41	3. 463 × 27	4. 504 × 32	5. 761 × 22
6. 757 × 38	7. 904 × 36	8. 283 × 79	9. 418 × 52	10. 536 × 65
11. 316 × 41	12. 186 × 93	13. 483 × 62	14. 247 × 36	15. 908 × 23

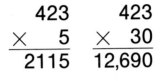 **Calculate**

Multiply.

16. 173 × 2	17. 173 × 4	18. 173 × 8	19. 173 × 16	20. 173 × 32
21. 427 × 2	22. 427 × 4	23. 427 × 8	24. 427 × 16	25. 427 × 32

Toy Store Problems

1. Norman's Toy Store has 10 shelves of dolls with 35 dolls on each shelf. How many dolls in all? **350**

2. Joellen's Toys sold 34 boxes of whistles. Each box had 16 whistles. How many whistles were sold?

3. Okano's Toy Store has 15 baskets of rubber balls. Each basket holds 60 balls. How many balls in all?

4. Gem Toy Store sells 200 model car kits each month. How many model car kits will the store sell in 27 months?

5. Fong's Toys had 3 racks of jump ropes with 48 jump ropes on each rack. How many jump ropes in all?

6. Jess bought 3 yo-yos for $0.59 each, 5 bags of marbles for $1.39 each, and 20 balloons for $0.10 each. How much did Jess spend in all?

7. Laura Isaacs sells 175 bicycles a year. How many bicycles will she sell in 3 years?

8. Sally Perez bought 24 games for $6.99 each. How much did Sally spend?

9. Huey's Toy Store sells 140 different stuffed animals. The store has 25 of each animal. How many animals in all?

10. George Smith bought 2 puzzles for $11.99 each and 3 toy cars for $1.59 each. How much did George spend in all?

11. The fifth-grade class bought 27 packages of balloons. There were 26 balloons in each package. How many balloons did they buy in all?

12. Ralph McCarthy ordered 50 boxes of baseballs. There are 36 baseballs in each box. How many baseballs did Mr. McCarthy order?

Chapter Review

Multiply.   (ex. 1-3: p. 89),   (ex. 4-6: p. 91),   (ex. 7-10: p. 92),
(ex. 11-15: p. 94),   (ex. 16-20: p. 95)

1. 41
    × 3

2. 23
    × 2

3. 33
    × 3

4. 65
    × 4

5. 77
    × 3

6. 19
    × 6

7. 30×6×4

8. 7×8×2

9. 10×4×9

10. 8×5×9

11. 221
    × 3

12. 432
    × 2

13. 604
    × 2

14. 811
    × 4

15. 612
    × 3

16. 857
    × 4

17. 625
    × 7

18. 649
    × 3

19. 785
    × 2

20. 435
    × 6

Multiply.   (ex. 21-23: p. 98),   (ex. 24-25: p. 99),   (ex. 26-28: p. 102),
(ex. 29-31: p. 103),   (ex. 32-35: p. 104)

21. 1436
    × 6

22. 8743
    × 5

23. 7642
    × 8

24. $35.26
    × 2

25. $47.09
    × 7

26. 500
    × 6

27. 7000
    × 4

28. 60
    × 9

29. 40
    ×20

30. 600
    × 60

31. 50
    ×20

32. 29
    ×30

33. 65
    ×400

34. 87
    ×3000

35. 75
    ×60

Multiply.   (ex. 36-38: p. 105),   (ex. 39-40: p. 106),   (ex. 41-45: p. 112)

36. 85×16

37. 41×15

38. 26×11

39. 25×74

40. 46×65

41. 654
    × 31

42. 480
    × 65

43. 303
    × 79

44. 297
    × 43

45. 776
    × 52

Chapter Test

Multiply.

1. 63
   × 2

2. 41
   × 5

3. 73
   × 3

4. 98
   × 4

5. 603
   × 6

6. 346
   × 7

7. $20 \times 4 \times 3$

8. $6 \times 9 \times 7$

9. $10 \times 9 \times 4$

10. $3 \times 5 \times 2$

Multiply.

11. 1639
    × 4

12. 7062
    × 3

13. 8754
    × 6

14. $16.87
    × 9

15. $10.47
    × 6

16. 60
    × 3

17. 5000
    × 9

18. 700
    × 50

19. 93
    × 90

20. 57
    × 300

Multiply.

21. 29
    × 14

22. 65
    × 17

23. 83
    × 16

24. 379
    × 46

25. 761
    × 39

Brush Up

Add, subtract, multiply, or divide.

1. 6 +6	2. 7 +4	3. 15 − 6	4. 11 − 3	5. 6 +7	6. 12 − 7
7. 13 − 9	8. 9 +5	9. 5 +6	10. 14 − 8	11. 17 − 9	12. 8 +7

13. 7×4 14. 8×7 15. $72 \div 8$ 16. 9×3 17. $16 \div 2$

18. 5×8 19. $36 \div 9$ 20. 4×9 21. 7×7 22. $28 \div 4$

Write the numbers.

23. sixteen thousand, eight

24. two hundred thousand, one hundred six

25. eighty million

26. thirty-two thousand, one hundred

Add or subtract.

27. 55 −48	28. 3765 +8342	29. 700 −284	30. 280 +128	31. 62 −56
32. 76 −50	33. 611 +237	34. 94 −58	35. 407 −197	36. 5463 −2574

Multiply.

37. 722 × 2	38. 600 × 5	39. 20 ×40	40. 35 ×16	41. 469 × 64

42. 846×7 43. 55×15 44. 46×95 45. 4000×3 46. 99×18

CHAPTER 5

Division

Using Division at Work

Al Turner owns a tow truck business. In one day
the company towed 72 cars. There were 4 drivers working
that day. Al works the problem 72 ÷ 4 to find the average
number of cars each driver towed. Each tow truck driver
towed an average of 18 cars that day.

Fair Share Dividing

27 equals 6 fair shares with 4 in each share and 3 left over.

17 equals 3 fair shares with 5 in each share and 2 left over.

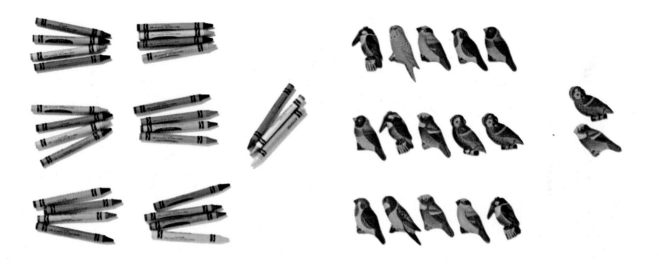

Find the answers. Use markers or pieces of paper if you need help.

1. John has 27 marbles. He makes 5 fair shares.
   a. How many in each share? 5
   b. How many left over? 2

2. Agnes has 22 magazines. She makes 3 fair shares.
   a. How many in each share?
   b. How many left over?

3. Susie has 18 baseball trading cards. She makes 4 fair shares.
   a. How many in each share?
   b. How many left over?

4. Rick has 19 bottles of poster paint. He makes 7 fair shares.
   a. How many in each share?
   b. How many left over?

5. Alfred has 34 old colored bottles. He makes 8 fair shares.
   a. How many in each share?
   b. How many left over?

6. Mary has 31 small toy cars. She makes 6 fair shares.
   a. How many in each share?
   b. How many left over?

Remainders

A multiplication table can help you divide. Try $3\overline{)16}$.

16 is between 15 and 18, so the quotient is between 5 and 6.

×	1	2	3	4	5	6	7	8	9
2	2	4	6	8	10	12	14	16	18
3	3	6	9	12	15	18	21	24	27
4	4	8	12	16	20	24	28	32	36

quotient **5 r1** remainder

divisor **3**$\overline{)\textbf{16}}$ dividend

$\underline{-\ \textbf{15}}$ $5 \times 3 = 15$

1   The **remainder** is the number left over when you divide.

Use the multiplication table. Divide. The remainder must be less than the divisor.

1. $4\overline{)18}$ 2. $3\overline{)28}$ 3. $2\overline{)15}$ 4. $3\overline{)22}$ 5. $4\overline{)34}$

6. $3\overline{)25}$ 7. $4\overline{)15}$ 8. $2\overline{)11}$ 9. $4\overline{)21}$ 10. $2\overline{)19}$

11. $2\overline{)13}$ 12. $3\overline{)19}$ 13. $3\overline{)17}$ 14. $4\overline{)35}$ 15. $3\overline{)20}$

16. $3\overline{)23}$ 17. $4\overline{)23}$ 18. $2\overline{)17}$ 19. $4\overline{)25}$ 20. $3\overline{)29}$

21. $4\overline{)17}$ 22. $3\overline{)11}$ 23. $4\overline{)29}$ 24. $3\overline{)16}$ 25. $3\overline{)26}$

⭐ Challenge

Write all the numbers that can be remainders when you divide by each of these. Remember that the remainder must be less than the divisor.

26. 2   27. 3   28. 4   29. 5   30. 6

Multiply to Divide

To divide 53 by 8, think $\square \times 8$ is close to 53.

$6 \times 8 = 48$

$7 \times 8 = 56$ 56 is more than 53, so 7 is too big.

$$\begin{array}{r} 6 \text{ r}5 \\ 8\overline{)53} \\ -48 \\ \hline 5 \end{array}$$

Divide.

1. $8\overline{)61}$ → 7 r5
2. $9\overline{)70}$
3. $6\overline{)55}$
4. $6\overline{)40}$
5. $7\overline{)51}$

6. $8\overline{)23}$
7. $9\overline{)62}$
8. $6\overline{)17}$
9. $5\overline{)44}$
10. $9\overline{)32}$

11. $7\overline{)60}$
12. $7\overline{)27}$
13. $8\overline{)51}$
14. $6\overline{)46}$
15. $8\overline{)35}$

16. $6\overline{)39}$
17. $5\overline{)29}$
18. $7\overline{)26}$
19. $8\overline{)29}$
20. $6\overline{)15}$

21. $5\overline{)23}$
22. $9\overline{)23}$
23. $8\overline{)41}$
24. $5\overline{)37}$
25. $9\overline{)50}$

Copy and complete.

26. $7\overline{)34}$ → $\square$ r6
27. $6\overline{)47}$ → 7 r$\square$
28. $3\overline{)29}$ → $\square$ r2
29. $8\overline{)71}$ → 8 r$\square$
30. $4\overline{)31}$ → 7 r$\square$

31. $2\overline{)15}$ → $\square$ r1
32. $5\overline{)49}$ → 9 r$\square$
33. $9\overline{)71}$ → $\square$ r8
34. $7\overline{)57}$ → 8 r$\square$
35. $9\overline{)59}$ → $\square$ r5

Two-Digit Quotients

Step 1
Divide tens.
Multiply. Subtract.

$$\begin{array}{r} 2 \\ 3\overline{)69} \\ -6 \\ \hline 0 \end{array}$$

Step 2
Bring down ones.

$$\begin{array}{r} 2 \\ 3\overline{)69} \\ -6\downarrow \\ \hline 09 \end{array}$$

Step 3
Divide ones.
Multiply. Subtract.

$$\begin{array}{r} 23 \\ 3\overline{)69} \\ -6 \\ \hline 09 \\ -9 \\ \hline 0 \end{array}$$

Divide.

1. $4\overline{)84}$ *21*

2. $2\overline{)68}$

3. $3\overline{)96}$

4. $5\overline{)55}$

5. $2\overline{)88}$

6. $4\overline{)48}$

7. $3\overline{)63}$

8. $2\overline{)84}$

9. $7\overline{)77}$

10. $2\overline{)86}$

11. $3\overline{)99}$

12. $2\overline{)44}$

13. $2\overline{)66}$

14. $3\overline{)69}$

15. $8\overline{)88}$

16. $3\overline{)93}$

17. $2\overline{)48}$

18. $2\overline{)82}$

19. $3\overline{)39}$

20. $3\overline{)66}$

21. George Lang is planting a garden. He has 66 tomato plants. He wants to plant 6 plants in a row. How many rows can he make?

22. Susan Shaw has 48 strawberry plants. She wants to plant 4 plants in a row. How many rows can she make?

More Two-Digit Quotients

Step 1
Divide tens. Multiply.
Subtract. Bring down
ones.

$$\begin{array}{r} 1 \\ 4\overline{)76} \\ -4\downarrow \\ \hline 36 \end{array}$$

Step 2
Divide ones. Multiply.
Subtract.

$$\begin{array}{r} 19 \\ 4\overline{)76} \\ -4 \\ \hline 36 \\ -36 \\ \hline 0 \end{array}$$

Check
Multiply the quotient by the
divisor. The answer should
be the same as the dividend.

$$\begin{array}{r} 19 \\ \times4 \\ \hline 76 \end{array}$$

Divide. Multiply to check the first row.

1. $2\overline{)76}$ 38
2. $6\overline{)96}$
3. $2\overline{)92}$
4. $3\overline{)42}$
5. $5\overline{)85}$

6. $8\overline{)96}$
7. $4\overline{)72}$
8. $3\overline{)87}$
9. $4\overline{)52}$
10. $4\overline{)92}$

11. $2\overline{)38}$
12. $3\overline{)84}$
13. $5\overline{)55}$
14. $7\overline{)84}$
15. $6\overline{)66}$

16. $4\overline{)68}$
17. $5\overline{)95}$
18. $6\overline{)78}$
19. $2\overline{)52}$
20. $3\overline{)54}$

21. $2\overline{)64}$
22. $3\overline{)33}$
23. $6\overline{)84}$
24. $5\overline{)65}$
25. $4\overline{)48}$

26. $3\overline{)69}$
27. $7\overline{)98}$
28. $6\overline{)72}$
29. $5\overline{)75}$
30. $4\overline{)96}$

Calculate
Work each problem from left to right.

31. $56 \div 7 \times 2 + 3 - 7 + 2$

32. $81 \div 9 + 6 \times 7 - 4 + 10$

Two-Digit Quotients with Remainders

Step 1
Divide tens. Multiply.
Subtract. Divide ones.
Multiply. Subtract.

```
      27
  3)82
  − 6
    22
  − 21
     1
```

Step 2
Write the
remainder.

```
      27 r1
  3)82
  − 6
    22
  − 21
     1
```

Check
Multiply the quotient
by the divisor.
Then add the remainder.

```
      27
  ×    3
      81
  +    1
      82
```

Divide. Multiply and then add to check the first row.

1. 8)97   12 r1
2. 6)68
3. 3)74
4. 4)93
5. 6)91

6. 4)97
7. 2)87
8. 3)79
9. 5)64
10. 2)27

11. 8)91
12. 4)47
13. 3)98
14. 6)87
15. 2)23

Rewrite these problems using ⟌ . Divide.

16. $86 \div 7$
17. $97 \div 8$
18. $93 \div 2$
19. $79 \div 5$
20. $81 \div 5$

21. $74 \div 6$
22. $95 \div 8$
23. $31 \div 2$
24. $85 \div 3$
25. $92 \div 8$

26. $85 \div 6$
27. $92 \div 6$
28. $64 \div 3$
29. $69 \div 4$
30. $87 \div 6$

31. $33 \div 2$
32. $76 \div 5$
33. $47 \div 2$
34. $87 \div 6$
35. $41 \div 4$

36. $89 \div 7$
37. $65 \div 3$
38. $77 \div 4$
39. $83 \div 6$
40. $62 \div 5$

Remainders in Word Problems

47 people want to go to a play. Only 6 people can ride in each car. How many cars do they need?

$$\begin{array}{r} 7\text{ r}5 \quad \text{cars} \\ 6\overline{)47} \quad \text{people} \end{array}$$

They will need 8 cars, not 7. The 5 remaining people will need the extra car.

Solve each problem.

1. 30 people are going on a trip. 4 people can sleep in one room. How many rooms do they need?   8

2. 58 Girl Scouts are going on a camping trip. 5 girls can sleep in one tent. How many tents do they need?

3. Judith has 79 books to pack. She can pack 8 books in one box. How many boxes does she need?

4. Dan has 52 photos. He puts 6 photos on each page of his photo album. How many pages does he need?

5. 62 hot dogs are needed for a picnic. There are 8 hot dogs in a package. How many packages of hot dogs are needed?

6. Peggy Anaya's class baked 89 rolls for a bake sale. They decided to put 6 rolls in each bag. How many bags do they need?

Practicing Division

Practice the kinds of division you have learned.

```
      6 r2          12          18 r1
  7)44          3)36         4)73
  − 42          − 3          − 4
     2             06            33
                 − 6          − 32
                    0             1
```

Divide. Check the first row.

1. 7)64   9 r1
2. 5)95
3. 4)84
4. 4)45
5. 3)39

6. 9)86
7. 5)37
8. 7)82
9. 4)34
10. 5)55

11. 3)17
12. 2)48
13. 6)29
14. 4)42
15. 3)93

16. 81 ÷ 7
17. 69 ÷ 3
18. 65 ÷ 4
19. 77 ÷ 7
20. 25 ÷ 3

21. 47 ÷ 4
22. 87 ÷ 9
23. 53 ÷ 5
24. 64 ÷ 4
25. 38 ÷ 5

Challenge

Copy and correct each problem.

```
      7 r2            21 r5           9 r2           25 r3
26. 6)43        27. 4)89        28. 5)37       29. 3)75
    −42             −8              −35            −6
      1              09               2             15
                    − 4                            −12
                       5                              3
```

Three-Digit Quotients

Step 1
Divide hundreds.
Multiply. Subtract.
Bring down tens.

$$
\begin{array}{r}
2 \\
4\overline{)848} \\
-8 \\
\hline
04 \\
\end{array}
$$

Step 2
Divide tens.
Multiply. Subtract.
Bring down ones.

$$
\begin{array}{r}
21 \\
4\overline{)848} \\
-8 \\
\hline
04 \\
-4 \\
\hline
08 \\
\end{array}
$$

Step 3
Divide ones.
Multiply. Subtract.

$$
\begin{array}{r}
212 \\
4\overline{)848} \\
-8 \\
\hline
04 \\
-4 \\
\hline
08 \\
-8 \\
\hline
0 \\
\end{array}
$$

Divide.

1. $3\overline{)963}$ 2. $4\overline{)444}$ 3. $3\overline{)936}$ 4. $2\overline{)628}$ 5. $2\overline{)648}$

6. $3\overline{)996}$ 7. $4\overline{)448}$ 8. $5\overline{)555}$ 9. $2\overline{)486}$ 10. $3\overline{)666}$

11. $884 \div 4$ 12. $666 \div 6$ 13. $369 \div 3$ 14. $448 \div 4$ 15. $846 \div 2$

16. Andrews' Frame Shop charges $8 to frame one picture. If they took in $888 during January, how many pictures did they frame?

Three-Digit Quotients with Remainders

Divide.

$$\begin{array}{r} 144\ r3 \\ 6\overline{)867} \\ -\ 6 \\ \hline 26 \\ -\ 24 \\ \hline 27 \\ -\ 24 \\ \hline 3 \end{array}$$

Check.

$$\begin{array}{r} 144 \\ \times\ \ 6 \\ \hline 864 \\ +\ \ \ 3 \\ \hline 867 \end{array}$$

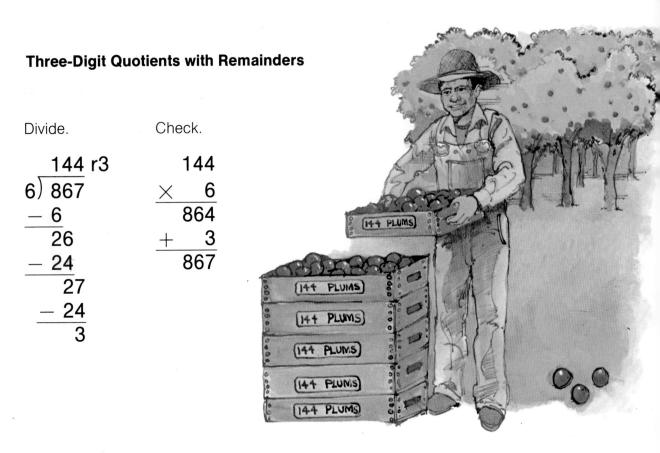

Divide. Check the first row.

1. 219 r1
   4)877

2. 5)917

3. 7)849

4. 2)967

5. 3)848

6. 4)683

7. 3)976

8. 5)747

9. 4)591

10. 6)908

11. 6)705

12. 8)911

13. 5)773

14. 6)885

15. 3)713

16. 4)853

17. 3)653

18. 2)547

19. 5)806

20. 6)954

21. 797 ÷ 2

22. 849 ÷ 4

23. 427 ÷ 3

24. 698 ÷ 5

25. 409 ÷ 3

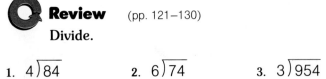 **Review** (pp. 121–130)

Divide.

1. 4)84

2. 6)74

3. 3)954

4. 5)563

5. 2)464

Dividing Hundreds

$8\overline{)257}$ Look at the hundreds. There are not enough hundreds to divide, so divide tens.

Step 1
Divide tens.
Multiply. Subtract.
Bring down ones.

$$\begin{array}{r} 3 \\ 8\overline{)\ 257} \\ -\ 24 \\ \hline 17 \end{array}$$

Write 3 in the tens place of the quotient.

Step 2
Divide ones.
Multiply. Subtract.
Write the remainder.

$$\begin{array}{r} 32\ \text{r1} \\ 8\overline{)\ 257} \\ -\ 24 \\ \hline 17 \\ -\ 16 \\ \hline 1 \end{array}$$

Divide. Check the first row.

1. $\overset{72\ \text{r5}}{6\overline{)437}}$
2. $8\overline{)348}$
3. $5\overline{)318}$
4. $4\overline{)237}$
5. $9\overline{)703}$

6. $3\overline{)206}$
7. $2\overline{)177}$
8. $6\overline{)448}$
9. $7\overline{)549}$
10. $8\overline{)716}$

11. $9\overline{)523}$
12. $5\overline{)417}$
13. $4\overline{)374}$
14. $6\overline{)195}$
15. $8\overline{)642}$

16. Jose has collected 237 colored bottles. He can fit 8 bottles on a shelf. How many shelves can he fill? How many bottles left over?

17. Stephanie has collected 146 pennies. She can fit 9 pennies on each page in an album. How many pages can she fill? How many pennies left over?

Placing the First Digit in the Quotient

Before you divide, decide where the first digit should go.

$\frac{2}{4\overline{)843}}$ There are enough hundreds to divide, so the first digit will go above the **hundreds** place.

$\frac{8}{6\overline{)492}}$ There are not enough hundreds to divide, so the first digit will go above the **tens** place.

Write the first digit for each quotient in the correct place. Do not complete the problem.

1. $6\overline{)154}$ (²)
2. $7\overline{)830}$
3. $5\overline{)426}$
4. $7\overline{)812}$
5. $8\overline{)729}$

6. $5\overline{)731}$
7. $5\overline{)462}$
8. $9\overline{)945}$
9. $4\overline{)348}$
10. $4\overline{)813}$

11. $3\overline{)121}$
12. $4\overline{)261}$
13. $2\overline{)913}$
14. $6\overline{)482}$
15. $6\overline{)777}$

16. $3\overline{)714}$
17. $8\overline{)711}$
18. $9\overline{)281}$
19. $3\overline{)916}$
20. $3\overline{)267}$

21. $5\overline{)478}$
22. $7\overline{)612}$
23. $8\overline{)841}$
24. $9\overline{)329}$
25. $6\overline{)476}$

Choose the correct answer.

26. $3\overline{)254}$
    (84 r2 or 842 r1)
27. $2\overline{)408}$
    (24 or 204)
28. $6\overline{)587}$
    (975 or 97 r5)

29. $4\overline{)861}$
    (215 r1 or 25 r5)
30. $7\overline{)329}$
    (470 or 47)
31. $3\overline{)982}$
    (327 r1 or 37 r2)

Zero in the Quotient

Step 1
Divide hundreds.
Multiply. Subtract.
Bring down tens.

$$
\begin{array}{r}
2 \\
4\overline{)837} \\
-8 \\
\hline
03 \\
\end{array}
$$

Step 2
Divide tens.
Multiply. Subtract.
Bring down ones.

$$
\begin{array}{r}
20 \\
4\overline{)837} \\
-8 \\
\hline
03 \\
-0 \\
\hline
37 \\
\end{array}
$$

Step 3
Divide ones.
Multiply. Subtract.
Write the remainder.

$$
\begin{array}{r}
209 \text{ r1} \\
4\overline{)837} \\
-8 \\
\hline
03 \\
-0 \\
\hline
37 \\
-36 \\
\hline
1 \\
\end{array}
$$

Divide. Check the first row.

1. 106 r1
   6)637

2. 5)548

3. 4)817

4. 3)928

5. 4)431

6. 3)614

7. 8)869

8. 9)928

9. 7)744

10. 2)819

11. 6)641

12. 7)739

13. 5)514

14. 8)819

15. 4)436

16. 5)543

17. 2)407

18. 6)649

19. 3)914

20. 3)319

21. 3)325

22. 4)831

23. 5)543

24. 9)965

25. 3)634

 Calculate

Find the missing numbers.

26. ?÷7＝108

27. ?÷7＝108 r1

28. ?÷7＝108 r5

29. ?÷7＝108 r6

Gift-Making Problems

1. Perry spent 320 minutes making 8 pencil holders. How many minutes did he take to make each one?   40

2. Tony made 4 hand puppets. It took him 544 minutes. How many minutes did it take to make each puppet?

3. Jana spent 705 minutes making 5 pot holders. How many minutes did she take to make each one?

4. Bob spent 153 minutes making 9 greeting cards. How many minutes did he take to make each one?

5. Lynn spent 306 minutes painting 9 sheets of wrapping paper. How many minutes did she take to paint each one?

6. Cerita needed 9 marbles to make one paperweight. If she used 495 marbles, how many paperweights did she make?

7. Yoshiro made sets of coasters with 8 coasters in each set. If he used 128 coasters, how many sets did he make?

8. Paula needed 8 balls of yarn to knit a sweater. If she used 144 balls of yarn, how many sweaters did she make?

9. Elaine made wooden puzzles with 6 pieces in each puzzle. If she used 864 pieces, how many puzzles did she make?

10. Anwar needed 3 bottles of paint to paint a toy boat. If he used 108 bottles of paint, how many toy boats did he paint?

11. Larry spent 192 minutes making 8 pot hangers. How many minutes did he take to make each one?

12. Will made bunches of paper flowers with 7 flowers in each bunch. If he used 294 flowers, how many bunches did he make?

Dividing Thousands

$3\overline{)4628}$ There are enough thousands to divide.

```
      1542 r2
3)  4628
   − 3
     16
   − 15
     12
   − 12
      08
   −  6
      2
```

Divide. Check the first row.

1. $4\overline{)7529}$ 1882 r1
2. $5\overline{)8614}$
3. $3\overline{)8627}$
4. $7\overline{)9874}$
5. $2\overline{)7613}$

6. $8\overline{)9714}$
7. $4\overline{)8915}$
8. $6\overline{)8714}$
9. $7\overline{)8381}$
10. $7\overline{)8081}$

11. $6\overline{)8132}$
12. $2\overline{)5179}$
13. $3\overline{)4588}$

14. $4763 \div 3$
15. $9046 \div 7$
16. $8919 \div 4$

17. $3475 \div 2$
18. $6187 \div 6$
19. $6741 \div 4$

20. A bicycle company has to ship 8103 bicycles. The packers put 6 bicycles in each crate. How many crates do they fill? How many bicycles left over?

More Dividing Thousands

$3\overline{)2587}$ Look for the thousands. There are not enough thousands to divide, so divide hundreds.

```
    862 r1
3)2587
 − 24
   18
 − 18
    07
 −   6
     1
```

Divide. Check the first row.

1. 953 r2
   $4\overline{)3814}$

2. $7\overline{)6413}$

3. $5\overline{)4812}$

4. $3\overline{)2113}$

5. $8\overline{)7612}$

6. $5\overline{)4413}$

7. $2\overline{)1517}$

8. $6\overline{)4813}$

9. $6\overline{)5813}$

10. $9\overline{)8572}$

Now do these.

11. $7\overline{)6023}$

12. $3\overline{)3824}$

13. $9\overline{)8418}$

14. $8\overline{)8617}$

15. $6\overline{)5753}$

16. $9652 \div 3$

17. $6460 \div 7$

18. $8746 \div 4$

19. $3615 \div 4$

20. $4109 \div 2$

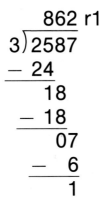 **Review** (pp. 121–137)

Divide.

1. $6\overline{)92}$

2. $7\overline{)653}$

3. $5\overline{)626}$

4. $6\overline{)5462}$

5. $4\overline{)8977}$

Dividing Money

Lionel and Linda earned $12.60 mowing lawns. They divided the money equally. How much did each of them earn?

Remember to line up decimals.

```
   $6.30
2)$12.60
 - 12
   06
 -  6
    0
```

Divide. Remember $ and . in your answers.

1. $0.66 over 3)$1.98

2. 4)$36.24

3. 8)$16.32

4. 5)$5.20

5. 6)$69.24

6. 4)$9.28

7. 5)$14.50

8. 4)$1.16

9. 9)$3.33

10. 8)$79.28

11. 3)$4.35

12. 7)$14.70

13. 2)$38.54

14. 8)$12.16

15. 3)$16.77

16. Beth earned $16.25 in 5 hours. How much did she earn each hour?

17. 5 tickets to a football game cost $62.50. How much for each ticket?

18. 8 cartons of milk cost $6.56. How much for each carton?

19. Mark earned $8.82 in 7 hours. How much did he earn each hour?

Rare Book Club Problems

Solve each problem.

1. The Rare Book Club divides its 870 members into 6 equal groups to help with club activities. How many people in each group? 145

2. The club is having a show of 146 rare books. If 9 books fit on one bookrack, how many bookracks will they fill? How many books left over?

3. The book club library is open 6 hours a day. Frank Novak promises to spend 246 hours working in the library. How many 6-hour days is that?

4. A speaker is coming to talk about rare books. The club has 532 chairs. If 8 chairs are put in each row, how many rows will there be? How many chairs left over?

5. The speaker has 74 slides to show. If she puts the same number of slides in each of 2 trays, how many slides will be in each tray?

6. Lucy Moin repairs old books. If she can repair 7 books a week, how many weeks will it take her to repair 133 books?

Bowling Averages

Natalie bowled 5 games in one day. Here is how to find the **average** of her 5 scores.

Step 1
Add the scores.

Step 2
Divide the sum by the number of scores.

$$
\begin{array}{r}
138 \\
92 \\
111 \\
118 \\
+ \quad 96 \\
\hline
555
\end{array}
$$

$$
\begin{array}{r}
111 \\
5\overline{)555}
\end{array}
$$

The average score is 111.

Find Natalie's average score for each day.

1. Monday: 120, 144, 133, 152, 141
   138

2. Tuesday: 112, 142, 134, 132, 120

3. Thursday: 140, 142, 136, 130, 132

4. Friday: 90, 110, 94, 114, 122

 **Challenge**

5. What was Natalie's average score for the 4 days?
   Hint: Start by adding the averages for each day.

Traveling Averages

The Van Louck family went on a four-week vacation. They recorded the number of kilometers they drove each day.

Day	Week 1	Week 2	Week 3	Week 4
Sunday	212	85	308	216
Monday	46	392	144	55
Tuesday	315	115	96	411
Wednesday	187	28	35	136
Thursday	98	284	288	204
Friday	233	188	103	83
Saturday	57	203	76	71

For each week, find the average number of kilometers they drove each day.

1. week 1 164

2. week 2

3. week 3

4. week 4

Short Division—Dividing Tens

In short division, you do some of the work in your head.

Step 1
Divide tens.

$$3 \overline{)79} \quad 2$$

Step 2
Put the left over ten with the ones.

$$3 \overline{)7^19} \quad 2$$

Think: 7 tens
          −6 tens
          1 ten left over

Step 3
Divide ones.
Write the remainder.

$$3 \overline{)7^19} \quad 2\ 6\ r1$$

Think: 19
         −18
          1 left over

Divide. Use short division.

1. $4\overline{)65}$ 16 r1
2. $3\overline{)71}$
3. $5\overline{)96}$
4. $6\overline{)86}$
5. $2\overline{)57}$

6. $7\overline{)86}$
7. $3\overline{)85}$
8. $3\overline{)95}$
9. $5\overline{)73}$
10. $6\overline{)91}$

11. $2\overline{)87}$
12. $2\overline{)93}$
13. $4\overline{)75}$
14. $6\overline{)83}$
15. $7\overline{)94}$

16. $2\overline{)71}$
17. $3\overline{)56}$
18. $6\overline{)79}$
19. $4\overline{)61}$
20. $2\overline{)65}$

21. Alex's Gym is having a picnic. 45 people are going. 5 people can go in 1 car. How many cars are needed?

22. Olga drove 98 kilometers in 2 hours. She drove the same number of kilometers each hour. How many kilometers did she drive each hour?

Short Division—Dividing Hundreds

Any division problem with a one-digit divisor can be done using short division.

Step 1
Divide hundreds.
Put the left over
hundred with the tens.

$$\frac{2}{3\overline{)7^143}}$$

Think: 7 hundreds
        −6 hundreds
         1 hundred left over

Step 2
Divide tens.
Put the left over
ten with the ones.

$$\frac{2\ 4}{3\overline{)7^14^23}}$$

Think: 14 tens
        −12 tens
          2 tens left over

Step 3
Divide ones.
Write the
remainder.

$$\frac{2\ 4\ 7\ r2}{3\overline{)7^14^23}}$$

Think: 23
        −21
          2 left over

Divide. Use short division. Check the first row.

1. $\overset{249\ r1}{3\overline{)748}}$

2. $4\overline{)697}$

3. $5\overline{)784}$

4. $7\overline{)859}$

5. $2\overline{)937}$

6. $6\overline{)932}$

7. $5\overline{)564}$

8. $3\overline{)826}$

9. $4\overline{)845}$

10. $3\overline{)656}$

11. $7\overline{)949}$

12. $8\overline{)897}$

13. $6\overline{)718}$

14. $2\overline{)427}$

15. $4\overline{)538}$

16. $2\overline{)465}$

17. $4\overline{)698}$

18. $3\overline{)725}$

19. $6\overline{)981}$

20. $9\overline{)996}$

 **Challenge**

Divide. Use short division.

21. $904 \div 3$

22. $562 \div 5$

23. $477 \div 2$

24. $308 \div 3$

25. $689 \div 4$

26. $721 \div 6$

27. $469 \div 3$

28. $844 \div 8$

29. $652 \div 6$

30. $605 \div 3$

Short Division with Hundreds

In long division, you write out all your work. In short division, you do some of the work mentally.

long division

$$\begin{array}{r} 112\text{ r}3 \\ 4\overline{)451} \\ -\,4 \\ \hline 05 \\ -\,4 \\ \hline 11 \\ -\,8 \\ \hline 3 \end{array}$$

short division

$$4\overline{)45^{1}1}\; {\small 11\ 2\text{ r}3}$$

Divide. Use long or short division.

1. 3)347   115 r2
2. 8)911
3. 6)944
4. 4)686
5. 2)737

6. 3)815
7. 5)763
8. 6)848
9. 3)419
10. 7)817

11. 4)845
12. 2)477
13. 3)493
14. 5)718
15. 6)667

Find each quotient and remainder.

16. $937 \div 2$
17. $737 \div 3$
18. $914 \div 4$
19. $805 \div 6$
20. $861 \div 4$

21. $679 \div 6$
22. $445 \div 3$
23. $608 \div 5$
24. $637 \div 3$
25. $767 \div 2$

26. $437 \div 3$
27. $865 \div 7$
28. $309 \div 2$
29. $689 \div 5$
30. $249 \div 2$

Zero in Short Division

Sometimes in short division
you get zeros in the quotient.

$$\begin{array}{r} 208 \text{ r1} \\ 4\overline{)833} \end{array}$$

$$\begin{array}{r} 1090 \text{ r2} \\ 4\overline{)4362} \end{array}$$

Divide. Use short division. Watch out for zeros in the quotient.

1. $\begin{array}{r} 1035 \text{ r2} \\ 4\overline{)4142} \end{array}$
2. $6\overline{)6515}$
3. $3\overline{)907}$
4. $5\overline{)1023}$
5. $7\overline{)9944}$

6. $7\overline{)731}$
7. $6\overline{)9643}$
8. $4\overline{)5239}$
9. $5\overline{)506}$
10. $6\overline{)6167}$

11. $3\overline{)901}$
12. $2\overline{)8073}$
13. $9\overline{)940}$
14. $3\overline{)7211}$
15. $5\overline{)503}$

16. $6\overline{)7841}$
17. $5\overline{)5462}$
18. $3\overline{)620}$
19. $4\overline{)831}$
20. $2\overline{)8011}$

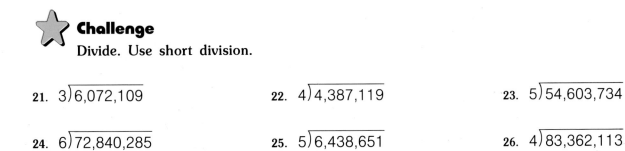

⭐ Challenge
Divide. Use short division.

21. $3\overline{)6,072,109}$
22. $4\overline{)4,387,119}$
23. $5\overline{)54,603,734}$

24. $6\overline{)72,840,285}$
25. $5\overline{)6,438,651}$
26. $4\overline{)83,362,113}$

Chapter Review

Divide. (ex. 1-5: pp. 122–123), (ex. 6-10: pp. 124–125),
(ex. 11-15: p. 126)

1. $4\overline{)37}$
2. $2\overline{)17}$
3. $3\overline{)25}$
4. $7\overline{)46}$
5. $6\overline{)31}$

6. $3\overline{)39}$
7. $2\overline{)24}$
8. $4\overline{)92}$
9. $6\overline{)72}$
10. $5\overline{)95}$

11. $3\overline{)23}$
12. $5\overline{)64}$
13. $4\overline{)69}$
14. $6\overline{)77}$
15. $7\overline{)86}$

Divide. (ex. 16-20: p. 129), (ex. 21-25: p. 130)

16. $4\overline{)448}$
17. $3\overline{)639}$
18. $2\overline{)268}$
19. $5\overline{)555}$
20. $4\overline{)844}$

21. $5\overline{)617}$
22. $6\overline{)876}$
23. $4\overline{)549}$
24. $7\overline{)816}$
25. $3\overline{)651}$

Divide. (ex. 26-30: p. 131), (ex. 31-35: p. 133)

26. $8\overline{)542}$
27. $6\overline{)295}$
28. $3\overline{)187}$
29. $4\overline{)365}$
30. $7\overline{)643}$

31. $5\overline{)713}$
32. $2\overline{)816}$
33. $7\overline{)769}$
34. $6\overline{)654}$
35. $3\overline{)927}$

Divide. (ex. 36-40: p. 136), (ex. 41-45: p. 137),
(ex. 46-50: p. 138)

36. $5\overline{)7463}$
37. $6\overline{)8179}$
38. $3\overline{)4482}$
39. $4\overline{)6189}$
40. $9\overline{)9892}$

41. $7\overline{)6140}$
42. $6\overline{)5462}$
43. $4\overline{)2996}$
44. $6\overline{)4187}$
45. $8\overline{)6733}$

46. $2\overline{)\$12.60}$
47. $5\overline{)\$16.25}$
48. $7\overline{)\$8.82}$
49. $8\overline{)\$24.16}$
50. $9\overline{)\$9.99}$

Chapter Test

Divide.

1. $3\overline{)25}$ 2. $4\overline{)17}$ 3. $2\overline{)31}$ 4. $4\overline{)48}$ 5. $8\overline{)88}$

6. $3\overline{)63}$ 7. $8\overline{)92}$ 8. $2\overline{)37}$ 9. $3\overline{)65}$ 10. $7\overline{)98}$

Divide.

11. $4\overline{)844}$ 12. $3\overline{)636}$ 13. $2\overline{)224}$ 14. $4\overline{)879}$ 15. $6\overline{)806}$

Divide.

16. $6\overline{)295}$ 17. $6\overline{)758}$ 18. $6\overline{)548}$ 19. $5\overline{)315}$ 20. $4\overline{)372}$

Divide.

21. $8\overline{)8194}$ 22. $7\overline{)5083}$ 23. $2\overline{)3749}$ 24. $6\overline{)3826}$ 25. $4\overline{)3015}$

Brush Up

Add.

1. 38
+98

2. 565
+392

3. 1099
+5677

4. 465
+3926

5. 5523
+6119

6. $2.79
+ 4.50

7. $3.45
+ 6.98

8. $4.46
+ 3.12

9. $7.95
+ 1.08

10. $8.62
+ 0.44

Subtract.

11. 62
−56

12. 314
− 80

13. 407
−192

14. 800
−374

15. 5688
−2397

16. $8.31
− 3.26

17. $5.00
− 3.99

18. $7.51
− 4.06

19. $9.81
− 6.39

20. $6.07
− 4.52

Multiply.

21. 469
× 6

22. 5070
× 8

23. 700
× 50

24. 26
×52

25. 347
× 41

26. $11.41
× 7

27. $36.72
× 5

28. $84.30
× 8

29. $0.33
× 6

30. $90.02
× 5

Divide.

31. 4)96

32. 5)773

33. 6)448

34. 4)6741

35. 3)4588

36. 3)$1.98

37. 8)$12.16

38. 8)$79.28

39. 5)$14.50

40. 4)$9.28

CHAPTER 6

Problem Solving

Using Problem Solving at Work

Laura Hillman is a basketball coach. New uniforms for the team
cost $340. One sponsor donated $200; another donated $50.
Laura works the problem $200 + $50 = $250 to find how much she
has so far. Then she works $340 − $250 to find how much she
still needs to raise. Laura needs $90 more for the uniforms.

Choosing the Operation

Before you solve a problem, think:
- What is the question?
- What are the important facts?
- Will you add, subtract, multiply, or divide?

Answer the questions about each problem.

1. One week 248 planes landed at the airport. 342 planes took off. How many more took off than landed?
   a. What are the important facts?
      248 planes landed, 342 took off
   b. Will you add, subtract, multiply, or divide?
   c. Solve the problem.

2. The airplane pilots fly 28 hours each week. How many hours do they fly in 8 weeks?
   a. What are the important facts?
   b. Will you add, subtract, multiply, or divide?
   c. Solve the problem.

3. 168 planes landed on Saturday. 79 planes landed on Sunday. How many planes landed on those two days?
   a. What are the important facts?
   b. Will you add, subtract, multiply, or divide?
   c. Solve the problem.

4. A helicopter takes 4 people on each trip. One month 356 people took the helicopter. How many trips was that?
   a. What are the important facts?
   b. Will you add, subtract, multiply, or divide?
   c. Solve the problem.

5. About 300 suitcases can be unloaded in an hour. How many suitcases can be unloaded in 8 hours?
   a. What are the important facts?
   b. Will you add, subtract, multiply, or divide?
   c. Solve the problem.

Choosing the Operation

Tell whether you will **add, subtract, multiply,** or **divide.** Then solve the problem.

1. The Wildlife Park has 24 lions. Each eats 2 bags of food a day. How many bags do all the lions eat in a day? multiply, 48

2. Art spent 20 minutes seeing the lions, 35 minutes seeing the bears, and 15 minutes seeing the tigers. How many minutes was that in all?

3. Kathy spent $1.19 on food for the monkeys and $0.89 on food for the birds. How much did she spend in all?

4. The park has 275 camels with one hump and 384 camels with two humps. How many more camels with two humps?

5. The park got 432 new turtles. If 8 turtles are put in each turtle tank, how many turtle tanks are needed?

6. The park is open for 6 hours a day. How many hours is it open in 35 days?

7. The park has 349 white bears, 685 brown bears, and 492 black bears. How many bears in all?

8. The park puts 7 snakes in each snake tank. If they have 273 snakes, how many tanks are needed?

9. The park has 785 foxes and 864 weasels. How many more weasels than foxes?

10. The park had 697 tigers. It gave 250 of them to another wildlife park. How many tigers were left?

11. Susan went to the park 6 times in one year. If she paid $2.25 to get in each time, how much did she spend going to the park that year?

12. Manuel has 90 more minutes to spend at the park. If he spends 10 minutes seeing each kind of animal, how many more kinds of animals can he see?

 **Calculate**

13. The park train makes 28 trips a day. If the park is open 208 days a year, how many trips does the train make in 3 years?

Writing Problems

Writing problems can help you solve problems. Write a question about each. Then answer the question.

1. A movie ticket costs $3.50. Sukie went to the movies 3 times in April. *How much did she spend on movies in April?* *$10.50*

2. During a double feature, the first movie lasts 126 minutes, the cartoon lasts 4 minutes, and the second movie lasts 165 minutes.

3. 859 people went to the movie theater on Friday. 945 people went on Saturday.

4. The movie theater shows a movie for 2 weeks. There are 52 weeks in a year.

5. The movie theater has 85 rows of seats with 20 seats in each row.

6. Al and Sarah started out to the movies with $20. They spent $5.80.

7. Pam, Chuck, and Len spent $7.50 on movie tickets and juice drinks. They shared the cost equally.

8. One night, the theater collected $948.75 for adults' tickets and $995.75 for children's tickets.

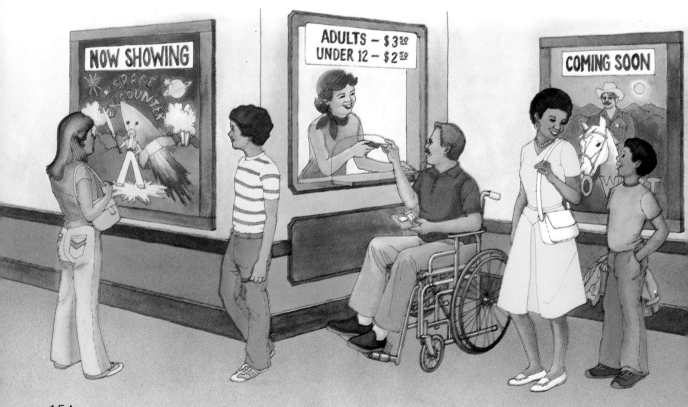

Making an Easier Problem

You can write an easier problem to help solve a harder problem.

Write an easier problem for each. Then solve both the easier problem and the harder problem.

1. There are 7421 cars in Clift and 8985 cars in Hardis. How many cars in both cities?

   There are 7 cars in Clift and 9 cars in Hardis. How many cars in both cities?

   $$
   \begin{array}{r} 7 \\ +9 \\ \hline 16 \end{array}
   \qquad
   \begin{array}{r} 7421 \\ +8985 \\ \hline 16{,}406 \end{array}
   $$

2. There are 13 schools in Clift. Each school has room for 875 children. How many children can go to all 13 schools?

3. Harwood has a population of 6043. Melville has a population of 3783. What is the population of both towns?

4. Lewis has an area of 1687 square kilometers. Centerville has 1349 square kilometers. How much larger is Lewis?

5. Townsville has 7859 kilometers of paved roads. Shaw has 4587 kilometers of paved roads. How many more kilometers of paved roads does Townsville have?

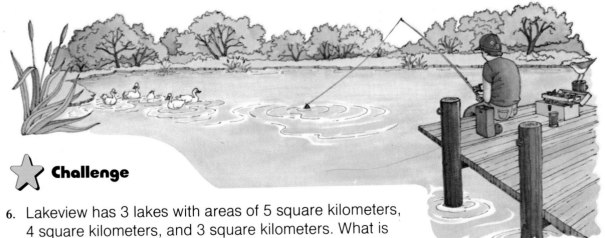

⭐ **Challenge**

6. Lakeview has 3 lakes with areas of 5 square kilometers, 4 square kilometers, and 3 square kilometers. What is the average area of the 3 lakes?

Too Much Information

If you have more information than you need, think:
- Do you have too much information? Choose only the information you need.

For each problem, tell what information is not needed. Then solve the problem.

1. It costs $7.50 per person to rent a canoe. 42 people rent canoes and 76 people rent sailboats. How much does the boathouse collect for renting canoes?   76 people, $315

2. A bicycle race around the lake will last for 2 hours. 68 adults and 95 children are in the race. How many more children than adults are in the race?

3. One month the boathouse sold 465 red kites, 369 yellow kites, and 721 green kites at $1.79 each. How many kites were sold that month?

4. $360 was spent to plant new trees. There were 7 different types of trees, and each tree cost $8. How many trees were planted?

5. 86 people swim on Friday, 356 people swim on Saturday, and 497 people swim on Sunday. How many more people swim on Sunday than on Saturday?

6. One Sunday 96 people went fishing. 84 people each caught 3 fish. How many fish did they catch in all?

⭐ **Challenge**

7. The boathouse is open 6 hours on weekdays and 8 hours on Saturdays and Sundays. There are 4 lifeguards who each make $8.50 an hour. Joan works as a lifeguard during June and July and makes $525 each month. How much does she make in all?

Too Little Information

Sometimes you do not have enough information to solve a problem.
- Decide what facts you need.

What do you need to know before you can solve each problem?

1. There are 583 brown seals on Rock Island. How many more brown seals than gray seals?   the number of gray seals

2. One spring 68 female sea lions had pups. A few females had twins. How many sea lion pups were born that spring?

3. Rock Island has 435 gray seals, 583 brown seals, and sea lions. How many seals and sea lions in all?

4. On East Island there are 285 adult seals. How many more adults than babies?

5. How many fish do 75 seals eat in a day?

6. A seal swam for 3 hours. How far did he swim?

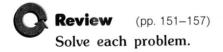 **Review**   (pp. 151–157)
Solve each problem.

1. One rainy day 578 students at Rockport School had umbrellas. 349 had raincoats. There were 645 students at school that day. How many did not have umbrellas?

2. One year the town of Rockport had 46 rainy days. The next year there were 56 rainy days. How many rainy days in those two years?

Solving Two-Step Problems

Sometimes you must do two steps to solve a problem.

Rick buys 3 paperback books for $1.95 each and gives the clerk $10.00. What is his change?

Step 1
Multiply.

$$\begin{array}{r} \$1.95 \\ \times 3 \\ \hline \$5.85 \end{array}$$

Step 2
Subtract.

$$\begin{array}{r} \$10.00 \\ -5.85 \\ \hline \$4.15 \end{array}$$

Rick's change is $4.15.

Finish solving each problem. Step 1 has been done for you.

1. Eddie has $4.25 to buy books. His father gives him another $5.75. How many paperback books can he buy for $2.00 each?

   Step 1: Add.

   $$\begin{array}{r} \$4.25 \\ +5.75 \\ \hline \$10.00 \end{array}$$

   Step 2: Divide.

   $$\begin{array}{r} 5 \text{ books} \\ 2\overline{)10} \end{array}$$

2. Betty's Bookstore orders 6 boxes of books. There are 24 books in a box and each book costs $2.00. How much does Betty spend for the order?

   Step 1: Multiply.

   $$\begin{array}{r} 24 \\ \times6 \\ \hline 144 \end{array}$$

3. Betty gets 900 new books. She puts 375 on tables and divides the rest equally among 5 bookcases. How many books does Betty put in each bookcase?

   Step 1: Subtract.

   $$\begin{array}{r} 900 \\ -375 \\ \hline 525 \end{array}$$

4. Elena buys each of her 3 friends a book for $1.85 and a bookmark for $0.49. How much does she spend in all?

   Step 1: Add.

   $$\begin{array}{r} \$1.85 \\ +0.49 \\ \hline \$2.34 \end{array}$$

Solving Two-Step Problems

Use two steps to solve each problem.

1. Fred has $10.90. He saves $7.50 and spends the rest on 4 paperback books. How much does each paperback cost? $0.85

2. Betty Sue has $15.80 and spends $6.75 on books. Then she earns $4.50 raking leaves. How much money does she have then?

3. Betty's Bookstore has a sale and takes $0.75 off the price of every book. Liana buys two copies of a book that was $5.65 before the sale. How much does she spend?

4. Paul and Ernie earn $3.75 an hour for spending 6 hours cleaning up Betty's Bookstore. If they divide their earnings equally, how much does each make?

5. Jennie spends $8.70 for 6 copies of *Sportslife. Sports* costs $1.75 a copy. How much more does one copy of *Sports* cost than *Sportslife*?

6. Paul buys a book for $3.75 and a magazine for $1.35. He gives the clerk $20. What is his change?

 **Calculate**

7. A school has $300 to buy books. They order 35 copies of a book that costs $2.79 and 58 copies of a book that costs $3.48. How much money does the school have left?

Solving Two-Step Problems

Use two steps to solve each problem.

1. Six people are planting a garden. They spend $85 for seeds, $44 for fertilizer, and divide the amount equally. How much does each spend? $21.50

2. They need 12 meters of garden hose. They have two hoses that are 4 meters and 3 meters long. How many more meters of hose do they need?

3. They buy 176 bean plants. Mike plants 85 on Saturday and the rest on Sunday. It takes 5 minutes for each plant. How much time does he spend planting on Sunday?

4. The 6 people pick about 2 boxes of beans from each of their 15 bean plants. If they divide the beans equally, how many boxes does each get?

5. Margaret buys 2 wheelbarrows for $28.98 each. The total sales tax is $3.48. What is the total bill?

6. They have 6 rows of tomato plants with 8 plants in each row. Each plant cost $0.85. How much for all the plants?

⭐ Challenge

7. Jim weeded for 210 minutes a day on 6 Saturdays and 75 minutes a day on 5 Sundays. There are 60 minutes in one hour. How many hours did he weed in all?

Using Rounding to Check Answers

You can use rounding to be sure that your answers are sensible.

There are 42 people in the Checkers Club. Each pays $2.75 in dues a month. How much is collected each month?

Step 1
Find the exact answer.

$$\begin{array}{r} \$2.75 \\ \times\ \ \ \ 42 \\ \hline \$115.50 \end{array}$$

Step 2
Round to the nearest ten. Then multiply.

$$\begin{array}{r} \$2.80 \\ \times\ \ \ \ 40 \\ \hline \$112.00 \end{array}$$

$115.50 is a sensible answer.

Solve each problem. Then round the numbers to the nearest ten and solve again to see if your answer is sensible.

1. The Checkers Club has $789. They spent $432 to repaint the Club's room. How much was left?
   $789 − $432 = $357
   $790 − $430 = $360

2. Eileen played 3 games of checkers. She spent 18 minutes on the first game, 24 minutes on the second game and 17 minutes on the third. How many minutes in all?

3. The Checkers Club bought 21 new checkerboards. Each board cost $7.31. How much did the club spend?

4. In a set of checkers, there are 24 playing pieces. How many pieces in 26 sets of checkers?

 **Challenge**

5. Armand won 8 checkers games in these number of minutes: 24, 29, 27, 24, 25, 32, 19, and 23. Round each time to the nearest ten. Then find the average time.

Estimating Answers

You can use rounding to estimate answers.

The Kitchen Supply Company ships
6 frying pans in a box. Can they ship
478 pans in 78 boxes?

Think: Round 478 to 480,
        $480 \div 6 = 80$.
They cannot ship 478 pans in 78 boxes.

Round to estimate an answer to each question. Write yes or no.

1. The Kitchen Supply Company ships
   5 electric mixers in one carton.
   Can they ship 67 mixers in
   14 cartons?   yes

2. The Kitchen Place has 71 boxes of
   spoons with 36 spoons in each box.
   Are there enough spoons to fill an
   order of 3000?

3. 8 sets of dishes fit in one large
   drawer. Can 158 sets of dishes fit
   in 22 drawers?

4. 3 mixing bowls fit in one box. Can
   243 mixing bowls fit in 84 boxes?

5. You have $10 to spend at the Kitchen
   Place. You want to buy a mixing bowl
   that costs $4.99 and a potholder that
   costs $1.49. Can you buy both?

6. You have $20 to spend at the Kitchen
   Place. You want to buy a teapot that
   costs $8.99 and a cutting board that
   costs $11.79. Can you buy both?

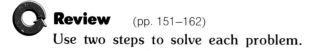

Review   (pp. 151–162)
Use two steps to solve each problem.

1. Monita buys 3 dish towels that each
   cost $2.49. She gives the clerk $10.00.
   What is her change?

2. Darrell buys a tablecloth for $11.49
   and a frying pan for $6.50. He gives
   the clerk $20.00. What is his change?

Using Diagrams

A **diagram** or drawing can help you solve a problem. To solve
the problem below, you need the information in the diagram.
In the diagrams on this page, km stands for kilometers.

● Decide what facts you need. Find those facts in the diagram.

Janet goes from the office building to the bus station, then to
the post office, and back to the office building. How far does she go?

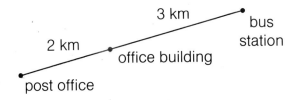

office building to bus station	3 km
bus station to post office	5 km
post office to office building	+ 2 km
Janet has gone 10 kilometers.	10 km

**Solve each problem. Find any needed information in the
diagram.**

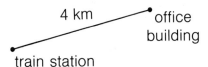

1. Janet and Wally deliver packages.
    Wally starts at the office building and
    makes 3 trips back and forth to the
    train station. How far does he go?
    24 kilometers

2. Janet is going from the post office to
    the train station. She has gone
    4 kilometers. How much farther does
    she have to go?

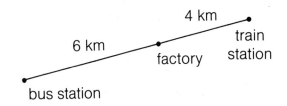

3. Wally leaves the post office just as
    Janet leaves the factory. They meet
    after Janet has gone 4 kilometers.
    How far has Wally gone?

4. Janet and Wally start at the factory.
    She goes to the bus station and he
    goes to the train station. How far
    apart are they then?

Making Diagrams

Make a diagram to help solve each problem.

1. An office building has several elevators. Two elevators leave the 30th floor. The first stops at the 33rd floor and the other stops at the 28th floor. How many floors are between the elevators?   4

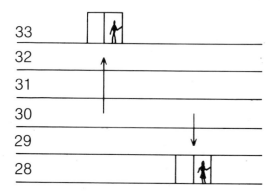

2. There are 2 flights of stairs between floors. How many flights between the 6th floor and the 13th floor?

3. An elevator leaves the 14th floor and goes down 4 floors, up 3 floors down 6 floors, and then up 8 floors. On what floor does it stop?

4. An elevator starts on the 14th floor, goes down to the 8th floor, and then halfway back up to the 14th floor. On what floor does it stop?

5. One elevator is on the 17th floor and another elevator is on the 23rd floor. They move toward each other and meet when the first elevator has gone up 3 floors. How many floors up or down has the second elevator gone?

6. An elevator goes up 6 floors and then down 9 floors. It stops at the 48th floor. On what floor did it start?

Making Diagrams

Make a diagram to help solve each problem.

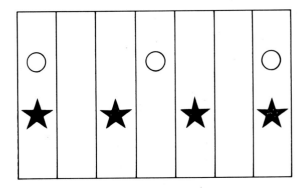

1. A flag has 7 stripes. The first, fourth, and seventh stripes have circles. The first, third, fifth, and seventh stripes have stars. How many stripes have no shapes?   2

2. A flag has 50 stars with either 5 or 6 stars in a row. The top row has 6 stars, the next row has 5 stars, the next has 6, the next has 5, and so on. How many rows?

3. A flag has 15 rows of stars with either 3 or 4 stars in each row. The top row has 4 stars, the next row has 3, and so on. How many stars in all?

4. A long banner has 19 stripes in this pattern: 1 red, then 3 blue, then 2 yellow. Then the pattern repeats. What color is the middle stripe?

5. A banner has 26 stripes in this pattern: 2 green, then 1 white, then 3 red, then 2 black. What color is the last stripe?

6. A banner has 30 stripes in this pattern: 1 blue, then two red, then 1 white. How many times is the complete pattern repeated?

7. A banner has 24 stripes in this pattern: one red, then two green, then one red. What color is the fifteenth stripe?

Chapter Review

Tell whether you will **add, subtract, multiply,** or **divide.** Then solve the problem.   (ex. 1-4: p. 152)

1. A pet shop keeps 6 fish in each tank. If they have 96 fish, how many tanks do they have?

2. There are 31 parrots and 67 parakeets in a bird cage. How many more parakeets than parrots?

3. The shop has 238 canaries and 187 finches. How many canaries and finches in all?

4. There are 24 turtle tanks with 13 turtles in each tank. How many turtles in all?

For each problem, tell what information is not needed. Then solve the problem.   (ex. 5-6: p. 156)

5. 87 people rented canoes, 45 people rented sailboats, and 65 people rented rowboats. How many more people rented canoes than rowboats?

6. Ron bought 4 magazines for $1.45 each and a pair of sunglasses for $6.75. How much did he spend for the magazines?

Use two steps to solve each problem.   (ex. 7-8: p. 159)

7. Paula buys two books for $4.75 each and a magazine for $1.35. How much does she spend in all?

8. Bert buys a book for $4.25 and a magazine for $0.85. He gives the clerk $10. What is his change?

Make a diagram to help solve each problem.
(ex. 9-10: p. 164)

9. A factory and an office building are 14 kilometers apart. Janet goes from the office building to the factory, and then halfway back to the office building. How far does she go?

10. Two trains leave a station going in opposite directions. After one train has gone 8 kilometers and the other has gone 6 kilometers, how far apart are the trains?

Chapter Test

Tell whether you will add, subtract, multiply, or divide. Then solve the problem.

1. Nick has 24 kilograms of luggage and June has 21 kilograms. How many kilograms do they have together?

2. A taxicab ride to the airport cost $8.65. What was the change from $20.00?

3. One week 456 planes landed. 678 took off. How many more took off than landed?

4. The airport restaurant is open 18 hours a day. How many hours is it open in 14 days?

For each problem, tell what information is not needed. Then solve the problem.

5. There were 8 rainy days in April, 7 rainy days in May, and 9 rainy days in June. How many more rainy days in June than in May?

6. It took 3 days to repair the leaking roof. It cost $150 for materials and $475 for labor. How much did it cost in all?

Use two steps to solve each problem.

7. There are 12 rows of pepper plants with 15 plants in each row. Each plant costs $0.45. How much for all the plants?

8. Joyce buys 3 pairs of gardening gloves for $3.87 a pair. The sales tax is $0.70. What is the total bill?

Make a diagram to help solve each problem.

9. An office building is 8 kilometers from the post office. Wally leaves the office building just as Janet leaves the post office. They meet after Wally has gone 3 kilometers. How far has Janet gone?

10. Two trains move toward each other from stations 15 kilometers apart. They meet after one train has gone 9 kilometers. How far has the other train gone?

Brush Up

Write > or < to order the numbers.

1. 5969 ◯ 5914
2. 7010 ◯ 7101
3. 37,654 ◯ 37,459
4. 24,398 ◯ 24,389
5. 148,025 ◯ 148,003
6. 7,567,000 ◯ 7,765,000

Write the answers.

7. Round 889 to the nearest hundred.
8. Round 444 to the nearest ten.
9. Round 6989 to the nearest thousand.
10. Round 3457 to the nearest thousand.
11. Round 735 to the nearest hundred.
12. Round 2672 to the nearest ten.

Add or subtract.

13. $\begin{array}{r} 163,465 \\ +725,232 \end{array}$

14. $\begin{array}{r} 83 \\ -59 \end{array}$

15. $\begin{array}{r} 466 \\ +435 \end{array}$

16. $\begin{array}{r} 790 \\ -\ 56 \end{array}$

17. $\begin{array}{r} 505 \\ -136 \end{array}$

18. $\begin{array}{r} 786 \\ 41 \\ +\ 59 \end{array}$

19. $\begin{array}{r} 89,957 \\ -43,725 \end{array}$

20. $\begin{array}{r} 8000 \\ -2445 \end{array}$

21. $\begin{array}{r} 6179 \\ 850 \\ +\ 493 \end{array}$

22. $\begin{array}{r} 22,998 \\ -\ \ \ 539 \end{array}$

Multiply or divide.

23. $\begin{array}{r} 79 \\ \times\ 7 \end{array}$

24. $\begin{array}{r} 441 \\ \times\ \ 3 \end{array}$

25. $\begin{array}{r} 87 \\ \times 20 \end{array}$

26. $\begin{array}{r} 68 \\ \times 28 \end{array}$

27. $\begin{array}{r} 707 \\ \times\ 39 \end{array}$

28. $6\overline{)67}$
29. $4\overline{)884}$
30. $7\overline{)49}$
31. $4\overline{)64}$
32. $7\overline{)982}$

33. $33 \div 4$
34. 23×6
35. 71×9
36. $65 \div 7$
37. $84 \div 3$

CHAPTER 7

Geometry

Using Geometry at Work

Nancy George is a sculptor. She is making a steel sculpture
out of similar triangles. One triangle has sides that measure
3 meters, 4 meters, and 5 meters. A second triangle has
the same angles and sides of 1.5 meters, 2 meters, and 2.5
meters. Nancy can use both triangles because they are similar.

Rays and Angles

A **ray** is named with two letters.
A ray starts at a point and continues
in one direction. Ray AB starts at
point A and continues through point B.

Two rays that start at the same point
form an angle. The common point is
called the **vertex**. Ray YX and Ray YZ
form angle XYZ. It can also be named
angle ZYX. ∠ is the symbol for angle.

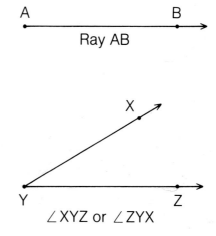

∠XYZ or ∠ZYX

Name each angle.

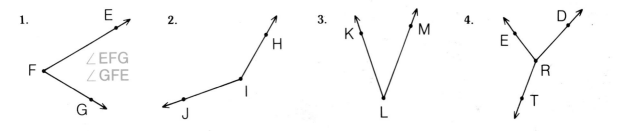

1. ∠EFG
   ∠GFE

2.

3.

4.

Name the vertex of these angles.

5. ∠GHI   6. ∠CBA   7. ∠RPO   8. ∠STV   9. ∠MNO

⭐ **Challenge**

Name each angle in these shapes.

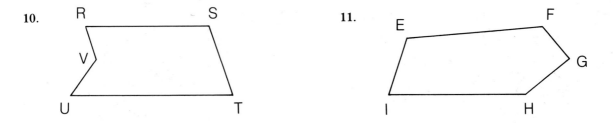

10.

11.

Right Angles

A **right angle** is shaped like the square corner of a sheet of paper.

Answer the questions. You can use a square corner to find right angles.

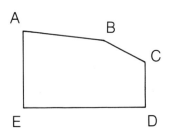

1a. Name the right angles.   ∠ AED, ∠ EDC
b. Name the angle that is smaller than a right angle.
c. Name the angles that are larger than a right angle.

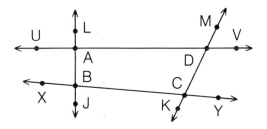

2a. Name four right angles.
b. Name six angles that are smaller than a right angle.
c. Name six angles that are larger than a right angle.

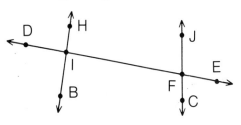

3a. Name the right angles.
b. Name two angles that are smaller than a right angle.
c. Name two angles that are larger than a right angle.

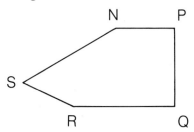

4a. Name the right angles.
b. Name the angle that is smaller than a right angle.
c. Name the angles that are larger than a right angle.

5. Draw a shape with only one right angle.

6. Draw a shape with exactly two right angles.

Types of Angles

An **acute angle** is smaller than a right angle.

An **obtuse angle** is larger than a right angle.

Tell whether each angle is **right, acute,** or **obtuse.** You can use a square corner or a protractor to help you decide.

1. 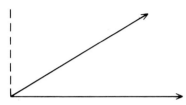 obtuse

2.

3.

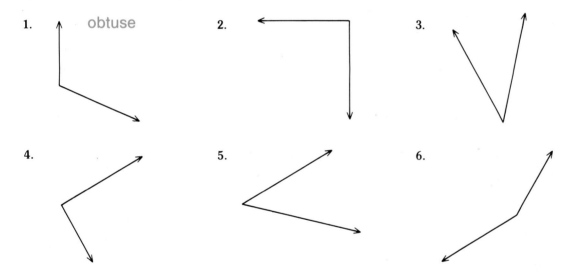

4.

5.

6.

Name each angle in these shapes. Then tell whether each is **right, acute,** or **obtuse.**

7. A   B
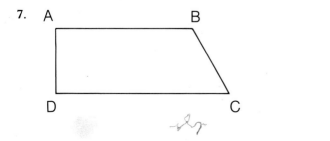
D   C

8. R   S
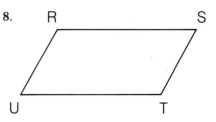
U   T

Types of Lines

Lines are named with two letters.

Line MY

A **line segment** is part of a line.

Lines AB and CD are **parallel** lines.
Parallel lines never meet.
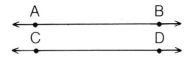

Lines EF and GH are **intersecting** lines.
Intersecting lines meet or cross each other.

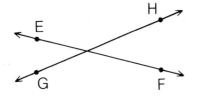

Lines IJ and JK are **perpendicular** lines.
Perpendicular lines form a right angle.

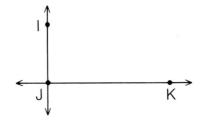

Write **parallel**, **perpendicular**, or **intersecting** for each pair of
lines. Some pairs have two answers.

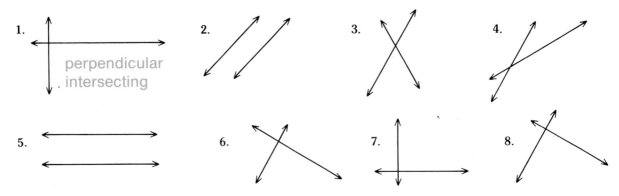

1.

perpendicular
intersecting

2.

3.

4.

5.

6.

7.

8.

Naming Lines

Name all of the pairs of parallel line segments in each shape.

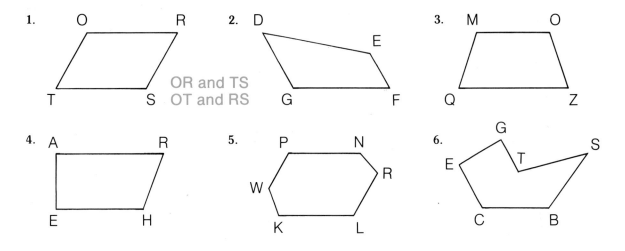

1. O R
   T S
   OR and TS
   OT and RS

2. D E
   G F

3. M O
   Q Z

4. A R
   E H

5. P N
   W R
   K L

6. G
   E T S
   C B

Name all of the pairs of intersecting line segments in each shape.

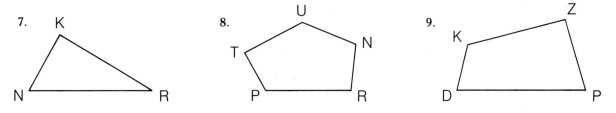

7. K
   N R

8. U
   T N
   P R

9. Z
   K
   D P

Name all of the pairs of perpendicular line segments in each shape.

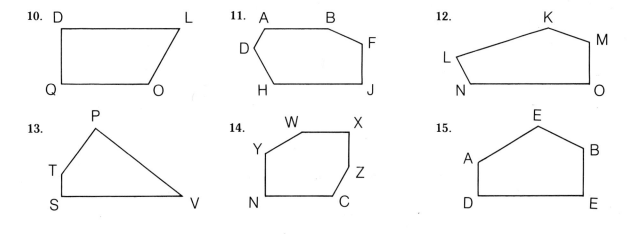

10. D L
    Q O

11. A B
    D F
    H J

12. K
    M
    L
    N O

13. P
    T
    S V

14. W X
    Y
    Z
    N C

15. E
    A B
    D E

Polygons

A **polygon** is a closed shape formed by straight line segments.
A polygon is made of three or more sides.

These are polygons.

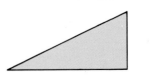 

Triangle   Hexagon

These are not polygons.

Pentagon   Octagon

Is the shape a polygon? Write yes or no.

1. 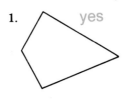 yes
2.
3.
4.

5.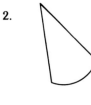
6.
7.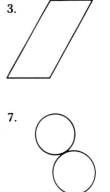
8.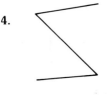
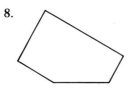

How many sides does each polygon have?

9. triangle   10. hexagon   11. pentagon   12. octagon

Quadrilaterals

A polygon with four sides is a **quadrilateral**. Some quadrilaterals have special names.

A **trapezoid** is a quadrilateral with only one pair of parallel sides.

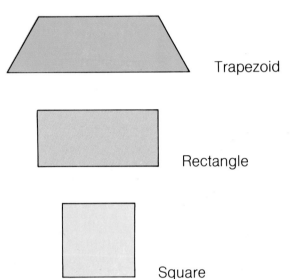

Trapezoid

A **rectangle** has four right angles. Opposite sides of a rectangle are parallel.

Rectangle

A **square** is a rectangle with all of its sides the same length.

Square

Tell whether each quadrilateral is a trapezoid, a square, or a rectangle. (Some shapes have two names.)

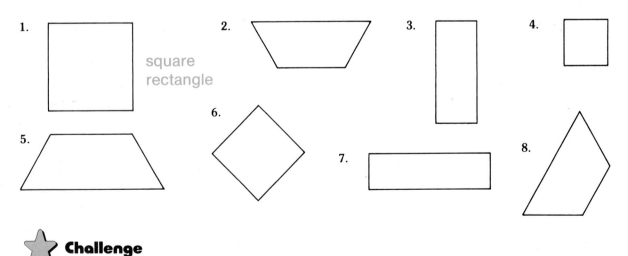

1.

square
rectangle

2.

3.

4.

5.

6.

7.

8.

⭐ **Challenge**

9. Draw a quadrilateral with only one pair of parallel sides.

10. Draw a quadrilateral with two pairs of parallel sides.

Parallelograms

A **parallelogram** is a quadrilateral with two pairs of parallel sides. Here are three special kinds of parallelograms.

A **rhombus** is a parallelogram with no right angles and all of its sides the same length.

Rectangles and squares are parallelograms with four right angles.

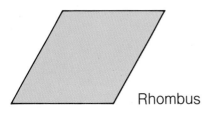
Rhombus

Rectangle   Square

Tell whether each parallelogram is a rectangle, a square, or a rhombus. (Some shapes have two names.)

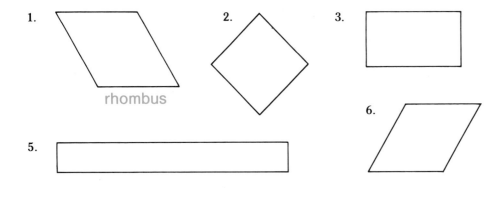

1.

rhombus

2.

3.

4.

6.

5.

 Review   (pp. 171–178)

Use this shape to find the answers.

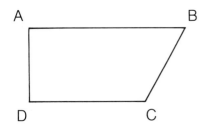

A   B

D   C

1. Name each angle. Then tell whether each is **right**, **obtuse**, or **acute**.

2. Name a pair of parallel line segments.

3. Name two pairs of intersecting line segments.

Circles

Point A is the center of circle A.

A **radius** connects the center of a circle with a point on a circle. All the **radii** of a circle are the same length. AF, AB, AC, and AG are radii of this circle.

A **chord** connects two points on a circle. DE and FG are chords.

A **diameter** is a chord that goes through the center of a circle. FG is a diameter of this circle. A diameter of a circle is twice as long as its radius.

Circle A

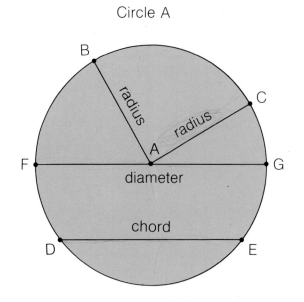

Write the answers.

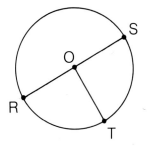

1a. Name the center.   point O
  b. Name three radii.
  c. Name a diameter.

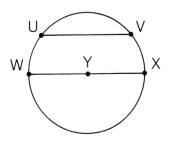

2a. Name a diameter.
  b. Name two chords.
  c. Which chord is longer?

 **Challenge**

3. Radius ED of a circle is 7 centimeters long. How long is radius EF of the same circle? Make a drawing of the circle and label the radii.

4. A circle has a radius that is 8 centimeters long. How long is the diameter of the circle?

More Circles

Circle T

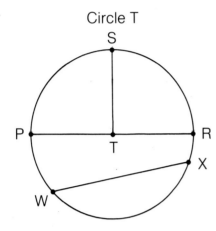

Circle B

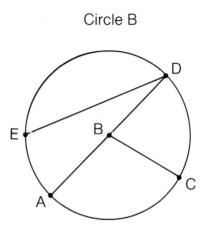

Use the circles to find the answers.

1. Name three radii of circle T.   TP, TS, TR

2. Name a diameter of circle T.

3. Name three radii of circle B.

4. Name two chords of circle T.

5. Name a diameter of circle B.

6. Name two angles in circle T.

7. Name two chords of circle B.

Review   (pp. 171–180)

Use this circle to find the answers.

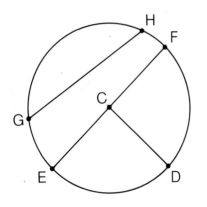

1. Are EF and CD parallel or intersecting?

2. Name two angles.

3. Name two chords.

4. Name a diameter.

5. Name three radii.

Congruent Shapes

Shapes that have the same size and shape are **congruent**.

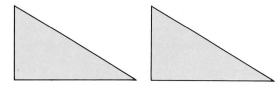

These are congruent.

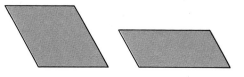

These are not congruent.

Are the shapes congruent? Write yes or no.

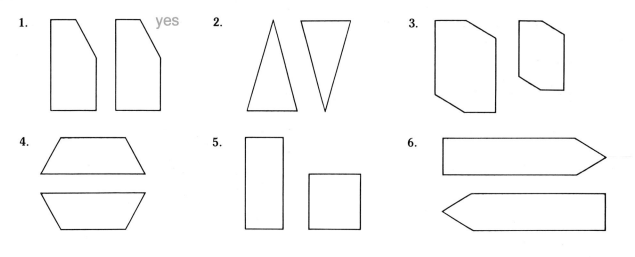

1. yes

2.

3.

4.

5.

6.

7. Write the letters of the pairs of congruent trapezoids.

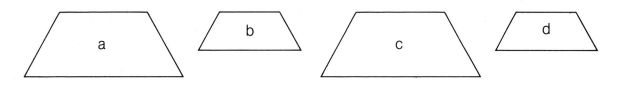

 **Challenge**

8. Draw a pair of congruent line segments.

Finding Congruent Parts

Tell whether each shape is divided into congruent parts.

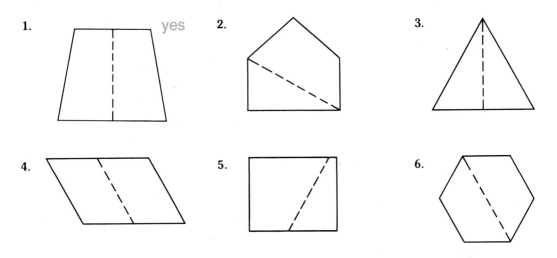

1. yes   2.   3.

4.   5.   6.

Tell whether each rectangle is divided into congruent parts.

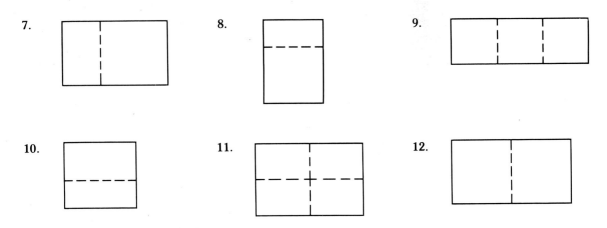

7.   8.   9.

10.   11.   12.

⭐ Challenge

13. Draw a rectangle. Show three ways to divide it into two congruent parts.

14. Draw a line segment. Divide it into two congruent parts.

Similar Shapes

Shapes that have the same shape are **similar**.

These are similar.

These are not similar.

Are the shapes similar? Write yes or no.

1. 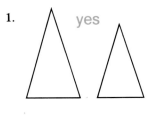 yes

2.

3.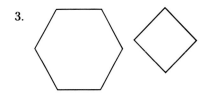

4.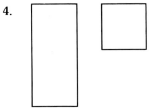

5.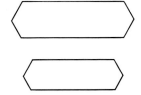

6.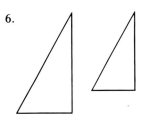

Calculate

7. A parallelogram has sides that measure 465 centimeters, 589 centimeters, 465 centimeters, and 589 centimeters. What is the distance around this parallelogram?

Folding Lines of Symmetry

Make a square. Fold it in half. Unfold.

The fold line is a **line of symmetry.**

It divides the square into two parts that are the same size and shape.

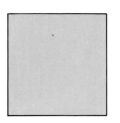

Fold across. Unfold. This fold line is a line of symmetry, too.

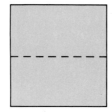

Use the same square. Make these folds, too.

1. How many new lines of symmetry have you made?   2

2. Are there any other lines of symmetry in the square?

3. How many lines of symmetry does the square have in all?

4. Do all lines of symmetry pass through the center of the square?

5. Are the lines of symmetry parallel or intersecting?

 **Challenge**

6. Draw a shape other than a square. How many lines of symmetry can you find?

Symmetry in Letters and Words

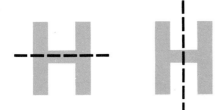

Both dotted lines are
lines of symmetry.

Copy each letter. Draw the line of symmetry.

1. U 2. C 3. M 4. V 5. D

The line of symmetry divides each word in half. Write the word.

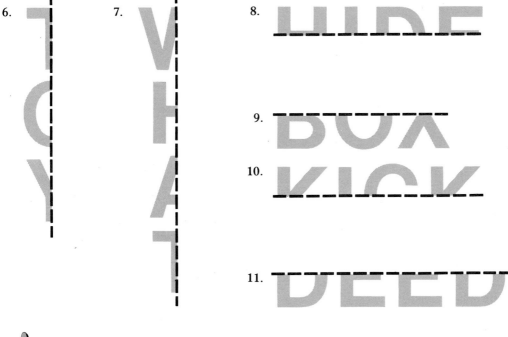

6.

7.

8. HIDE

9. BOX

10. KICK

11. DEED

⭐ Challenge

12. Which letters of the alphabet have at least one line of symmetry?

13. Write two words that have a line of symmetry.

Solid Shapes

Each flat surface of a solid is a **face**.

Two faces meet at an **edge**.

Edges meet at a **vertex**.

A cube has six faces, twelve edges, and eight **vertices**.

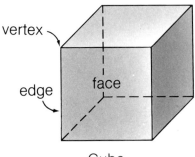

Cube

Count the numbers of edges, faces, and vertices for each solid shape.

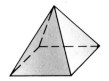

1a. ⬚ edges   9
 b. ⬚ faces
 c. ⬚ vertices

2a. ⬚ edges
 b. ⬚ faces
 c. ⬚ vertices

3a. ⬚ edges
 b. ⬚ faces
 c. ⬚ vertices

 **Calculate**

4. This solid has six faces. Find the area of each face. Then add to find the total surface area of the solid.

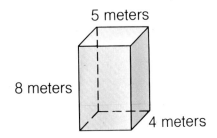

5 meters

8 meters

4 meters

More Solid Shapes

Cube

Cone

Cylinder

Sphere

Pyramid   Rectangular Prism   Triangular Prism

Write the name of a solid shape to answer each question.

1. Which shape has six square faces?
   cube

2. Which shape has four triangular faces and one four-sided face?

3. Which shape has no flat faces?

4. Which shape has only two flat faces?

5. Which two shapes have six quadrilaterals for faces?

6. Which shape has two triangles and three rectangles for faces?

7. Which shape has eight edges?

8. Which shape has nine edges?

9. Which shape has only one vertex?

10. Which shape has six vertices?

11. Which four shapes have no curved faces or edges?

12. In what ways is the sphere different from the other solids?

Chapter Review

Name each angle in these shapes. Then tell whether each angle is **right**, **acute**, or **obtuse**. (ex. 1-2: p. 173)

1.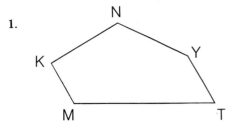

2.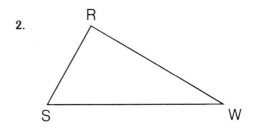

Write the name of each shape. (ex. 3-5: p. 178), (ex. 6-8: p. 187)

3.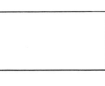

4.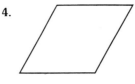

5.

6.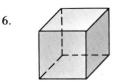

7.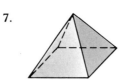

8.

Use this circle to find the answers. (ex. 9: p. 179)

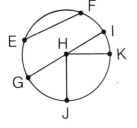

9a. Name the center.
  b. Name a diameter.
  c. Name four radii.
  d. Name two chords.

Tell whether each pair of shapes is **similar**, **congruent**, or **both**. (ex. 10-12: pp. 181, 183)

10. 11. 12.

Chapter Test

Name each angle in these shapes. Then tell whether each angle is **right, acute,** or **obtuse.**

1.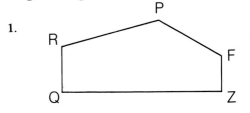

2.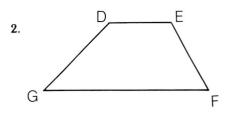

Write the name of each shape.

3.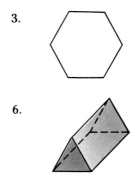

4.

5.

6.

7.

8.

Use this circle to find the answers.

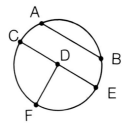

9a. Name the center.
 b. Name two chords.
 c. Name a diameter.
 d. Name three radii.

Tell whether each pair of shapes is **similar, congruent,** or **both.**

10.

11.

12.

Brush Up

Add.

1. 59
+36

2. 11
  5
+89

3. 172
+ 81

4. 906
161
+ 27

5. 488
+ 93

6. 3375
+ 650

7. 3976
+1424

8. 5906
+3139

9. 8877
+4325

10. 1969
432
+3655

Subtract.

11. 88
−29

12. 60
−34

13. 713
− 64

14. 361
− 85

15. 749
−637

16. 500
−308

17. 303
−284

18. 9254
−3858

19. 7884
−3947

20. 2000
−1176

Multiply.

21. 64
× 5

22. 98
× 6

23. 402
× 8

24. 674
× 3

25. 562
× 7

26. 5432
× 4

27. 8459
× 6

28. 750
× 10

29. 94
×21

30. 483
× 91

Divide.

31. $4\overline{)37}$

32. $3\overline{)19}$

33. $8\overline{)50}$

34. $6\overline{)66}$

35. $2\overline{)448}$

36. $8\overline{)96}$

37. $3\overline{)47}$

38. $9\overline{)624}$

39. $6\overline{)541}$

40. $7\overline{)931}$

41. 78 ÷ 6

42. 63 ÷ 4

43. 148 ÷ 4

44. 206 ÷ 2

45. 843 ÷ 6

CHAPTER 8

Fractions and Decimals

Using Decimals at Work

Ann Kellogg is a machinist. She uses drill bits to drill holes in metal. The drill bits come in different sizes and are marked with decimals. Ann wants to use the largest of three bits marked 5.5 mm, 5.15 mm, and 5.35 mm. Because she knows how to order decimals, Ann knows the bit marked 5.5 mm is the largest.

Parts of Shapes

This circle is divided into 3 equal parts, or thirds. One-third of the circle is shaded.

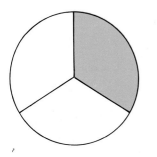

You can write one-third as a **fraction**.

1 ← **numerator**: number of shaded parts
3 ← **denominator**: number of equal parts

Write the fraction for the shaded part.

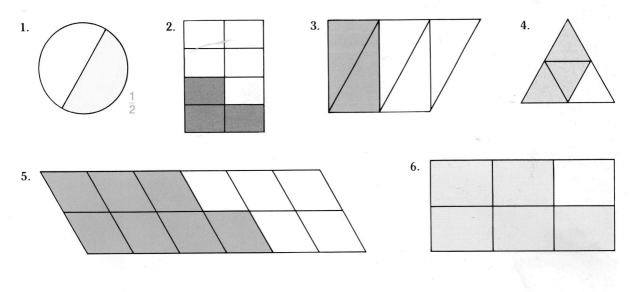

1. $\frac{1}{2}$

2.

3.

4.

5.

6.

Write a fraction for each.

7. three-fifths

8. one-half

9. seven-eighths

10. four-sixths

11. five-tenths

12. three-ninths

13. one-fourth

14. three-eighths

15. one-sixth

16. two-thirds

17. three-fourths

18. nine-tenths

Parts of Groups

There are 6 eggs in this group. Each egg is one-sixth of the whole group.

$\dfrac{5}{6}$ ← number of speckled eggs
← total number of eggs

Write a fraction for each.

1. $\dfrac{?}{?}$ of the toys are toy cars. $\dfrac{3}{5}$

2. $\dfrac{?}{?}$ of the flowers are red.

3. $\dfrac{?}{?}$ of the animals are cats.

4. $\dfrac{?}{?}$ of the fruit are bananas.

Write the fraction.

5. There are 5 birds. 3 are blue jays. $\dfrac{?}{?}$ of the birds are blue jays.

6. There are 9 coins. 4 are nickels. $\dfrac{?}{?}$ of the coins are nickels.

7. There are 6 balloons. 2 are purple. $\dfrac{?}{?}$ of the balloons are purple.

8. There are 15 bottles. 9 are glass. $\dfrac{?}{?}$ of the bottles are glass.

Parts of Shapes and Groups

a, 11, 12

One-third or $\frac{1}{3}$ is shaded.
Two-thirds or $\frac{2}{3}$ is not shaded.
Three-thirds or $\frac{3}{3}$ equals one whole.

Two-fifths or $\frac{2}{5}$ are limes.
Three-fifths or $\frac{3}{5}$ are lemons.
Five-fifths or $\frac{5}{5}$ equals one whole.

Write a fraction for each.

1a. Shaded: $\frac{2}{3}$
b. Not shaded:
c. Whole:

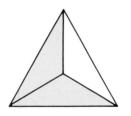

2a. Toy cats:
b. Toy dogs:
c. Whole:

3a. Shaded:
b. Not shaded:
c. Whole:

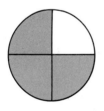

Write a fraction for each.

4. Numerator is 3.
   Denominator is 10.

5. Numerator is 7.
   Denominator is 10.

6. Numerator is 5.
   Denominator is 10.

7. Denominator is 8.
   Numerator is 3.

8. Denominator is 6.
   Numerator is 2.

9. Denominator is 9.
   Numerator is 5.

10. Denominator is 8.
    Numerator is 5.

11. Numerator is 1.
    Denominator is 4.

12. Denominator is 5.
    Numerator is 3.

Fraction Problems

These are fuel gauges. They show how much gasoline there is in a car's fuel tank. Use the fuel gauges to answer the questions.

a  b 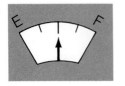 c 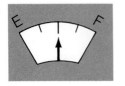 d

1. Each fuel gauge is divided into ⬚ parts.   4

2. How full is tank **a**? Write a fraction.

3. How full is tank **b**? Write a fraction.

4. How full is tank **c**? Write a fraction.

5. Tank **d** is empty. Show this with a fraction.

6. Write the fraction for a full fuel tank.

The fraction strip is divided into 9 equal parts. Use the fraction strip. Write the answers.

A	B	C	D	E	F	G	H	I	J

$\frac{0}{9}$ $\frac{1}{9}$ $\frac{2}{9}$ $\frac{3}{9}$ $\frac{4}{9}$ $\frac{5}{9}$ $\frac{6}{9}$ $\frac{7}{9}$ $\frac{8}{9}$ $\frac{9}{9}$

0   1

7. A to C is $\frac{?}{?}$. $\frac{2}{9}$

8. A to F is $\frac{?}{?}$.

9. A to B is $\frac{?}{?}$.

10. A to D is $\frac{?}{?}$.

11. A to E is $\frac{?}{?}$.

12. A to G is $\frac{?}{?}$.

13. A to I is $\frac{?}{?}$.

14. A to J is $\frac{?}{?}$.

15. A to H is $\frac{?}{?}$.

16. How many ninths are equal to 0?

17. How many ninths are equal to 1?

Equal Fractions

The whole shapes are the same. The kinds of parts are different.

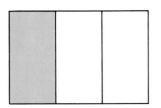

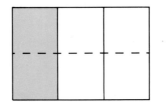

$\frac{1}{3}$ of the rectangle is shaded.

$\frac{2}{6}$ of the rectangle is shaded.

$\frac{1}{3}$ and $\frac{2}{6}$ are **equal fractions**. They name the same number.

Copy and complete.

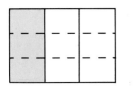

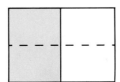

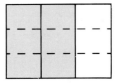

1. $\frac{2}{3} = \frac{?}{6}$ $\frac{2}{3} = \frac{4}{6}$

2. $\frac{1}{4} = \frac{?}{8}$

3. $\frac{3}{4} = \frac{?}{8}$

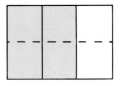

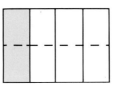

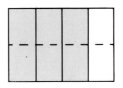

4. $\frac{1}{3} = \frac{?}{9}$

5. $\frac{1}{2} = \frac{?}{4}$

6. $\frac{2}{3} = \frac{?}{9}$

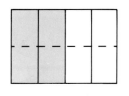

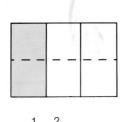

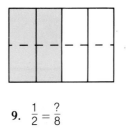

7. $\frac{2}{4} = \frac{?}{8}$

8. $\frac{1}{3} = \frac{?}{6}$

9. $\frac{1}{2} = \frac{?}{8}$

Multiplying and Dividing to Find Equal Fractions

You can multiply or divide both the numerator and denominator of a fraction by the same number to find an equal fraction.

$$\frac{2}{3} = \frac{2 \times 4}{3 \times 4} \text{ or } \frac{8}{12}$$

$$\frac{10}{15} = \frac{10 \div 5}{15 \div 5} \text{ or } \frac{2}{3}$$

Find the equal fractions.

1. $\frac{3}{6} = \frac{3 \div 3}{6 \div 3}$ or $\frac{?}{?}$ $\frac{1}{2}$

2. $\frac{3}{7} = \frac{3 \times 3}{7 \times 3}$ or $\frac{?}{?}$

3. $\frac{12}{18} = \frac{12 \div 6}{18 \div 6}$ or $\frac{?}{?}$

4. $\frac{2}{6} = \frac{2 \times 3}{6 \times 3}$ or $\frac{?}{?}$

5. $\frac{30}{40} = \frac{30 \div 10}{40 \div 10}$ or $\frac{?}{?}$

6. $\frac{2}{3} = \frac{2 \times 4}{3 \times 4}$ or $\frac{?}{?}$

Multiply or divide to find any two equal fractions for each.

7. $\frac{5}{8}$

8. $\frac{1}{2}$

9. $\frac{20}{36}$

10. $\frac{1}{4}$

11. $\frac{12}{20}$

12. $\frac{24}{48}$

13. $\frac{6}{9}$

14. $\frac{12}{18}$

15. $\frac{1}{3}$

16. $\frac{2}{10}$

17. $\frac{6}{8}$

18. $\frac{8}{16}$

19. Cynthia and Robert go fishing. They catch 8 fish. Robert cooks $\frac{2}{4}$ of the fish. Cynthia cooks $\frac{4}{8}$ of the fish. Did they cook the same number of fish?

Completing Equal Fractions

You can multiply to find a missing numerator.

Step 1
5 is multiplied by 4 to get 20.

Step 2
Multiply 2 by 4 to find the missing numerator.

$$\frac{2}{5} = \frac{?}{20}$$
×4

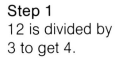
$$\frac{2}{5} = \frac{8}{20}$$

You can divide to find a missing numerator.

Step 1
12 is divided by 3 to get 4.

Step 2
Divide 9 by 3 to find the missing numerator.

$$\frac{9}{12} = \frac{?}{4}$$
÷3

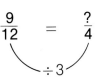
$$\frac{9}{12} = \frac{3}{4}$$

Copy and complete.

1.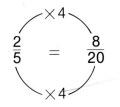
$$\frac{4}{5} = \frac{8}{10}$$

2.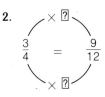
$$\frac{3}{4} = \frac{9}{12}$$

3.
$$\frac{8}{20} = \frac{2}{5}$$

4.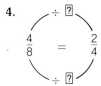
$$\frac{4}{8} = \frac{2}{4}$$

Copy and complete.

5. $\frac{3}{7} = \frac{?}{14}$

6. $\frac{5}{9} = \frac{?}{36}$

7. $\frac{3}{8} = \frac{?}{40}$

8. $\frac{8}{9} = \frac{?}{27}$

9. $\frac{4}{8} = \frac{?}{2}$

10. $\frac{12}{15} = \frac{?}{5}$

11. $\frac{10}{12} = \frac{?}{6}$

12. $\frac{8}{20} = \frac{?}{5}$

13. $\frac{3}{5} = \frac{?}{10}$

14. $\frac{15}{25} = \frac{?}{5}$

15. $\frac{2}{6} = \frac{?}{3}$

16. $\frac{9}{24} = \frac{?}{8}$

17. $\frac{3}{27} = \frac{?}{9}$

18. $\frac{1}{6} = \frac{?}{24}$

19. $\frac{2}{5} = \frac{?}{15}$

20. $\frac{2}{14} = \frac{?}{7}$

21. $\frac{1}{2} = \frac{?}{10}$

22. $\frac{4}{6} = \frac{?}{3}$

23. $\frac{10}{15} = \frac{?}{3}$

24. $\frac{5}{6} = \frac{?}{12}$

Simplifying Fractions

When you divide the numerator and the denominator by the largest possible number, the fraction is in **simplest form**.

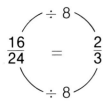

$$\frac{16}{24} = \frac{2}{3}$$

with $\div 8$ on numerator and $\div 8$ on denominator

8 is the largest number that both 16 and 24 can be divided by.

$\frac{2}{3}$ is the simplest form of $\frac{16}{24}$.

$\frac{1}{3}$ $\frac{2}{3}$

Is the fraction in simplest form? Write yes or no.

1. $\frac{9}{12}$ no   2. $\frac{4}{5}$ 3. $\frac{10}{14}$ 4. $\frac{15}{20}$ 5. $\frac{2}{3}$ 6. $\frac{12}{18}$

7. $\frac{2}{16}$ 8. $\frac{9}{15}$ 9. $\frac{3}{6}$ 10. $\frac{7}{10}$ 11. $\frac{8}{12}$ 12. $\frac{30}{40}$

Match each fraction to its simplest form. Write the letter.

13. $\frac{5}{10}$ 14. $\frac{12}{16}$ 15. $\frac{20}{80}$ 16. $\frac{10}{15}$ 17. $\frac{70}{80}$ 18. $\frac{2}{12}$

A. $\frac{1}{6}$ B. $\frac{2}{3}$ C. $\frac{1}{2}$ D. $\frac{7}{8}$ E. $\frac{1}{4}$ F. $\frac{3}{4}$

Write each fraction in simplest form.

19. $\frac{8}{12}$ 20. $\frac{6}{8}$ 21. $\frac{15}{24}$ 22. $\frac{3}{6}$ 23. $\frac{9}{15}$ 24. $\frac{2}{14}$

25. $\frac{12}{18}$ 26. $\frac{15}{20}$ 27. $\frac{10}{16}$ 28. $\frac{9}{12}$ 29. $\frac{8}{10}$ 30. $\frac{40}{50}$

Whole Numbers and Fractions

The simplest form of a fraction may be a whole number.
A fraction with 1 as the denominator equals a whole number.

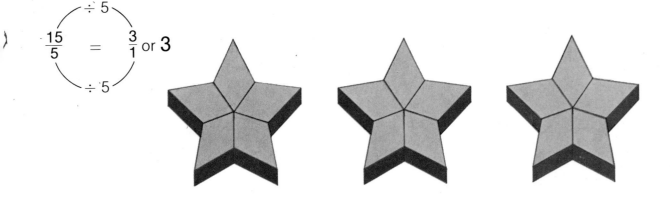

$$\frac{15}{5} = \frac{3}{1} \text{ or } 3$$

($\div 5$ ... $\div 5$)

Choose the simplest form for each fraction.

1. $\frac{15}{3}$ $\left(\frac{5}{2}, \frac{1}{5}, \text{ or } 5\right)$ 5

2. $\frac{20}{10}$ $\left(2, \frac{1}{2}, \text{ or } \frac{2}{5}\right)$

3. $\frac{16}{8}$ $\left(\frac{1}{8}, 2, \text{ or } \frac{3}{8}\right)$

4. $\frac{25}{5}$ $\left(\frac{1}{5}, 5, \text{ or } \frac{3}{5}\right)$

5. $\frac{49}{7}$ $\left(7, \frac{1}{7}, \text{ or } \frac{7}{7}\right)$

6. $\frac{81}{9}$ $\left(9, \frac{1}{9}, \text{ or } \frac{8}{9}\right)$

Write each fraction in simplest form.

7. $\frac{14}{7}$

8. $\frac{8}{8}$

9. $\frac{16}{4}$

10. $\frac{40}{10}$

11. $\frac{32}{8}$

12. $\frac{12}{6}$

13. $\frac{36}{6}$

14. $\frac{24}{8}$

15. $\frac{9}{9}$

16. $\frac{49}{7}$

17. $\frac{18}{2}$

18. $\frac{6}{3}$

⭐ **Challenge**

Write each fraction in simplest form.

19. $\frac{144}{24}$

20. $\frac{50}{10}$

21. $\frac{100}{10}$

22. $\frac{300}{30}$

23. $\frac{324}{18}$

24. $\frac{225}{15}$

Comparing Numerators to Order Fractions

To order fractions with the same denominators, compare
the numerators.

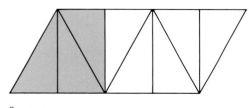

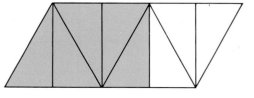

$\frac{3}{8}$ of the parts are shaded.

3 is less than 5.

$\frac{3}{8}$ is less than $\frac{5}{8}$.

$\frac{3}{8} < \frac{5}{8}$

$\frac{5}{8}$ of the parts are shaded.

5 is greater than 3.

$\frac{5}{8}$ is greater than $\frac{3}{8}$.

$\frac{5}{8} > \frac{3}{8}$

Look at the rectangles. Which fraction is greater?

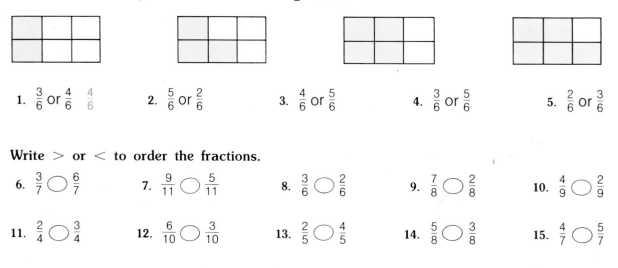

1. $\frac{3}{6}$ or $\frac{4}{6}$ $\frac{4}{6}$

2. $\frac{5}{6}$ or $\frac{2}{6}$

3. $\frac{4}{6}$ or $\frac{5}{6}$

4. $\frac{3}{6}$ or $\frac{5}{6}$

5. $\frac{2}{6}$ or $\frac{3}{6}$

Write > or < to order the fractions.

6. $\frac{3}{7} \bigcirc \frac{6}{7}$

7. $\frac{9}{11} \bigcirc \frac{5}{11}$

8. $\frac{3}{6} \bigcirc \frac{2}{6}$

9. $\frac{7}{8} \bigcirc \frac{2}{8}$

10. $\frac{4}{9} \bigcirc \frac{2}{9}$

11. $\frac{2}{4} \bigcirc \frac{3}{4}$

12. $\frac{6}{10} \bigcirc \frac{3}{10}$

13. $\frac{2}{5} \bigcirc \frac{4}{5}$

14. $\frac{5}{8} \bigcirc \frac{3}{8}$

15. $\frac{4}{7} \bigcirc \frac{5}{7}$

Calculate

Add or subtract from left to right to find the
numerator and denominator.

16. $\frac{8 + 5 - 2 - 3 + 6 + 3}{9 - 7 + 8 + 4 - 2 + 8}$

17. $\frac{16 + 8 - 15 - 6 + 9 - 11}{30 - 9 + 19 - 4 + 16 - 10}$

Comparing Denominators to Order Fractions

To order fractions when the numerators are 1, compare the denominators.

1 whole

| $\frac{1}{2}$ | $\frac{1}{2}$ |

| $\frac{1}{4}$ | $\frac{1}{4}$ | $\frac{1}{4}$ | $\frac{1}{4}$ |

| $\frac{1}{8}$ | $\frac{1}{8}$ | $\frac{1}{8}$ | $\frac{1}{8}$ | $\frac{1}{8}$ | $\frac{1}{8}$ | $\frac{1}{8}$ | $\frac{1}{8}$ |

| $\frac{1}{3}$ | $\frac{1}{3}$ | $\frac{1}{3}$ |

| $\frac{1}{6}$ | $\frac{1}{6}$ | $\frac{1}{6}$ | $\frac{1}{6}$ | $\frac{1}{6}$ | $\frac{1}{6}$ |

Compare denominators. Halves are greater than fourths. $\frac{1}{2} > \frac{1}{4}$

Compare denominators. Sixths are less than thirds. $\frac{1}{6} < \frac{1}{3}$

Look at the fraction bars. Use $>$ or $<$ to order the fractions.

1. $\frac{1}{3} \bigcirc< \frac{1}{2}$ 2. $\frac{1}{4} \bigcirc \frac{1}{6}$ 3. $\frac{1}{8} \bigcirc \frac{1}{2}$ 4. $\frac{1}{6} \bigcirc \frac{1}{3}$ 5. $\frac{1}{3} \bigcirc \frac{1}{4}$

Write $>$ or $<$ to order the fractions.

6. $\frac{1}{4} \bigcirc \frac{1}{5}$ 7. $\frac{1}{8} \bigcirc \frac{1}{6}$ 8. $\frac{1}{9} \bigcirc \frac{1}{10}$ 9. $\frac{1}{10} \bigcirc \frac{1}{9}$ 10. $\frac{1}{3} \bigcirc \frac{1}{7}$

11. $\frac{1}{6} \bigcirc \frac{1}{7}$ 12. $\frac{1}{2} \bigcirc \frac{1}{4}$ 13. $\frac{1}{8} \bigcirc \frac{1}{3}$ 14. $\frac{1}{11} \bigcirc \frac{1}{13}$ 15. $\frac{1}{8} \bigcirc \frac{1}{10}$

⭐ **Challenge**

Write the fractions in order from least to greatest.

16. $\frac{1}{3}, \frac{1}{6}, \frac{1}{8}$ 17. $\frac{1}{10}, \frac{1}{2}, \frac{1}{6}$ 18. $\frac{1}{7}, \frac{1}{9}, \frac{1}{3}$ 19. $\frac{1}{2}, \frac{1}{8}, \frac{1}{3}$ 20. $\frac{1}{6}, \frac{1}{4}, \frac{1}{9}$

More Comparing Denominators to Order Fractions

To order fractions when the numerators are the same, compare the denominators. The fraction with the smaller denominator is the larger fraction.

1 whole		
$\frac{1}{3}$	$\frac{1}{3}$	$\frac{1}{3}$

$\frac{1}{8}$	$\frac{1}{8}$	$\frac{1}{8}$	$\frac{1}{8}$	$\frac{1}{8}$	$\frac{1}{8}$	$\frac{1}{8}$	$\frac{1}{8}$

3 thirds make 1 whole.

8 eighths make 1 whole.

Thirds are greater than eighths, so $\frac{2}{3} > \frac{2}{8}$.

Look at the denominators. Order the fractions.

1. $\frac{2}{3} \bigcirc\!\!\!> \frac{2}{4}$

2. $\frac{7}{10} \bigcirc \frac{7}{8}$

3. $\frac{5}{6} \bigcirc \frac{5}{8}$

4. $\frac{2}{6} \bigcirc \frac{2}{3}$

5. $\frac{3}{4} \bigcirc \frac{3}{8}$

6. $\frac{4}{10} \bigcirc \frac{4}{5}$

7. $\frac{6}{7} \bigcirc \frac{6}{10}$

8. $\frac{2}{3} \bigcirc \frac{2}{6}$

9. $\frac{2}{10} \bigcirc \frac{2}{9}$

10. $\frac{9}{15} \bigcirc \frac{9}{18}$

11. $\frac{15}{20} \bigcirc \frac{15}{16}$

12. $\frac{8}{10} \bigcirc \frac{8}{16}$

13. $\frac{5}{12} \bigcirc \frac{5}{11}$

14. $\frac{6}{8} \bigcirc \frac{6}{18}$

15. $\frac{9}{12} \bigcirc \frac{9}{10}$

16. $\frac{4}{7} \bigcirc \frac{4}{9}$

17. $\frac{7}{16} \bigcirc \frac{7}{20}$

18. $\frac{3}{10} \bigcirc \frac{3}{6}$

19. $\frac{8}{12} \bigcirc \frac{8}{15}$

20. $\frac{6}{9} \bigcirc \frac{6}{15}$

Review   (pp. 193–204)

Write > or < to order the fractions.

1. $\frac{5}{7} \bigcirc \frac{5}{9}$

2. $\frac{1}{8} \bigcirc \frac{1}{12}$

3. $\frac{6}{10} \bigcirc \frac{4}{10}$

4. $\frac{1}{4} \bigcirc \frac{3}{4}$

5. $\frac{1}{5} \bigcirc \frac{1}{3}$

6. $\frac{2}{8} \bigcirc \frac{1}{8}$

7. $\frac{6}{12} \bigcirc \frac{6}{7}$

8. $\frac{2}{3} \bigcirc \frac{2}{6}$

9. $\frac{1}{6} \bigcirc \frac{1}{8}$

10. $\frac{3}{5} \bigcirc \frac{2}{5}$

Fractions Greater Than One

You can write the fraction $\frac{7}{4}$ as $1\frac{3}{4}$.

$1\frac{3}{4}$ is a **mixed number**.

$1\frac{3}{4}$ is read *one and three-fourths*.

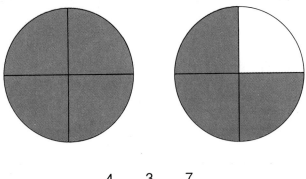

$$\frac{4}{4} + \frac{3}{4} = \frac{7}{4}$$

Write a fraction and a mixed number for the number of shaded parts.

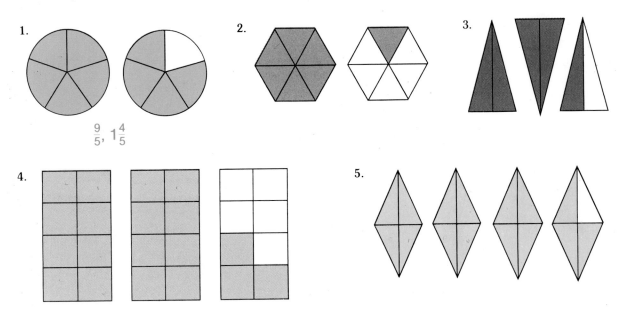

1.

$\frac{9}{5}, 1\frac{4}{5}$

2.

3.

4.

5.

Change each fraction to a whole number. Make drawings if you need help.

6. $\frac{12}{6}$ 7. $\frac{10}{5}$ 8. $\frac{8}{8}$ 9. $\frac{14}{7}$ 10. $\frac{12}{4}$ 11. $\frac{3}{3}$

12. $\frac{6}{2}$ 13. $\frac{9}{3}$ 14. $\frac{9}{9}$ 15. $\frac{4}{2}$ 16. $\frac{2}{2}$ 17. $\frac{8}{4}$

Changing Fractions to Mixed Numbers

Follow these steps to change $\frac{8}{3}$ to a mixed number.

Step 1
Make as many wholes as you can.

$$\frac{8}{3} = \frac{6}{3} + \frac{2}{3}$$

$$\frac{6}{3} = 2 \text{ wholes}$$

Step 2
Write the whole number and the leftover fraction as a mixed number.

$$2 + \frac{2}{3} = 2\frac{2}{3}$$

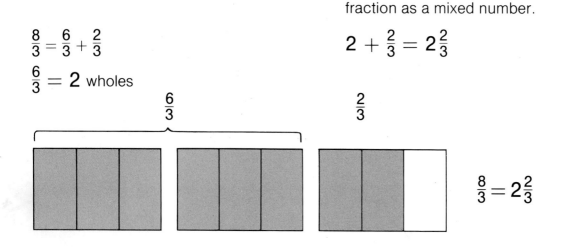

$\frac{6}{3}$ $\frac{2}{3}$

$$\frac{8}{3} = 2\frac{2}{3}$$

Complete these mixed numbers. Make drawings if you need help.

1. $\frac{7}{6} = ?\frac{1}{6}$ $1\frac{1}{6}$ 2. $\frac{8}{5} = ?\frac{3}{5}$ 3. $\frac{9}{4} = ?\frac{1}{4}$ 4. $\frac{7}{2} = ?\frac{1}{2}$ 5. $\frac{5}{2} = ?\frac{1}{2}$

6. $\frac{5}{3} = 1\frac{?}{3}$ 7. $\frac{6}{4} = 1\frac{?}{4}$ 8. $\frac{13}{6} = 2\frac{?}{6}$ 9. $\frac{10}{3} = 3\frac{?}{3}$ 10. $\frac{6}{5} = 1\frac{?}{5}$

11. $\frac{11}{4} = ?\frac{?}{4}$ 12. $\frac{15}{8} = ?\frac{?}{8}$ 13. $\frac{12}{5} = ?\frac{?}{5}$ 14. $\frac{7}{3} = ?\frac{?}{3}$ 15. $\frac{12}{7} = ?\frac{?}{7}$

Change each fraction to a whole number or a mixed number.

16. $\frac{11}{6}$ 17. $\frac{8}{4}$ 18. $\frac{9}{3}$ 19. $\frac{6}{5}$ 20. $\frac{4}{2}$ 21. $\frac{8}{2}$

22. $\frac{7}{3}$ 23. $\frac{6}{4}$ 24. $\frac{7}{5}$ 25. $\frac{9}{4}$ 26. $\frac{5}{5}$ 27. $\frac{18}{6}$

28. $\frac{9}{2}$ 29. $\frac{10}{3}$ 30. $\frac{4}{4}$ 31. $\frac{10}{5}$ 32. $\frac{7}{2}$ 33. $\frac{8}{7}$

Dividing to Change Fractions to Mixed Numbers

You have learned one way to change $\frac{11}{4}$ to a mixed number.

$$\frac{11}{4} = \frac{8}{4} + \frac{3}{4} \qquad 2 + \frac{3}{4} = 2\frac{3}{4}$$

You can also divide to change $\frac{11}{4}$ to a mixed number.

Step 1
Divide the numerator
by the denominator.

Step 2
Show the answer as a mixed number.
The remainder is the numerator.
The divisor is the denominator.

$$\begin{array}{r} 2\ r3 \\ 4)\overline{11} \\ -\ 8 \\ \hline 3 \end{array}$$

$$\frac{11}{4} = 2\frac{3}{4}$$

Divide to complete the mixed numbers.

1. $\frac{10}{3} = ?\frac{1}{3}$ $3\frac{1}{3}$

2. $\frac{5}{4} = ?\frac{1}{4}$

3. $\frac{8}{3} = 2\frac{?}{3}$

4. $\frac{5}{2} = ?\frac{1}{2}$

5. $\frac{9}{4} = 2\frac{?}{4}$

6. $\frac{7}{3} = ?\frac{1}{3}$

7. $\frac{10}{4} = ?\frac{?}{4}$

8. $\frac{8}{5} = ?\frac{?}{5}$

9. $\frac{9}{8} = ?\frac{?}{8}$

10. $\frac{11}{3} = ?\frac{?}{3}$

Divide to change the fractions to mixed numbers.

11. $\frac{21}{10}$

12. $\frac{13}{5}$

13. $\frac{13}{4}$

14. $\frac{9}{2}$

15. $\frac{7}{4}$

16. $\frac{10}{3}$

17. $\frac{15}{4}$

18. $\frac{7}{6}$

19. $\frac{9}{7}$

20. $\frac{15}{8}$

21. $\frac{17}{8}$

22. $\frac{13}{3}$

23. $\frac{9}{5}$

24. $\frac{11}{6}$

25. $\frac{13}{4}$

26. $\frac{11}{9}$

27. $\frac{14}{5}$

28. $\frac{8}{3}$

Changing Whole Numbers to Fractions

Multiply to change a whole number to a fraction.

$$2 = \frac{?}{3} \qquad 2 = \frac{6}{3} \qquad\qquad 4 = \frac{?}{9} \qquad 4 = \frac{36}{9}$$

Change each whole number to a fraction.

1. $4 = \frac{?}{3} \; \frac{12}{3}$

2. $5 = \frac{?}{2}$

3. $6 = \frac{?}{4}$

4. $7 = \frac{?}{6}$

5. $2 = \frac{?}{7}$

6. $7 = \frac{?}{8}$

7. $3 = \frac{?}{6}$

8. $4 = \frac{?}{8}$

9. $9 = \frac{?}{6}$

10. $5 = \frac{?}{5}$

Copy and complete.

11. $2\frac{1}{3} = \frac{?}{3} + \frac{1}{3}$

12. $4\frac{1}{5} = \frac{?}{5} + \frac{1}{5}$

13. $1\frac{1}{2} = \frac{?}{2} + \frac{1}{2}$

14. $5\frac{2}{3} = \frac{?}{3} + \frac{2}{3}$

15. $3\frac{1}{4} = \frac{?}{4} + \frac{1}{4}$

16. $6\frac{1}{3} = \frac{?}{3} + \frac{1}{3}$

17. $2\frac{1}{5} = \frac{?}{5} + \frac{1}{5}$

18. $1\frac{3}{5} = \frac{?}{5} + \frac{3}{5}$

 **Challenge**

19. Joan bought 6 sandwiches to serve at a party. She cut each sandwich into eight pieces. How many pieces were there in all?

Changing Mixed Numbers to Fractions

Follow these steps to change a mixed number to a fraction.

Step 1
Multiply the whole number by the denominator.

Step 2
Add the product to the numerator.

Step 3
Write the sum as the new numerator. Keep the same denominator.

$$10+3=13$$

$2\frac{3}{5}$

$2\frac{3}{5}$

$2\frac{3}{5} = \frac{13}{5}$

$2\times5=10$

Change each mixed number to a fraction.

1. $2\frac{1}{8}$ $\frac{17}{8}$

2. $1\frac{3}{8}$

3. $1\frac{5}{6}$

4. $2\frac{1}{3}$

5. $3\frac{1}{2}$

6. $3\frac{3}{4}$

7. $3\frac{3}{7}$

8. $3\frac{5}{8}$

9. $2\frac{4}{5}$

10. $1\frac{7}{11}$

11. $4\frac{1}{2}$

12. $1\frac{11}{12}$

13. $6\frac{1}{2}$

14. $3\frac{9}{10}$

15. $2\frac{5}{7}$

16. $3\frac{7}{8}$

17. $9\frac{5}{6}$

18. $4\frac{1}{3}$

19. $7\frac{1}{7}$

20. $8\frac{6}{7}$

21. $9\frac{2}{3}$

22. $5\frac{1}{2}$

23. $6\frac{2}{4}$

24. $3\frac{1}{3}$

25. $5\frac{2}{3}$

26. $1\frac{5}{9}$

27. $4\frac{3}{8}$

28. $6\frac{2}{7}$

29. $1\frac{1}{4}$

30. $3\frac{2}{9}$

⭐ **Challenge**
Write > or < to order the mixed numbers.

31. $4\frac{3}{4} \bigcirc 4\frac{1}{4}$

32. $6\frac{5}{6} \bigcirc 6\frac{1}{6}$

33. $2\frac{3}{8} \bigcirc 2\frac{7}{8}$

34. $8\frac{3}{5} \bigcirc 8\frac{2}{5}$

35. $3\frac{3}{5} \bigcirc 3\frac{3}{4}$

36. $5\frac{1}{7} \bigcirc 5\frac{1}{5}$

37. $1\frac{4}{5} \bigcirc 1\frac{4}{9}$

38. $7\frac{2}{3} \bigcirc 7\frac{2}{5}$

Reviewing Fractions and Mixed Numbers

Review what you have learned about fractions.

Copy and complete to find equal fractions.

1. $\frac{10}{16} = \frac{?}{8}$ $\frac{5}{8}$ 2. $\frac{3}{7} = \frac{?}{42}$ 3. $\frac{3}{15} = \frac{?}{30}$

4. $\frac{2}{3} = \frac{?}{9}$ 5. $\frac{20}{25} = \frac{?}{5}$ 6. $\frac{2}{3} = \frac{?}{12}$

7. $\frac{4}{5} = \frac{?}{15}$ 8. $\frac{1}{2} = \frac{?}{8}$ 9. $\frac{12}{24} = \frac{?}{2}$

Write each fraction in simplest form.

10. $\frac{8}{12}$ 11. $\frac{9}{18}$ 12. $\frac{4}{24}$ 13. $\frac{15}{35}$ 14. $\frac{4}{16}$ 15. $\frac{30}{60}$

16. $\frac{9}{24}$ 17. $\frac{5}{25}$ 18. $\frac{14}{7}$ 19. $\frac{25}{5}$ 20. $\frac{36}{6}$ 21. $\frac{49}{7}$

Write > or < to order these fractions.

22. $\frac{1}{6} \bigcirc \frac{1}{4}$ 23. $\frac{2}{8} \bigcirc \frac{6}{8}$ 24. $\frac{11}{12} \bigcirc \frac{9}{12}$ 25. $\frac{1}{6} \bigcirc \frac{1}{8}$

26. $\frac{7}{16} \bigcirc \frac{7}{11}$ 27. $\frac{4}{8} \bigcirc \frac{4}{5}$ 28. $\frac{1}{12} \bigcirc \frac{1}{16}$ 29. $\frac{3}{12} \bigcirc \frac{3}{6}$

Change each fraction to a mixed number.

30. $\frac{13}{4}$ 31. $\frac{25}{8}$ 32. $\frac{21}{4}$ 33. $\frac{25}{6}$ 34. $\frac{17}{10}$ 35. $\frac{9}{7}$

36. $\frac{3}{2}$ 37. $\frac{15}{8}$ 38. $\frac{11}{5}$ 39. $\frac{8}{3}$ 40. $\frac{11}{9}$ 41. $\frac{24}{5}$

42. $\frac{5}{3}$ 43. $\frac{11}{4}$ 44. $\frac{27}{7}$ 45. $\frac{4}{3}$ 46. $\frac{29}{6}$ 47. $\frac{73}{9}$

Kitchen Problems

Use what you have learned about fractions to solve each problem.

1. Winston puts $\frac{1}{2}$ of an apple in a fruit salad. He eats $\frac{1}{4}$ of the apple. Which is more, $\frac{1}{2}$ or $\frac{1}{4}$? $\frac{1}{2}$

2. Marcia uses $\frac{1}{8}$ carton of milk to make bread and $\frac{1}{2}$ carton to make muffins. Which took more milk?

3. Ben uses $\frac{1}{3}$ stick of butter to make gravy. Shanna uses $\frac{1}{4}$ stick of butter to make a casserole. Who uses more butter?

4. A salad recipe calls for $\frac{1}{8}$ of a pineapple. A dessert recipe calls for $\frac{3}{4}$ of a pineapple. Which recipe calls for more pineapple?

5. Theresa needs $\frac{3}{4}$ of a loaf of bread. The bread was already cut into eighths. How many eighths equals $\frac{3}{4}$?

6. A recipe calls for $\frac{2}{3}$ of a tomato. Arturo has already cut the tomato into sixths. How many sixths equals $\frac{2}{3}$?

Ratio

A **ratio** compares two quantities.

The ratio of mugs to plates is 2 to 3.
The ratio of plates to mugs is 3 to 2.

The ratio 2 to 3 can be written as the fraction $\frac{2}{3}$.

Write each ratio as a fraction.

1a. What is the ratio of 4 nickels to 6 pennies? $\frac{4}{6}$

b. of 6 pennies to 4 nickels? $\frac{6}{4}$

2a. What is the ratio of 9 dogs to 5 cats?

b. of 5 cats to 9 dogs?

3a. What is the ratio of 6 apples to 7 bananas?

b. of 7 bananas to 6 apples?

4a. What is the ratio of 7 chairs to 1 table?

b. of 1 table to 7 chairs?

5a. What is the ratio of 5 birds to 10 turtles?

b. of 10 turtles to 5 birds?

6a. What is the ratio of 2 dimes to 8 quarters?

b. of 8 quarters to 2 dimes?

7. 1 to 6   **8.** 5 to 8   **9.** 4 to 1   **10.** 3 to 7   **11.** 6 to 20

12. 7 to 5   **13.** 12 to 14   **14.** 2 to 10   **15.** 11 to 17   **16.** 6 to 5

17. 1 to 3   **18.** 6 to 8   **19.** 7 to 9   **20.** 14 to 18   **21.** 9 to 6

22. 4 to 3   **23.** 2 to 9   **24.** 1 to 7   **25.** 7 to 14   **26.** 12 to 3

Writing Ratios

It takes 3 tugboats to tow 1 ocean liner.

The ratio is $\frac{3}{1}$.

Give each ratio.

1. ratio: daisies to roses $\frac{2}{3}$

2. ratio: alligators to frogs

3. ratio: brown dogs to spotted dogs

4. ratio: pennies to quarters

5. ratio: starfish to snails

6. ratio: birds to cats

Equal Ratios

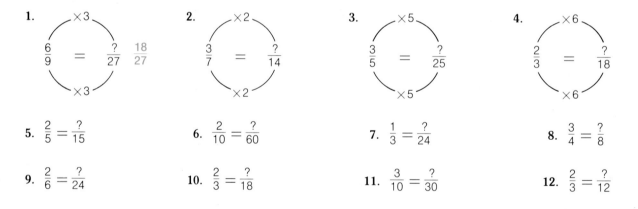

There are 2 people for every 3 seats.

There are 4 people for every 6 seats.

$\frac{2}{3}$ and $\frac{4}{6}$ are equal ratios. Two equal ratios can be written as a **proportion**. Read the proportion $\frac{2}{3} = \frac{4}{6}$ *two is to three as four is to six.*

Find equal ratios the same way you find equal fractions. Multiply to complete the equal ratios. Then write a proportion.

1. $\times 3$
    $\frac{6}{9} = \frac{?}{27}$ $\frac{18}{27}$
    $\times 3$

2. $\times 2$
    $\frac{3}{7} = \frac{?}{14}$
    $\times 2$

3. $\times 5$
    $\frac{3}{5} = \frac{?}{25}$
    $\times 5$

4. $\times 6$
    $\frac{2}{3} = \frac{?}{18}$
    $\times 6$

5. $\frac{2}{5} = \frac{?}{15}$

6. $\frac{2}{10} = \frac{?}{60}$

7. $\frac{1}{3} = \frac{?}{24}$

8. $\frac{3}{4} = \frac{?}{8}$

9. $\frac{2}{6} = \frac{?}{24}$

10. $\frac{2}{3} = \frac{?}{18}$

11. $\frac{3}{10} = \frac{?}{30}$

12. $\frac{2}{3} = \frac{?}{12}$

Use fractions to write a proportion. Then multiply to complete the proportion.

13. 5 is to 9 as ⍰ is to 45.

14. 2 is to 3 as ⍰ is to 9.

15. 3 is to 5 as ⍰ is to 15.

16. 4 is to 7 as ⍰ is to 56.

Tenths

You can use decimals to name tenths.

$\frac{7}{10}$ or 0.7 is shaded.
This decimal is read *seven-tenths.*

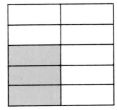

$1\frac{3}{10}$ or 1.3 is shaded.
This decimal is read *one and three-tenths.*

Write a fraction and a decimal for each.

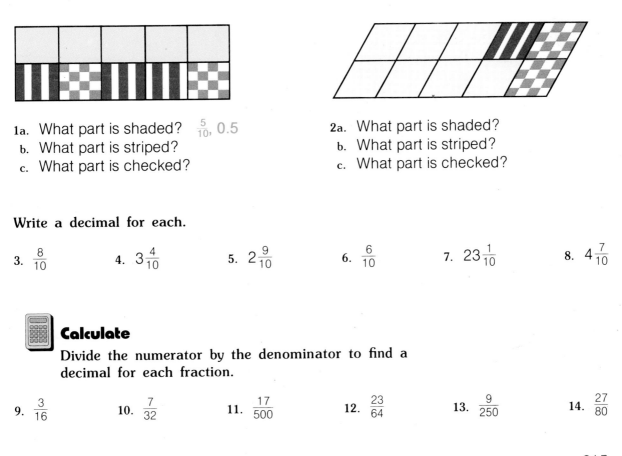

1a. What part is shaded? $\frac{5}{10}$, 0.5
 b. What part is striped?
 c. What part is checked?

2a. What part is shaded?
 b. What part is striped?
 c. What part is checked?

Write a decimal for each.

3. $\frac{8}{10}$
4. $3\frac{4}{10}$
5. $2\frac{9}{10}$
6. $\frac{6}{10}$
7. $23\frac{1}{10}$
8. $4\frac{7}{10}$

Calculate

Divide the numerator by the denominator to find a decimal for each fraction.

9. $\frac{3}{16}$
10. $\frac{7}{32}$
11. $\frac{17}{500}$
12. $\frac{23}{64}$
13. $\frac{9}{250}$
14. $\frac{27}{80}$

Hundredths

You can use decimals to name hundredths.

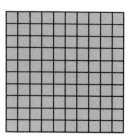

$\frac{65}{100}$ or 0.65 is shaded.
This decimal is read *sixty-five hundredths.*

$1\frac{35}{100}$ or 1.35 is shaded.
This decimal is read *one and thirty-five hundredths.*

Write a decimal for each.

1. $\frac{72}{100}$ 0.72
2. $\frac{14}{100}$
3. $\frac{35}{100}$
4. $\frac{78}{100}$
5. $\frac{92}{100}$
6. $\frac{46}{100}$

7. $2\frac{6}{100}$
8. $\frac{16}{100}$
9. $8\frac{89}{100}$
10. $3\frac{89}{100}$
11. $\frac{62}{100}$
12. $4\frac{29}{100}$

13. forty-eight hundredths
14. sixty-two hundredths
15. three-hundredths

16. seventy-one hundredths
17. nineteen-hundredths
18. thirty-hundredths

Write a fraction or mixed number for each.

19. 0.09
20. 0.20
21. 2.37
22. 0.51
23. 1.06
24. 0.89

25. 0.37
26. 2.46
27. 3.65
28. 0.97
29. 1.43
30. 6.14

31. twenty-one hundredths
32. forty-hundredths
33. seventy-six hundredths

34. ten-hundredths
35. sixty-four hundredths
36. ninety-five hundredths

Thousandths

You can use decimals to name thousandths.

$\frac{1}{1000}$ or 0.001   one-thousandth

$3\frac{245}{1000}$ or 3.245   three and two hundred forty-five thousandths

Write a decimal for each.

1. $\frac{136}{1000}$ 0.136   2. $\frac{278}{1000}$ 3. $\frac{86}{1000}$ 4. $\frac{76}{1000}$ 5. $\frac{7}{1000}$

6. $2\frac{137}{1000}$ 7. $4\frac{350}{1000}$ 8. $6\frac{6}{1000}$ 9. $5\frac{87}{1000}$ 10. $\frac{19}{1000}$

Write a fraction or mixed number for each.

11. 0.007   12. 0.023   13. 0.178   14. 0.607   15. 0.108

16. 4.207   17. 6.314   18. 0.009   19. 0.407   20. 1.058

Write a decimal and a fraction for each.

21. forty-seven thousandths

22. seven hundred three-thousandths

23. eighty-six thousandths

24. five hundred four-thousandths

25. three-thousandths

26. two hundred six-thousandths

27. two-thousandths

28. one hundred thirty-thousandths

29. seventy-two thousandths

30. six hundred eighty-one thousandths

Practicing Decimals

	Decimal	Fraction	Words
Tenths	1.4	$1\frac{4}{10}$	one and four-tenths
Hundredths	2.15	$2\frac{15}{100}$	two and fifteen-hundredths
Thousandths	3.045	$3\frac{45}{1000}$	three and forty-five thousandths

Write a decimal for each.

1. $\frac{5}{100}$ 0.05
2. $\frac{7}{10}$
3. $\frac{85}{1000}$
4. $1\frac{11}{100}$
5. $2\frac{5}{10}$
6. $\frac{89}{100}$

7. $3\frac{12}{100}$
8. $\frac{483}{1000}$
9. $\frac{6}{1000}$
10. $2\frac{3}{100}$
11. $\frac{99}{100}$
12. $5\frac{63}{1000}$

Write a fraction or a mixed number for each.

13. 0.02
14. 0.26
15. 0.13
16. 2.61
17. 0.103
18. 0.08

19. 1.119
20. 5.84
21. 0.005
22. 4.03
23. 7.65
24. 1.49

Write the words for each.

25. 7.1
26. 6.02
27. 0.015
28. 0.123
29. 1.9
30. 1.4

Review (pp. 193–218)

Write a decimal for each.

1. $\frac{7}{10}$
2. $\frac{86}{1000}$
3. $\frac{99}{100}$
4. $1\frac{5}{10}$
5. $\frac{6}{100}$
6. $8\frac{895}{1000}$

Decimals on a Number Strip

This number strip shows decimals in order.

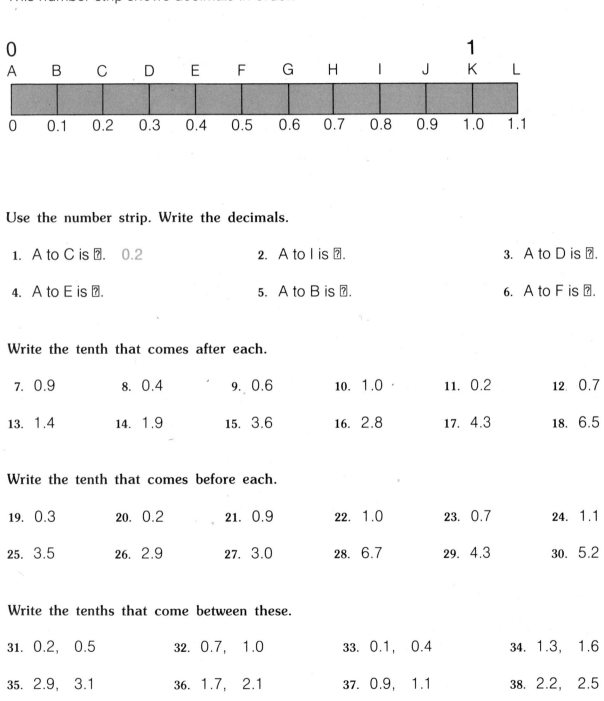

Use the number strip. Write the decimals.

1. A to C is ▨. 0.2

2. A to I is ▨.

3. A to D is ▨.

4. A to E is ▨.

5. A to B is ▨.

6. A to F is ▨.

Write the tenth that comes after each.

7. 0.9

8. 0.4

9. 0.6

10. 1.0

11. 0.2

12. 0.7

13. 1.4

14. 1.9

15. 3.6

16. 2.8

17. 4.3

18. 6.5

Write the tenth that comes before each.

19. 0.3

20. 0.2

21. 0.9

22. 1.0

23. 0.7

24. 1.1

25. 3.5

26. 2.9

27. 3.0

28. 6.7

29. 4.3

30. 5.2

Write the tenths that come between these.

31. 0.2, 0.5

32. 0.7, 1.0

33. 0.1, 0.4

34. 1.3, 1.6

35. 2.9, 3.1

36. 1.7, 2.1

37. 0.9, 1.1

38. 2.2, 2.5

Ordering Decimals

You compare digits to order decimals just as you do for whole numbers.

Compare 2.468 and 2.463.

The ones digits are the same.
The tenths digits are the same.
The hundredths digits are the same.
The thousandths digits are different.

8 is greater than 3, so 2.468 > 2.463.

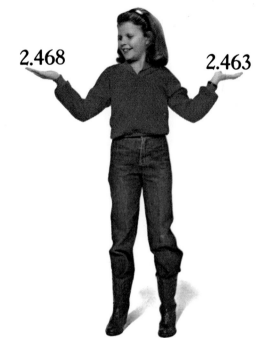

2.468   2.463

Write > or < to order the decimals.

1. 2.79 ⊘ 2.75   2. 2.680 ◯ 1.682   3. 4.981 ◯ 4.986   4. 5.810 ◯ 3.860

5. 0.7 ◯ 0.9   6. 0.12 ◯ 0.11   7. 1.6 ◯ 1.9   8. 3.54 ◯ 3.52

9. 7.91 ◯ 7.89   10. 0.56 ◯ 0.58   11. 6.4 ◯ 6.1   12. 0.987 ◯ 0.985

13. 51.7 ◯ 51.6   14. 35.4 ◯ 34.4   15. 14.62 ◯ 14.65   16. 27.39 ◯ 27.33

17. Hank broad jumped 1.83 meters.
George broad jumped 1.85 meters.
Who jumped farther?

18. Harriet high jumped 1.57 meters.
Monita high jumped 1.52 meters.
Who jumped higher?

More Ordering Decimals

Writing zeros to the right of a decimal does not change its value.

0.4 = 0.40

Remember, $\frac{4}{10} = \frac{40}{100}$.

4 tenths is the same as 40 hundredths.

To compare 0.4 and 0.27, change 0.4 to 0.40. 0.40 is greater than 0.27, so 0.4 > 0.27.

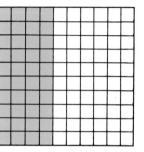

0.4   0.40

Write > or < to order the decimals.

1. 0.56 ⊘ 0.2
2. 0.3 ◯ 0.27
3. 0.8 ◯ 0.85
4. 0.49 ◯ 0.4

5. 0.76 ◯ 0.5
6. 0.9 ◯ 0.42
7. 0.1 ◯ 0.6
8. 0.5 ◯ 0.27

9. 1.79 ◯ 1.8
10. 3.4 ◯ 3.39
11. 4.7 ◯ 4.65
12. 9.6 ◯ 9.34

13. 8.06 ◯ 8.6
14. 3.6 ◯ 3.16
15. 7.4 ◯ 7.49
16. 6.15 ◯ 6.1

17. 2.3 ◯ 2.13
18. 7.03 ◯ 7.5
19. 0.6 ◯ 0.62
20. 0.35 ◯ 0.3

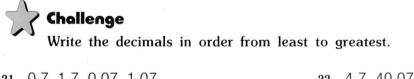 **Challenge**

Write the decimals in order from least to greatest.

21. 0.7, 1.7, 0.07, 1.07
22. 4.7, 40.07, 4.17, 40.7

23. 3.6, 0.6, 6.3, 3.06
24. 9.1, 0.19, 9.01, 1.9

25. 5.3, 5.03, 5.05, 3.35
26. 8.2, 2.80, 0.28, 8.02

Rounding to the Nearest Tenth

When you are rounding a decimal to the nearest tenth, you need to look only at the hundredths digit, no matter how many digits are in the decimal.

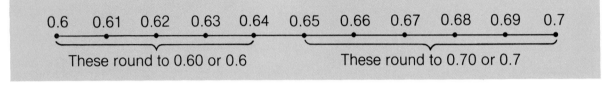

0.6   0.61   0.62   0.63   0.64   0.65   0.66   0.67   0.68   0.69   0.7

These round to 0.60 or 0.6   These round to 0.70 or 0.7

When the hundredths digit is 0, 1, 2, 3, or 4, the tenths digit stays the same.

When the hundredths digit is 5, 6, 7, 8, or 9, the tenths digit rounds to the next highest digit.

Round to the nearest tenth. Choose the correct answer.

1. 0.85
   (0.8 or 0.9)   0.9

2. 0.62
   (0.6 or 0.7)

3. 0.11
   (0.2 or 0.1)

4. 0.78
   (0.8 or 0.7)

5. 0.225
   (0.2 or 0.3)

6. 0.475
   (0.4 or 0.5)

7. 0.326
   (0.4 or 0.3)

8. 0.913
   (0.9 or 1.0)

Round to the nearest tenth.

9. 0.31   10. 0.67   11. 1.59   12. 1.23   13. 0.77

14. 0.138   15. 0.672   16. 1.226   17. 6.182   18. 1.896

19. A chemist measured 2.79 kilograms of soil. Round to the nearest tenth.

20. For an experiment, a scientist measured a distance of 0.734 meters. Round to the nearest tenth.

Rounding to the Nearest Hundredth

To round to the nearest hundredth, look at the thousandths digit.

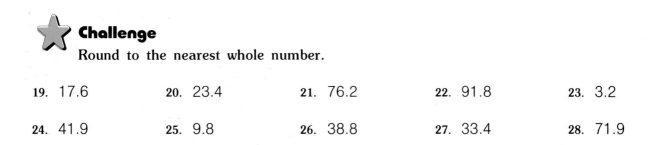

| 1.47 | 1.471 | 1.472 | 1.473 | 1.474 | 1.475 | 1.476 | 1.477 | 1.478 | 1.479 | 1.48 |

These round to 1.470 or 1.47   These round to 1.480 or 1.48

When the thousandths digit is 0, 1, 2, 3, or 4, the hundredths digit stays the same.

When the thousandths digit is 5, 6, 7, 8, or 9, the hundredths digit rounds to the next highest digit.

Round to the nearest hundredth. Choose the correct answer.

1. 2.804
   (2.80 or 2.81) 2.80

2. 0.157
   (0.16 or 0.15)

3. 0.338
   (0.33 or 0.34)

4. 1.463
   (1.47 or 1.46)

5. 0.189
   (0.19 or 0.18)

6. 0.669
   (0.66 or 0.67)

7. 3.421
   (3.41 or 3.42)

8. 0.927
   (0.93 or 0.92)

Round to the nearest hundredth.

9. 0.502

10. 1.445

11. 3.651

12. 4.211

13. 5.459

14. 0.755

15. 0.605

16. 3.228

17. 1.912

18. 7.434

⭐ Challenge
Round to the nearest whole number.

19. 17.6

20. 23.4

21. 76.2

22. 91.8

23. 3.2

24. 41.9

25. 9.8

26. 38.8

27. 33.4

28. 71.9

Chapter Review

Write each fraction in simplest form. (ex. 1-9: p. 200),
(ex. 10-12: p. 201)

1. $\frac{9}{24}$ 2. $\frac{4}{16}$ 3. $\frac{6}{21}$ 4. $\frac{9}{18}$ 5. $\frac{20}{36}$ 6. $\frac{8}{12}$

7. $\frac{12}{16}$ 8. $\frac{35}{45}$ 9. $\frac{2}{14}$ 10. $\frac{7}{7}$ 11. $\frac{36}{6}$ 12. $\frac{24}{3}$

Write $>$ or $<$ to order the fractions. (ex. 13-15: p. 202),
(ex. 16-18: p. 203), (ex. 19-20: p. 204)

13. $\frac{3}{5} \bigcirc \frac{2}{5}$ 14. $\frac{4}{7} \bigcirc \frac{6}{7}$ 15. $\frac{5}{10} \bigcirc \frac{2}{10}$ 16. $\frac{1}{3} \bigcirc \frac{1}{7}$

17. $\frac{1}{8} \bigcirc \frac{1}{2}$ 18. $\frac{1}{4} \bigcirc \frac{1}{5}$ 19. $\frac{4}{7} \bigcirc \frac{4}{8}$ 20. $\frac{3}{6} \bigcirc \frac{3}{9}$

Change each fraction to a whole number or a mixed number.
(ex. 21-26: p. 206)

21. $\frac{21}{8}$ 22. $\frac{9}{5}$ 23. $\frac{16}{7}$ 24. $\frac{23}{9}$ 25. $\frac{24}{4}$ 26. $\frac{12}{3}$

Change each mixed number to a fraction. (ex. 27-32: p. 209)

27. $2\frac{3}{8}$ 28. $3\frac{4}{5}$ 29. $1\frac{2}{7}$ 30. $1\frac{2}{6}$ 31. $4\frac{6}{8}$ 32. $5\frac{6}{7}$

Write a decimal for each. (ex. 33-38: p. 215), (ex. 39-44: p. 216),
(ex. 45-49: p. 217)

33. $\frac{3}{10}$ 34. $2\frac{1}{10}$ 35. $10\frac{6}{10}$ 36. $4\frac{2}{10}$ 37. $6\frac{4}{10}$ 38. $\frac{8}{10}$

39. $2\frac{46}{100}$ 40. $8\frac{51}{100}$ 41. $\frac{13}{100}$ 42. $1\frac{2}{100}$ 43. $\frac{89}{100}$ 44. $3\frac{66}{100}$

45. $\frac{75}{1000}$ 46. $\frac{3}{1000}$ 47. $3\frac{41}{1000}$ 48. $5\frac{273}{1000}$ 49. $3\frac{6}{1000}$

Chapter Test

Write each fraction in simplest form.

1. $\dfrac{3}{18}$ 2. $\dfrac{8}{24}$ 3. $\dfrac{6}{15}$ 4. $\dfrac{22}{38}$ 5. $\dfrac{10}{12}$ 6. $\dfrac{3}{9}$

7. $\dfrac{16}{40}$ 8. $\dfrac{12}{36}$ 9. $\dfrac{21}{7}$ 10. $\dfrac{35}{7}$ 11. $\dfrac{9}{9}$ 12. $\dfrac{56}{8}$

Write $>$ or $<$ to order the fractions.

13. $\dfrac{3}{6} \bigcirc \dfrac{5}{6}$ 14. $\dfrac{1}{8} \bigcirc \dfrac{1}{9}$ 15. $\dfrac{4}{8} \bigcirc \dfrac{4}{5}$ 16. $\dfrac{7}{9} \bigcirc \dfrac{7}{12}$

17. $\dfrac{4}{8} \bigcirc \dfrac{6}{8}$ 18. $\dfrac{1}{10} \bigcirc \dfrac{1}{13}$ 19. $\dfrac{5}{8} \bigcirc \dfrac{5}{10}$ 20. $\dfrac{9}{14} \bigcirc \dfrac{9}{10}$

Change each fraction to a whole number or mixed number.

21. $\dfrac{27}{3}$ 22. $\dfrac{15}{4}$ 23. $\dfrac{32}{8}$ 24. $\dfrac{17}{3}$ 25. $\dfrac{21}{6}$ 26. $\dfrac{9}{5}$

Change each mixed number to a fraction.

27. $1\dfrac{6}{8}$ 28. $3\dfrac{4}{9}$ 29. $2\dfrac{9}{10}$ 30. $1\dfrac{2}{3}$ 31. $4\dfrac{6}{7}$ 32. $5\dfrac{3}{4}$

Write a decimal for each.

33. $\dfrac{65}{100}$ 34. $1\dfrac{4}{10}$ 35. $2\dfrac{35}{100}$ 36. $\dfrac{62}{1000}$ 37. $7\dfrac{42}{1000}$

Brush Up

Write the numbers.

1. fifty-nine thousand, eight hundred forty-three

2. three million, two hundred seventy-six thousand, four hundred two

Add, subtract, multiply, or divide.

3. 90
   +48

4. 729
   + 86

5. 651
   +467

6. 598
   +369

7. 199
   +506

8. 99
   −39

9. 644
   − 75

10. 890
    −436

11. 377
    −208

12. 300
    −289

13. $6.50
    ×   4

14. $0.99
    ×   6

15. $4.57
    ×   3

16. $9.81
    ×   6

17. $0.33
    ×   9

18. 9)$8.19

19. 6)$12.36

20. 3)$5.85

21. 5)$24.50

22. 2)$22.12

Use shape VWXY to do these.

23. Name each angle in two ways.
    Then write **right, acute,** or **obtuse**
    for each angle.

24. Name a pair of parallel line segments
    in shape VWXY.

Write a whole number or mixed number for each fraction.

25. $\frac{9}{9}$

26. $\frac{8}{5}$

27. $\frac{14}{6}$

28. $\frac{12}{4}$

29. $\frac{15}{7}$

30. $\frac{34}{6}$

CHAPTER 9

Measurement

Using Measurement at Work

Paula Stuart is a pharmacist. She is preparing 50 bottles with 100 milliliters of medicine in each one. She multiplies 50 × 100 to find how many milliliters of medicine she will need in all. She will need 5000 milliliters in all.

Centimeters

A **centimeter** (**cm**) is a metric unit for measuring length.
This key is 5 cm long.

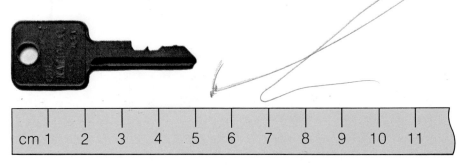

Use a ruler to measure the length of each object to the
nearest centimeter.

1.

11 cm

2.

3.

4.

Estimate in centimeters. Then measure each object to the
nearest centimeter.

5. the length of your pencil

6. the width of this book

7. the width of your thumbnail

8. the width of your hand

Meters

The **meter** (**m**) is the basic metric unit
for measuring length.
There are 100 centimeters in 1 meter.

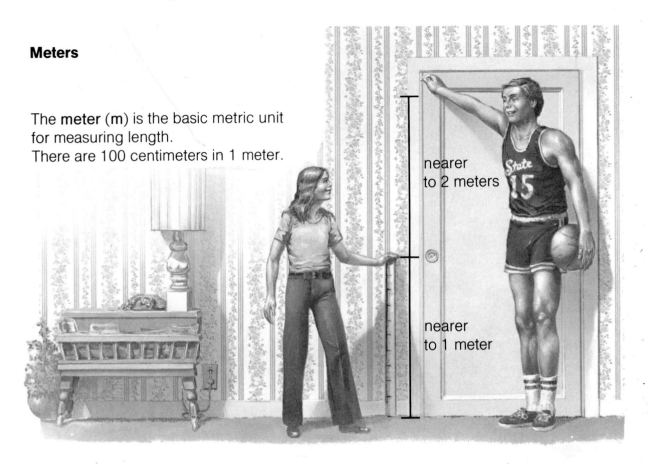

nearer
to 2 meters

nearer
to 1 meter

Copy and complete.

1. 400 cm=⬚ m   4 m

2. 700 cm=⬚ m

3. 500 cm=⬚ m

4. 1200 cm=⬚ m

5. 800 cm=⬚ m

6. 2400 cm=⬚ m

7. 3 m=⬚ cm

8. 6 m=⬚ cm

9. 9 m=⬚ cm

10. 14 m=⬚ cm

11. 7 m=⬚ cm

12. 2 m=⬚ cm

13. 26 m=⬚ cm

14. 19 m=⬚ cm

15. 38 m=⬚ cm

 **Challenge**

16. 1 m+13 cm=⬚ cm

17. 4 m+62 cm=⬚ cm

18. 3 m+41 cm=⬚ cm

19. 5 m+43 cm=⬚ cm

20. 2 m+70 cm=⬚ cm

21. 9 m+82 cm=⬚ cm

Decimeters and Millimeters

This ruler shows 10 centimeters or 1 **decimeter (dm)**.
It has **millimeter (mm)** markings.
There are 10 millimeters in 1 centimeter.

cm — 1 2 3 4 5 6 7 8 9 10

Remember, 1 m is the same as 10 dm, 100 cm, or 1000 mm.

Measure these. Write the lengths in millimeters.

1.

65 mm

2.

3.

4.

Copy and complete.

5. 5 dm = 🔲 cm

6. 2 dm = 🔲 cm

7. 6 dm = 🔲 cm

8. 30 cm = 🔲 dm

9. 40 cm = 🔲 dm

10. 60 cm = 🔲 dm

11. 9 cm = 🔲 mm

12. 8 cm = 🔲 mm

13. 4 cm = 🔲 mm

14. 50 mm = 🔲 cm

15. 20 mm = 🔲 cm

16. 30 mm = 🔲 cm

 **Calculate**

17. 79 m = 🔲 cm

18. 235 cm = 🔲 mm

19. 86 m = 🔲 mm

Kilometers

Long distances are measured in **kilometers** (**km**).
There are 1000 meters in 1 kilometer.

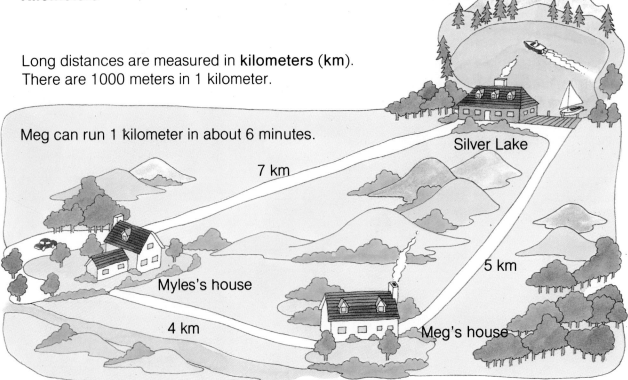

Meg can run 1 kilometer in about 6 minutes.

7 km

Silver Lake

5 km

Myles's house

4 km

Meg's house

Use the map to find the answers.

1. How many meters from Myles's house to the lake? *7000 meters*

2. How many meters from the lake to Meg's house?

3. How many kilometers from Meg's house to the lake by way of Myles's house?

4. How many kilometers from Myles's house to Meg's house by way of the lake?

Copy and complete.

5. 4000 m = ⬚ km

6. 9000 m = ⬚ km

7. 6000 m = ⬚ km

8. 7000 m = ⬚ km

9. 2000 m = ⬚ km

10. 3000 m = ⬚ km

11. 8 km = ⬚ m

12. 4 km = ⬚ m

13. 5 km = ⬚ m

14. 3 km = ⬚ m

15. 7 km = ⬚ m

16. 6 km = ⬚ m

Using a Map Drawn to Scale

This map is drawn to a **scale** of 1 cm to 2 km. This means that each centimeter on the map stands for a distance of 2 kilometers.

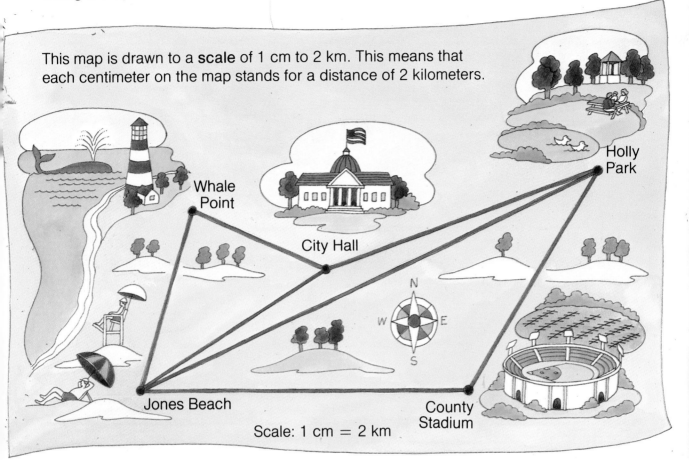

Whale Point

City Hall

Holly Park

Jones Beach

County Stadium

Scale: 1 cm = 2 km

Measure the distance between places on the map to the nearest centimeter. To find the actual distance, multiply the number of centimeters times 2.

	Places	Centimeters on Map	Actual Distance in Kilometers
1.	City Hall to Holly Park	8 cm	8 × 2 = 16 km
2.	County Stadium to Jones Beach		
3.	Whale Point to City Hall		
4.	Jones Beach to Holly Park		
5.	Holly Park to County Stadium		
6.	City Hall to Jones Beach		

Finding Perimeter

The **perimeter** of a shape is the distance around it. To find the perimeter of a shape, add the lengths of its sides.

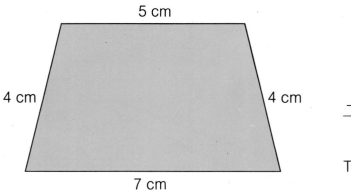

$$
\begin{array}{r}
5 \text{ cm} \\
4 \text{ cm} \\
4 \text{ cm} \\
+\ 7 \text{ cm} \\
\hline
20 \text{ cm}
\end{array}
$$

The perimeter of this shape is 20 cm.

Find the perimeters.

1.
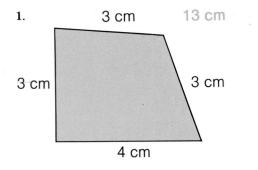

2.
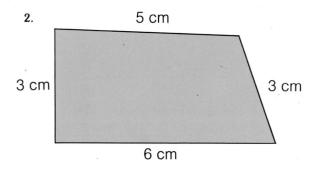

3. A triangle with sides of 7 meters, 6 meters, and 9 meters.

4. A rectangle with sides of 12 meters, 18 meters, 12 meters, and 18 meters.

5. A rectangle with sides of 8 meters, 10 meters, 8 meters, and 10 meters.

6. A triangle with sides of 8 meters, 6 meters, and 4 meters.

⭐ Challenge
Draw a shape that has each perimeter.

7. 42 cm

8. 18 cm

9. 36 cm

10. 15 cm

Multiplying to Find Perimeter

When all the sides of a shape are the same length, you can multiply to find the perimeter.

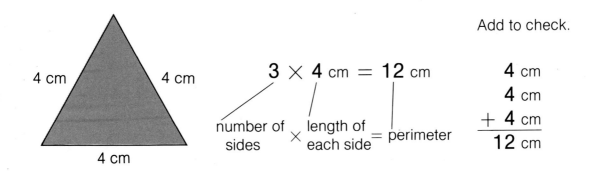

Add to check.

$$3 \times 4 \text{ cm} = 12 \text{ cm}$$

number of sides $\times$ length of each side = perimeter

$$\begin{array}{r} 4 \text{ cm} \\ 4 \text{ cm} \\ + \ 4 \text{ cm} \\ \hline 12 \text{ cm} \end{array}$$

Measure the length of each side to the nearest centimeter. Then multiply to find the perimeter.

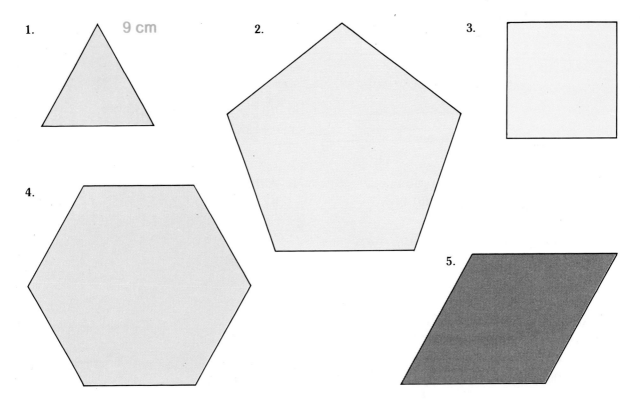

1. 9 cm

2.

3.

4.

5.

Perimeter Problems

There are two ways to find the perimeter of a rectangle.

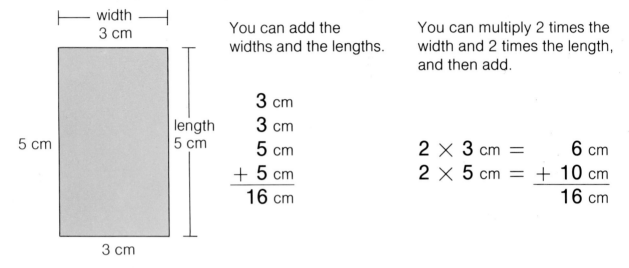

You can add the widths and the lengths.

$$
\begin{array}{r}
3 \text{ cm} \\
3 \text{ cm} \\
5 \text{ cm} \\
+\; 5 \text{ cm} \\
\hline
16 \text{ cm}
\end{array}
$$

You can multiply 2 times the width and 2 times the length, and then add.

$$
\begin{array}{r}
2 \times 3 \text{ cm} = \qquad 6 \text{ cm} \\
2 \times 5 \text{ cm} = +\; 10 \text{ cm} \\
\hline
16 \text{ cm}
\end{array}
$$

Add or multiply to find the perimeter of each rectangle. The shapes are shown smaller than actual size.

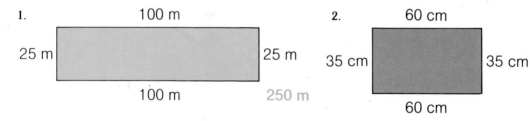

1. 100 m · 25 m · 25 m · 100 m · 250 m

2. 60 cm · 35 cm · 35 cm · 60 cm

3. A rectangle with a length of 37 centimeters and a width of 18 centimeters.

4. A rectangle with a length of 42 decimeters and a width of 34 decimeters.

⭐ Challenge

5. Fencing costs $2 a meter. A garden has a length of 24 meters and a width of 12 meters. How much will the fence cost if it goes all the way around the garden?

6. The perimeter of a rectangle is 72 centimeters. The length is 30 centimeters. What is the width of the rectangle?

Counting Squares to Find Area

The **area** of a shape is the number of square units that will fit inside it. The square unit shown here is a **square centimeter** (**square cm**).

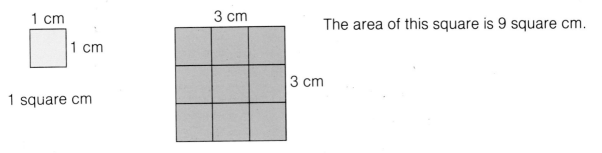

1 cm
1 cm

1 square cm

3 cm
3 cm

The area of this square is 9 square cm.

Count the square centimeters. What is the area of each shape?

1.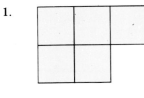

5 square cm

2.

3.

⭐ **Challenge**

Give the approximate area of each shape in square centimeters.

4.

5.

Multiplying to Find Area

To find the area of a rectangle, multiply length times width.

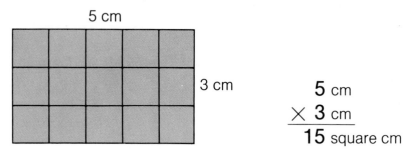

5 cm

3 cm

$$\begin{array}{r} 5 \text{ cm} \\ \times\ 3 \text{ cm} \\ \hline 15 \text{ square cm} \end{array}$$

Multiply to find the areas. These shapes are shown smaller than actual size.

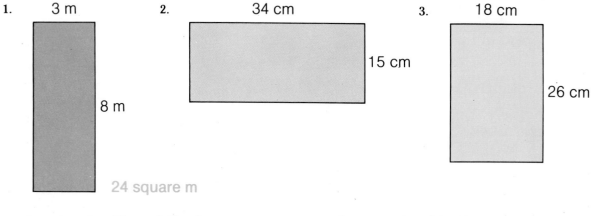

1.   3 m   8 m   24 square m

2.   34 cm   15 cm

3.   18 cm   26 cm

4. A rectangle with a width of 40 centimeters and a length of 52 centimeters.

5. A rectangle with a length of 32 millimeters and a width of 29 millimeters.

Review (pp. 229–238)

Write the answers.

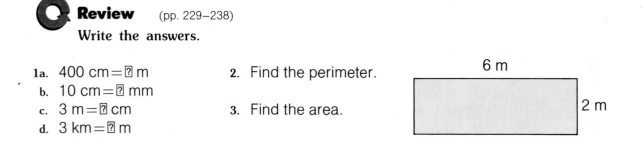

1a. 400 cm = ⬚ m
b. 10 cm = ⬚ mm
c. 3 m = ⬚ cm
d. 3 km = ⬚ m

2. Find the perimeter.

3. Find the area.

6 m

2 m

Cubic Centimeters

The **volume** of a solid shape is the number of cubic units that will fit inside it. The cubic unit shown here is a **cubic centimeter** (cubic cm).

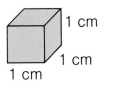

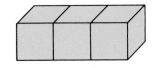

The volume of this solid is 3 cubic cm.

Count the cubic centimeters. What is the volume of each shape?

1.

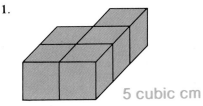

5 cubic cm

2.

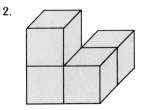

3.

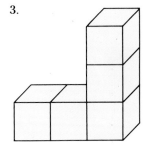

4.

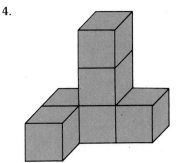

5.

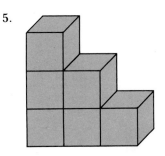

6.

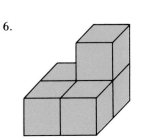

 **Calculate**

7. There are 1000 cubic millimeters in 1 cubic centimeter.
   a. How many cubic millimeters in 17.6 cubic centimeters?
   b. How many cubic millimeters in 315.21 cubic centimeters?

Volume

There are 6 cubic cm in each layer of this box. The box has two layers.

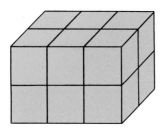

The volume of the box is 12 cubic cm.

Answer the questions.

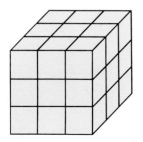

1a. How many cubic cm in one layer? 9
b. How many layers?
c. The volume of the box is
⬚ cubic cm.

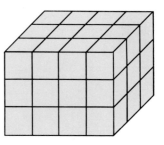

2a. How many cubic cm in one layer?
b. How many layers?
c. The volume of the box is
⬚ cubic cm.

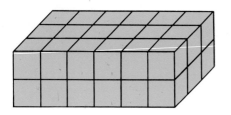

3a. How many cubic cm in one layer?
b. How many layers?
c. The volume of the box is
⬚ cubic cm.

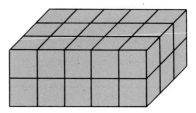

4a. How many cubic cm in one layer?
b. How many layers?
c. The volume of the box is
⬚ cubic cm.

Finding Volume

To find the volume of any box, multiply length times width times height.

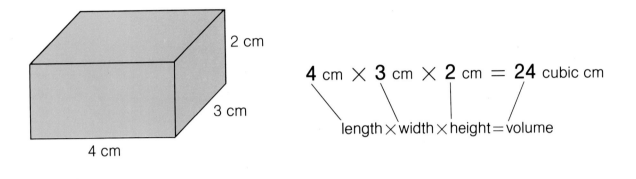

4 cm $\times$ 3 cm $\times$ 2 cm $=$ 24 cubic cm

length $\times$ width $\times$ height $=$ volume

Find the volume of each box.

1.

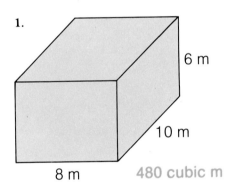

6 m

10 m

8 m   480 cubic m

2.

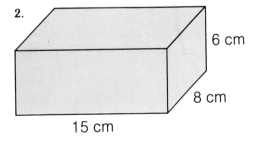

6 cm

8 cm

15 cm

3. A box with a length of 5 meters, a width of 3 meters, and a height of 2 meters.

4. A box with a length of 6 meters, a width of 4 meters, and a height of 7 meters.

Solve each problem.

5. Angie's room is 5 meters long, 4 meters wide, and 3 meters high. What is the volume of her room?

6. Doug's closet is 2 meters long, 1 meter wide, and 3 meters high. What is the volume of his closet?

Perimeter, Area, Volume

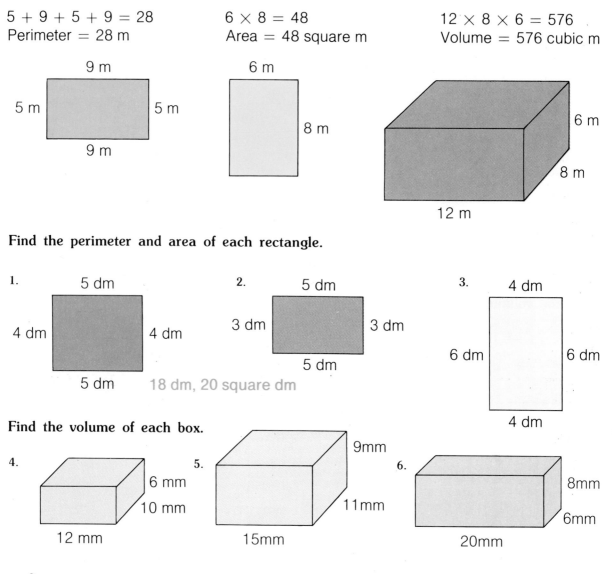

5 + 9 + 5 + 9 = 28
Perimeter = 28 m

9 m
5 m 5 m
9 m

6 × 8 = 48
Area = 48 square m

6 m
8 m

12 × 8 × 6 = 576
Volume = 576 cubic m

6 m
8 m
12 m

Find the perimeter and area of each rectangle.

1.
5 dm
4 dm   4 dm
5 dm
18 dm, 20 square dm

2.
5 dm
3 dm   3 dm
5 dm

3.
4 dm
6 dm   6 dm
4 dm

Find the volume of each box.

4.
6 mm
10 mm
12 mm

5.
9mm
11mm
15mm

6.
8mm
6mm
20mm

 **Challenge**

7. A square decimeter is 1 decimeter long and 1 decimeter wide. What is the area of a square decimeter in square centimeters? (Hint: Think 1 dm = ⬚ cm.)

8. A square centimeter is 10 millimeters long and 10 millimeters wide. What is the area of a square centimeter in square millimeters?

Milliliters

The amount a container will hold when filled is called its **capacity**. A **milliliter (ml)** is a metric unit for measuring capacity. A cubic centimeter has a capacity of 1 milliliter.

1 cubic cm

1 cm
1 cm
1 cm

soup spoon	30 ml
small glass	175 ml
thermos cup	250 ml
thermos bottle	750 ml

Use the pictures to answer these questions.

1. How many milliliters of fruit juice would you need to fill the thermos bottle 3 times?   2250 ml

2. About how many milliliters of fruit juice would the small glass hold? (175 ml or 75 ml)

3. About how many milliliters of water would the soup spoon hold? (30 ml or 90 ml)

4. How many milliliters of milk would you need to fill the thermos cup 4 times?

5. How many milliliters of milk in 6 small glasses?

6. How many milliliters of soup in 3 soup spoons?

Choose the best measure for each object.

7.

(30 ml, 3 ml, or 350 ml)

8.

(50 ml, 165 ml, or 300 ml)

9.

(8 ml, 83 ml, or 830 ml)

Liters

The **liter** (ℓ) is the basic metric unit for measuring capacity. There are 1000 milliliters in 1 liter. This large bottle holds about 19 liters. The glass holds about 300 milliliters.

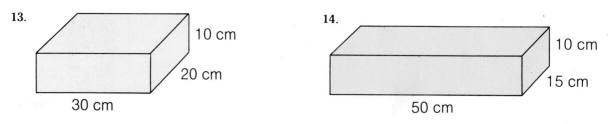

Copy and complete.

1. 3000 ml = ▢ ℓ 3 ℓ

2. 8000 ml = ▢ ℓ

3. 7000 ml = ▢ ℓ

4. 5000 ml = ▢ ℓ

5. 2000 ml = ▢ ℓ

6. 4000 ml = ▢ ℓ

7. 6 ℓ = ▢ ml

8. 5 ℓ = ▢ ml

9. 4 ℓ = ▢ ml

10. 8 ℓ = ▢ ml

11. 7 ℓ = ▢ ml

12. 9 ℓ = ▢ ml

⭐ **Challenge**

Find the volume of each box in cubic centimeters.
Then tell how many liters it holds. **1000 cubic cm = 1 liter**

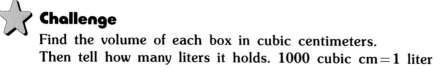

13.

10 cm

20 cm

30 cm

14.

10 cm

15 cm

50 cm

Grams

A **gram** (g) is a metric unit used to measure weight.

The paper clip weighs 2 grams.
The nickel weighs 5 grams.
The piece of chalk weighs 8 grams.
The eraser weighs 70 grams.

Use the pictures to answer these questions.

1. How much would 40 nickels weigh?   200 grams

2. How many paper clips weigh the same as 1 piece of chalk?

3. How many paper clips weigh as much as 10 nickels?

4. How many nickels weigh as much as 1 eraser?

5. 7 pieces of chalk weigh ▢ grams.

6. 32 paper clips weigh ▢ grams.

7. 12 erasers weigh ▢ grams.

8. 32 nickels weigh ▢ grams.

Choose the best measure for each object.

9.

(9 g, 80 g, or 100 g)

10.

(60 g, 600 g, or 6 g)

11.

(60 g, 10 g, or 200 g)

Kilograms

The **kilogram** (**kg**) is the basic metric unit for measuring weight. There are 1000 grams in 1 kilogram.

The girl weighs 40 kilograms.

Copy and complete.

1. 2000 g = ⬚ kg   **2 kg**

2. 5000 g = ⬚ kg

3. 4000 g = ⬚ kg

4. 6000 g = ⬚ kg

5. 9000 g = ⬚ kg

6. 3000 g = ⬚ kg

7. 8000 g = ⬚ kg

8. 2 kg = ⬚ g

9. 6 kg = ⬚ g

10. 3 kg = ⬚ g

11. A nickel weighs 5 grams. How many nickels weigh a kilogram?

12. A paper clip weighs 2 grams. How many paper clips weigh a kilogram?

Choose the best measure for each object.

13.

(10 g, 1 kg, or 1 g)

14.

(3 kg, 3 g, or 300 g)

15.

(120 g, 12 kg, or 1 kg)

Temperature in Celsius

Some thermometers measure temperature in degrees **Celsius** (°C). Each mark on this thermometer stands for 2 degrees. Temperatures can fall below zero degrees. 10°C below zero is shown as −10°C.

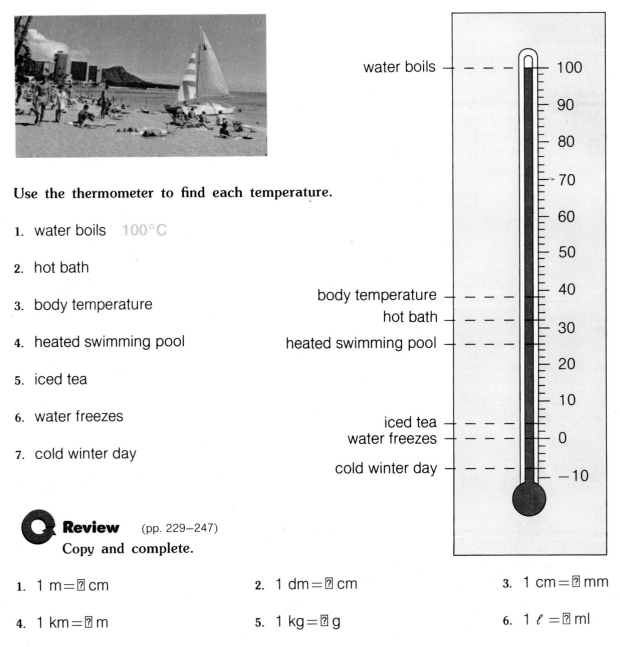

Use the thermometer to find each temperature.

1. water boils   100°C

2. hot bath

3. body temperature

4. heated swimming pool

5. iced tea

6. water freezes

7. cold winter day

Review   (pp. 229–247)
Copy and complete.

1. 1 m = ? cm

2. 1 dm = ? cm

3. 1 cm = ? mm

4. 1 km = ? m

5. 1 kg = ? g

6. 1 ℓ = ? ml

Measuring to the Nearest Inch

The **inch** (**in.**) is another unit for measuring length. This key is 2 in. long.

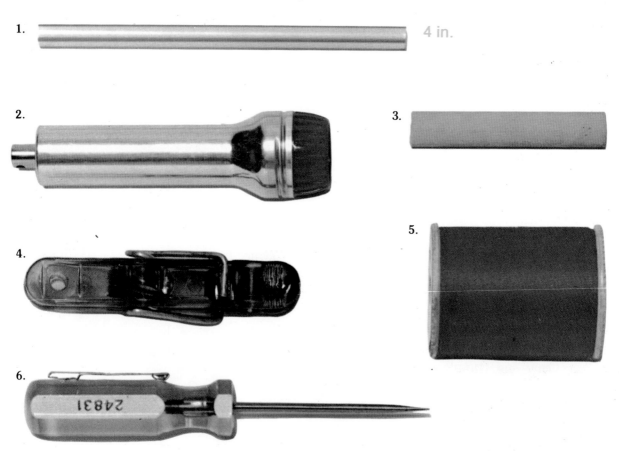

Estimate in inches. Then measure each object to the nearest inch.

1.   4 in.

2.

3.

4.

5.

6. 24831

Inches, Feet, Yards, and Miles

These units are also used for measuring length.

1 foot (ft) = 12 inches
1 yard (yd) = 3 feet
1 yard = 36 inches
1 mile (mi) = 1760 yards
1 mile = 5280 feet

To change larger units to smaller units, multiply.

7 feet = ▯ inches
Think: 1 foot = 12 inches
$7 \times 12 = 84$
7 feet = 84 inches

Copy and complete.

1. 4 ft = ▯ in. 48 in.

2. 9 ft = ▯ in.

3. 10 ft = ▯ in.

4. 8 yd = ▯ ft

5. 6 yd = ▯ ft

6. 14 yd = ▯ ft

7. 3 yd = ▯ in.

8. 10 yd = ▯ in.

9. 5 yd = ▯ in.

10. 5 mi = ▯ yd

11. 7 mi = ▯ yd

12. 4 mi = ▯ yd

13. 3 mi = ▯ ft

14. 10 mi = ▯ ft

15. 2 mi = ▯ ft

Which unit would you use to measure the length of each object? Write in., ft, yd, or mi.

16. a photograph

17. a toothbrush

18. a road between two cities

19. a car

Measuring Area

Area can be measured in square inches, square feet, square yards, or square miles.

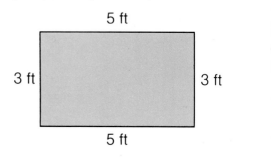

5 ft

3 ft   3 ft

5 ft

Remember, to find the area of a rectangle, multiply length times width.

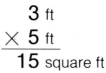

3 ft
× **5** ft
15 square ft

Solve the problems.

1. A room is 16 feet long and 12 feet wide. What is the area of the room?
192 square feet

2. A farmer's garden is 74 yards long and 25 yards wide. What is the area of the garden?

3. A sheet of drawing paper is 22 inches long and 19 inches wide. What is the area of the paper?

4. A one-story office building is 84 feet long and 63 feet wide. What is the floor area of the building?

5. A school district covers an area 32 miles long and 27 miles wide. What is the area of the school district?

6. A chalkboard measures 38 inches long and 33 inches wide. What is the area of the chalkboard?

 **Challenge**

7. Ron's porch is 7 yards long and 7 feet wide. What is the area of the porch?

Volume in Cubic Inches

Volume can be measured in cubic inches.

Remember, to find the volume of a box,
multiply length times width times height.
The volume is one cubic inch.

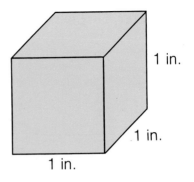

Find the volumes.

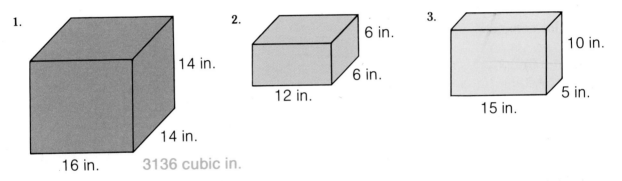

1. 14 in. / 14 in. / 16 in.   3136 cubic in.

2. 6 in. / 6 in. / 12 in.

3. 10 in. / 5 in. / 15 in.

4. A box with a length of 7 inches,
a width of 4 inches, and a height
of 2 inches.

5. A drawer with a length of 11 inches,
a width of 9 inches, and a height
of 5 inches.

6. A bread box with a length of
14 inches, a width of 8 inches, and
a height of 9 inches.

7. A marble box with a length of
9 inches, a width of 7 inches, and
a height of 2 inches.

8. A jewelry box with a length of
12 inches, a width of 10 inches, and
a height of 8 inches.

9. A cake pan with a length of
16 inches, a width of 12 inches, and
a height of 4 inches.

10. A drawer with a length of 12 inches,
a width of 8 inches, and a height
of 4 inches.

11. A box with a length of 6 inches,
a width of 3 inches, and a height
of 1 inch.

Cups, Pints, and Quarts

You can use these units to measure capacity.

1 pint (pt) = 2 cups
1 quart (qt) = 2 pints
1 quart = 4 cups

Cup   **Pint**   **Quart**

Copy and complete.

1. 8 pt = ▧ cups   *16 cups*

2. 19 pt = ▧ cups

3. 12 pt = ▧ cups

4. 7 qt = ▧ pt

5. 8 qt = ▧ pt

6. 17 qt = ▧ pt

7. 3 qt = ▧ cups

8. 6 qt = ▧ cups

9. 12 qt = ▧ cups

10. 7 pt = ▧ cups

11. 4 qt = ▧ pt

12. 8 qt = ▧ cups

13. 20 pt = ▧ cups

14. 14 qt = ▧ pt

15. 10 qt = ▧ cups

16. 2 pt = ▧ cups

17. 15 qt = ▧ pt

18. 11 qt = ▧ pt

 **Challenge**

19. Tim is making a fruit drink. He has
4 cups of orange juice, 2 pints of
pineapple juice, 1 pint of apple juice,
and 1 quart of grapefruit juice.
   a. How many cups of juice does Tim
      have in all?
   b. How much does he have in pints?

Cups, Pints, Quarts, and Gallons

Gallons are also used to measure capacity.

> 4 quarts = 1 gallon (gal)
> 8 pints = 1 gallon
> 16 cups = 1 gallon

To change smaller units to larger units, divide.

15 quarts = ▢ gallons ▢ quarts
Think: 4 quarts = 1 gallon

$$\begin{array}{r} 3 \text{ r}3 \\ 4\overline{)15} \end{array}$$ 15 quarts = 3 gallons 3 quarts

Copy and complete.

1. 27 qt = ▢ gal ▢ qt   6 gal 3 qt

2. 23 qt = ▢ gal ▢ qt

3. 6 qt = ▢ gal ▢ qt

4. 10 qt = ▢ gal ▢ qt

5. 35 pt = ▢ gal ▢ pt

6. 19 pt = ▢ gal ▢ pt

7. 34 cups = ▢ gal ▢ cups

8. 74 cups = ▢ gal ▢ cups

 Calculate

9. A paint store sold 78 gallons, 349 quarts, and 196 pints of paint in one month. How many pints of paint were sold in all?

Ounces, Pounds, and Tons

Ounces (oz), pounds (lb), and tons (T) can be used to measure weight. There are 16 ounces in 1 pound. There are 2000 pounds in one ton.

| 1 pound (lb) = 16 ounces (oz) |
| 1 ton (T) = 2000 pounds |

Copy and complete.

1. 5 lb = ⬚ oz 80 oz
2. 3 lb = ⬚ oz
3. 10 lb = ⬚ oz

4. 4 T = ⬚ lb
5. 8 T = ⬚ lb
6. 12 T = ⬚ lb

Copy and complete.

7. 38 oz = ⬚ lb ⬚ oz
8. 607 oz = ⬚ lb ⬚ oz
9. 18 oz = ⬚ lb ⬚ oz

10. 47 oz = ⬚ lb ⬚ oz
11. 100 oz = ⬚ lb ⬚ oz
12. 52 oz = ⬚ lb ⬚ oz

13. 3419 lb = ⬚ T ⬚ lb
14. 9654 lb = ⬚ T ⬚ lb
15. 3000 lb = ⬚ T ⬚ lb

 **Challenge**

16. Gary bought 3 pounds of topsoil, 4 pounds of sand, and 27 ounces of fertilizer for his plants. How many pounds and ounces of materials did he buy in all?

Temperature in Fahrenheit

Some thermometers measure temperature in degrees **Fahrenheit** (F°).
Each mark on this thermometer stands for 2 degrees. Temperatures
can fall below zero degrees. 10°F below zero is shown as −10°F.

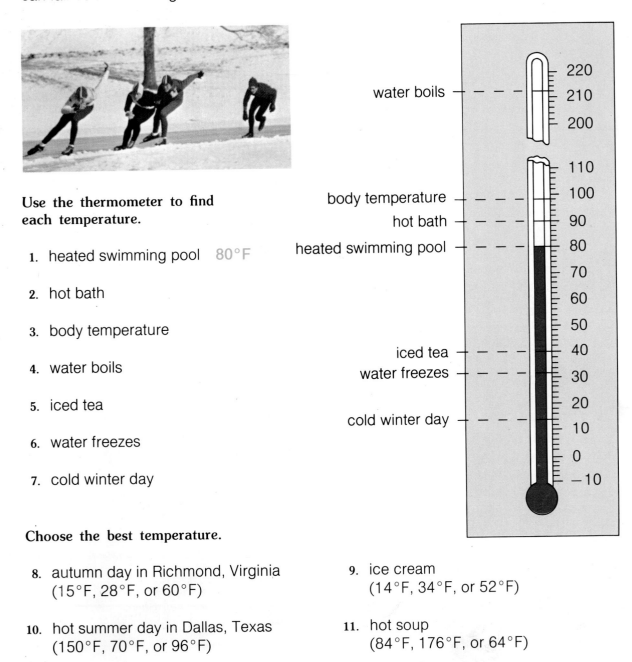

Use the thermometer to find each temperature.

1. heated swimming pool   80°F

2. hot bath

3. body temperature

4. water boils

5. iced tea

6. water freezes

7. cold winter day

Choose the best temperature.

8. autumn day in Richmond, Virginia
   (15°F, 28°F, or 60°F)

9. ice cream
   (14°F, 34°F, or 52°F)

10. hot summer day in Dallas, Texas
    (150°F, 70°F, or 96°F)

11. hot soup
    (84°F, 176°F, or 64°F)

Measuring Time

Some units for measuring time are hours (h), minutes (min), seconds (s), days (d), weeks (wk), months (mo), and years (yr).

60 seconds = 1 minute
60 minutes = 1 hour
24 hours = 1 day
7 days = 1 week
28 to 31 days = 1 month
12 months = 1 year
365 days = 1 year
52 weeks = 1 year

Copy and complete.

1. 3 d = ? h   72 h

2. 2 yr = ? wk

3. 180 s = ? min

4. 2 h = ? min

5. 96 h = ? d

6. 6 wk = ? d

7. 48 mo = ? yr

8. 3 yr = ? wk

9. 21 d = ? wk

10. 104 wk = ? yr

11. 300 s = ? min

12. 3 yr = ? mo

 **Challenge**

13. Scientists have studied the rates at which people breathe. They have found that most adults inhale (and exhale) about 15 times a minute.
   a. How many times would an adult inhale in 360 seconds?
   b. How many times would an adult inhale in 1 hour?
   c. How many times would an adult inhale in 3 hours?

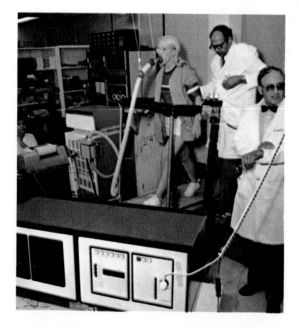

Time Problems

Ridgeview to Lakeville Train Schedule

Leave Ridgeview	Arrive Lakeville	
7:10 A.M.	7:55 A.M.	Daily except Saturday and Sunday
8:26 A.M.	9:14 A.M.	Daily except Sunday
10:50 A.M.	11:35 A.M.	Daily
12:10 P.M.	12:55 P.M.	Saturday only
3:02 P.M.	3:49 P.M.	Daily except Saturday and Sunday
6:15 P.M.	7:07 P.M.	Daily

Use the schedule to answer the questions.

1. How much time does each train take?
   a. the 8:26 A.M. train? 48 minutes
   b. the 7:10 A.M. train?
   c. the 6:15 P.M. train?
   d. the 3:02 P.M. train?
   e. the 12:10 P.M. train?
   f. the 10:50 A.M. train?

2. Karen and Wally are going from Ridgeview to Lakeville.
   a. Karen wants to arrive in Lakeville by 7:00 P.M. Sunday. How many trains can she take?
   b. Wally wants to arrive in Lakeville by 11:45 A.M. Monday. How many trains can he take?

Time Zones

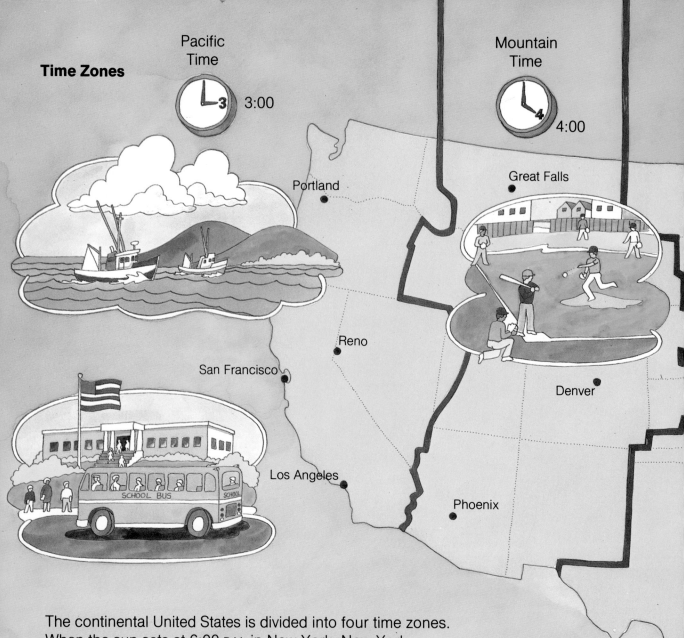

Pacific Time 3:00

Mountain Time 4:00

Portland

Reno

San Francisco

Los Angeles

Great Falls

Denver

Phoenix

The continental United States is divided into four time zones.
When the sun sets at 6:00 P.M. in New York, New York,
it is still 3:00 P.M. in Los Angeles, California.

Use the map to find the time zone for the following cities.

1. Reno, Nevada   Pacific

2. Cleveland, Ohio

3. Atlanta, Georgia

4. Phoenix, Arizona

5. Dallas, Texas

6. Boston, Massachusetts

7. Chicago, Illinois

8. Omaha, Nebraska

9. Los Angeles, California

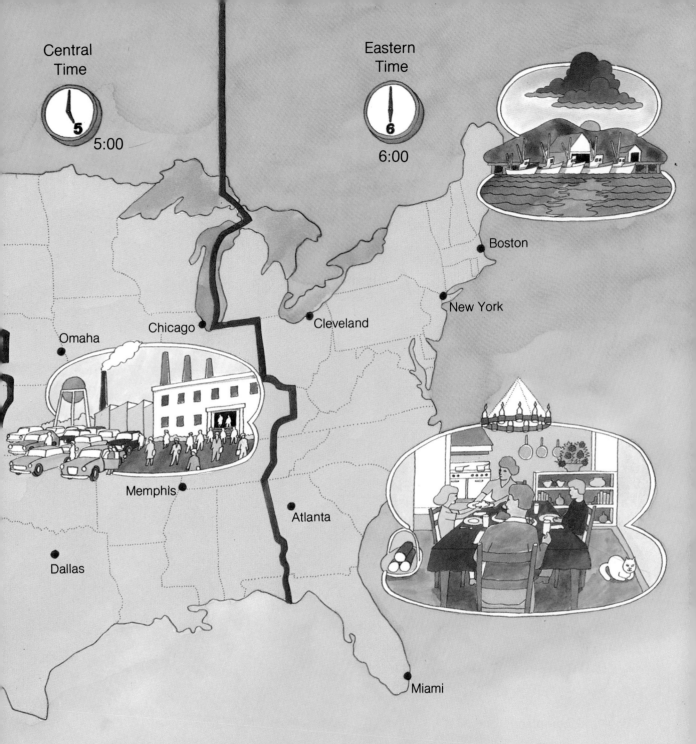

Central Time

5:00

Eastern Time

6:00

Boston

New York

Cleveland

Chicago

Omaha

Memphis

Atlanta

Dallas

Miami

10. If it is 3:00 P.M. Eastern time, what is the Central time?

11. If it is 11:00 A.M. Pacific time, what is the Mountain time?

12. If it is 10:00 A.M. Mountain time, what is the Eastern time?

13. If it is 8:00 A.M. Central time, what is the Pacific time?

Chapter Review

Copy and complete.   (ex. 1-2: p. 230),   (ex. 3-4: p. 231),   (ex. 5-6: p. 232)

1. 600 cm = ▢ m

2. 6 m = ▢ cm

3. 4 dm = ▢ cm

4. 80 mm = ▢ cm

5. 3000 m = ▢ km

6. 2000 m = ▢ km

Find the perimeter and the area of each shape.   (ex. 7–8: p. 234, p. 238)

7. 9 dm / 6 dm / 6 dm / 9 dm

8. 15 m / 11 m / 11 m / 15 m

Write the answers.   (ex. 9-10: p. 241)

9. What is the volume of a box with a length of 8 centimeters, a width of 3 centimeters, and a height of 4 centimeters?

10. What is the volume of a box with a length of 12 millimeters, a width of 6 millimeters, and a height of 7 millimeters?

Copy and complete.   (ex. 11-13: p. 244),   (ex. 14-16: p. 246)

11. 2000 ml = ▢ ℓ

12. 4000 ml = ▢ ℓ

13. 7000 ml = ▢ ℓ

14. 4000 g = ▢ kg

15. 5000 g = ▢ kg

16. 7 kg = ▢ g

Copy and complete.   (ex. 17-19: p. 249),   (ex. 20-22: p. 252),   (ex. 23-25: p. 254)

17. 9 ft = ▢ in.

18. 21 ft = ▢ in.

19. 6 yd = ▢ in.

20. 15 pt = ▢ cups

21. 14 pt = ▢ cups

22. 8 qt = ▢ pt

23. 4 lb = ▢ oz

24. 7 lb = ▢ oz

25. 6 T = ▢ lb

Chapter Test

Copy and complete.

1. 3 m = ⬚ cm

2. 800 cm = ⬚ m

3. 5 dm = ⬚ cm

4. 40 mm = ⬚ cm

5. 4000 m = ⬚ km

6. 7 m = ⬚ dm

Write the answers.

7. What is the perimeter of a rectangle with sides of 4 meters, 8 meters, 4 meters, and 8 meters? What is the area?

8. What is the perimeter of a rectangle with sides of 12 inches, 16 inches, 12 inches, and 16 inches? What is the area?

Find the volume of each box.

9.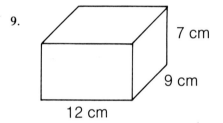
7 cm
9 cm
12 cm

10.
12 in.
7 in.
12 in.

Copy and complete.

11. 7 ℓ = ⬚ ml

12. 3 kg = ⬚ g

13. 4000 ml = ⬚ ℓ

14. 6 ℓ = ⬚ ml

15. 6000 g = ⬚ kg

16. 8 kg = ⬚ g

Copy and complete.

17. 10 ft = ⬚ in.

18. 5 mi = ⬚ yd

19. 12 yd = ⬚ ft

20. 8 d = ⬚ h

21. 7 lb = ⬚ oz

22. 4 qt = ⬚ gal

23. 3500 lb = ⬚ T ⬚ lb

24. 16 pt = ⬚ cups

25. 7 h = ⬚ min

Brush Up

Divide.

1. $24 \div 6$ 2. $81 \div 9$ 3. $36 \div 6$ 4. $54 \div 9$ 5. $32 \div 4$

6. $64 \div 8$ 7. $56 \div 7$ 8. $63 \div 7$ 9. $25 \div 5$ 10. $42 \div 7$

11. $3\overline{)399}$ 12. $7\overline{)86}$ 13. $4\overline{)25}$ 14. $5\overline{)987}$ 15. $2\overline{)651}$

16. $6\overline{)6123}$ 17. $5\overline{)526}$ 18. $3\overline{)4229}$ 19. $4\overline{)2100}$ 20. $9\overline{)3750}$

Multiply.

21. $\begin{array}{r} 30 \\ \times\ 5 \\ \hline \end{array}$ 22. $\begin{array}{r} 50 \\ \times\ 4 \\ \hline \end{array}$ 23. $\begin{array}{r} 80 \\ \times\ 3 \\ \hline \end{array}$ 24. $\begin{array}{r} 21 \\ \times\ 8 \\ \hline \end{array}$ 25. $\begin{array}{r} 48 \\ \times\ 9 \\ \hline \end{array}$

26. $\begin{array}{r} 17 \\ \times\ 3 \\ \hline \end{array}$ 27. $\begin{array}{r} 25 \\ \times\ 5 \\ \hline \end{array}$ 28. $\begin{array}{r} 55 \\ \times\ 6 \\ \hline \end{array}$ 29. $\begin{array}{r} 37 \\ \times\ 9 \\ \hline \end{array}$ 30. $\begin{array}{r} 51 \\ \times\ 8 \\ \hline \end{array}$

31. $\begin{array}{r} 35 \\ \times\ 6 \\ \hline \end{array}$ 32. $\begin{array}{r} 19 \\ \times\ 8 \\ \hline \end{array}$ 33. $\begin{array}{r} 64 \\ \times\ 3 \\ \hline \end{array}$ 34. $\begin{array}{r} 43 \\ \times\ 4 \\ \hline \end{array}$ 35. $\begin{array}{r} 75 \\ \times\ 5 \\ \hline \end{array}$

Subtract.

36. $\begin{array}{r} 379 \\ -250 \\ \hline \end{array}$ 37. $\begin{array}{r} 92 \\ -80 \\ \hline \end{array}$ 38. $\begin{array}{r} 58 \\ -50 \\ \hline \end{array}$ 39. $\begin{array}{r} 874 \\ -810 \\ \hline \end{array}$ 40. $\begin{array}{r} 713 \\ -640 \\ \hline \end{array}$

41. $\begin{array}{r} 218 \\ -192 \\ \hline \end{array}$ 42. $\begin{array}{r} 387 \\ -366 \\ \hline \end{array}$ 43. $\begin{array}{r} 989 \\ -965 \\ \hline \end{array}$ 44. $\begin{array}{r} 65 \\ -57 \\ \hline \end{array}$ 45. $\begin{array}{r} 497 \\ -468 \\ \hline \end{array}$

46. $\begin{array}{r} 194 \\ -180 \\ \hline \end{array}$ 47. $\begin{array}{r} 71 \\ -50 \\ \hline \end{array}$ 48. $\begin{array}{r} 268 \\ -250 \\ \hline \end{array}$ 49. $\begin{array}{r} 144 \\ -132 \\ \hline \end{array}$ 50. $\begin{array}{r} 581 \\ -576 \\ \hline \end{array}$

CHAPTER 10

Division

Using Division at Work

Brian Hicks is a shipping clerk at a foundry. He has an order for 832 copper bars. 16 bars can fit on a loading tray. He divides 832 by 16 to find how many loading trays he will need. He will need 52 loading trays for the bars.

Dividing by Tens

$30\overline{)85}$ $85 = 8$ tens $+ 5$ ones
To find the quotient, think: 8 tens divided by 3 tens is close
to 2 ones, so $30\overline{)85}$ is close to 2.

First write the quotient 2.
Then multiply: $2 \times 30 = 60$.
Then subtract: $85 - 60 = 25$.
Then write the remainder.

$$\text{quotient } \begin{array}{r} 2 \text{ r}25 \text{ remainder} \\ \text{divisor } 30\overline{)85} \\ -\ 60 \quad 30 \times 2 = 60 \\ \hline 25 \end{array}$$

Divide.

1. $40\overline{)94}$ 2 r14

2. $30\overline{)93}$

3. $20\overline{)59}$

4. $10\overline{)49}$

5. $40\overline{)98}$

6. $20\overline{)95}$

7. $50\overline{)67}$

8. $40\overline{)91}$

9. $50\overline{)63}$

10. $20\overline{)86}$

Rewrite these problems using $\overline{)}$. Divide.

11. $87 \div 30$

12. $97 \div 20$

13. $59 \div 10$

14. $53 \div 20$

15. $99 \div 50$

16. $85 \div 30$

17. $69 \div 50$

18. $71 \div 20$

19. $93 \div 40$

20. $47 \div 10$

21. A salesclerk sold 20 pairs of
sunglasses and collected $80.
What was the price of each pair
of sunglasses?

22. A part-time salesclerk earned
$50 one week. She worked
10 hours. How much did she
make each hour?

Dividing Hundreds

Step 1
Divide tens.
Write 2 in the tens place of the quotient.
Multiply. Subtract. Bring down ones.

$$
\begin{array}{r}
2 \\
30)\overline{829} \\
-\,60 \\
\hline
229 \\
\end{array}
$$

Step 2
Divide.
Write 7 in the ones place of the quotient.
Multiply. Subtract. Write the remainder.

$$
\begin{array}{r}
27 \text{ r}19 \\
30)\overline{829} \\
-\,60 \\
\hline
229 \\
-\,210 \\
\hline
19 \\
\end{array}
$$

Divide.

1. 30)‾606 (20 r6)
2. 40)‾977
3. 20)‾618
4. 10)‾217
5. 50)‾659

6. 40)‾893
7. 30)‾713
8. 80)‾959
9. 50)‾616
10. 10)‾172

11. 20)‾698
12. 70)‾914
13. 60)‾643
14. 80)‾993
15. 20)‾823

16. $998 \div 80$
17. $419 \div 20$
18. $665 \div 40$
19. $338 \div 30$
20. $913 \div 20$

21. $811 \div 70$
22. $731 \div 60$
23. $914 \div 30$
24. $911 \div 40$
25. $841 \div 80$

26. $514 \div 50$
27. $931 \div 20$
28. $845 \div 30$
29. $803 \div 70$
30. $925 \div 40$

Calculate
Work each problem from left to right.

31. $107 \times 2 \div 2 \times 150 \div 3$
32. $763 \times 8 \div 4 \times 6 \div 2$

33. $465 \times 5 \div 3 \times 6 \div 5$
34. $298 \times 6 \div 4 \times 4 \div 2$

Dividing Thousands

Divide thousands.
Watch for middle zeros.

```
      107 r8
40)4288
   − 40
     28
   −  0
    288
  − 280
      8
```

To check, multiply the
quotient by the divisor.
Then add the remainder.

```
    107   quotient
×    40   divisor
   4280
+     8   remainder
   4288
```

Divide. Check the first row.

1. $\overset{109 \ r24}{30\overline{)3294}}$

2. $20\overline{)6063}$

3. $40\overline{)8259}$

4. $30\overline{)9176}$

5. $20\overline{)8145}$

6. $50\overline{)5471}$

7. $10\overline{)6037}$

8. $30\overline{)9165}$

9. $60\overline{)6278}$

10. $20\overline{)4112}$

Now do these.

11. $60\overline{)6841}$

12. $30\overline{)9486}$

13. $20\overline{)5965}$

14. $50\overline{)5928}$

15. $40\overline{)8977}$

16. $20\overline{)8658}$

17. $80\overline{)9842}$

18. $10\overline{)3233}$

19. $40\overline{)7319}$

20. $20\overline{)9784}$

 **Challenge**

Copy and complete.

21. $\square \div 50 = 113 \ r37$

22. $\square \div 60 = 116 \ r7$

23. $\square \div 30 = 138 \ r27$

Farmers' Market Problems

James and Diana Johnson have a farm. Every Saturday they bring their produce to the farmers' market. Solve each problem.

1. One Saturday the Johnsons had 926 onions. Diana put 40 in each basket. How many baskets of onions? How many onions left over?   23, 6

2. The Johnsons had 6398 apples. They put 50 in each box. How many boxes of apples? How many apples left over?

3. The Johnsons had 753 ears of corn. They put 60 in each box. How many boxes of corn? How many ears of corn left over?

4. One week the Johnsons had 744 cucumbers. Diana put 70 in each box. How many boxes of cucumbers? How many cucumbers left over?

5. One Saturday they had 2231 potatoes. James put 20 in each bag. How many bags of potatoes? How many potatoes left over?

6. One week the Johnsons had 284 heads of lettuce. James put 20 in each box. How many boxes of lettuce? How many heads of lettuce left over?

One-Digit Quotients

$30\overline{)282}$ $282 = 28$ tens $+ 2$ ones
To find the quotient, think: 28 tens divided by 3 tens is close
to 9 ones, so $30\overline{)282}$ is close to 9. Write 9 as the
quotient in the ones place.

$$
\begin{array}{r}
9 \text{ r}12 \\
30\overline{)282} \\
-270 \\
\hline
12
\end{array}
$$
$30 \times 9 = 270$

Check
$$
\begin{array}{r}
30 \\
\times\ 9 \\
\hline
270 \\
+\ 12 \\
\hline
282
\end{array}
$$

Divide. Check the first row.

9 r5

1. $40\overline{)365}$
2. $30\overline{)179}$
3. $90\overline{)826}$
4. $60\overline{)523}$
5. $20\overline{)147}$

6. $70\overline{)218}$
7. $80\overline{)651}$
8. $50\overline{)482}$
9. $20\overline{)119}$
10. $40\overline{)168}$

11. $50\overline{)203}$
12. $40\overline{)283}$
13. $60\overline{)184}$
14. $90\overline{)357}$
15. $70\overline{)394}$

16. $365 \div 60$
17. $644 \div 90$
18. $273 \div 80$
19. $397 \div 40$
20. $521 \div 70$

21. $409 \div 80$
22. $153 \div 20$
23. $185 \div 30$
24. $461 \div 90$
25. $185 \div 50$

⭐ Challenge

Divide. Be careful where you place the first digit of
the quotient.

26. $874 \div 80$
27. $211 \div 30$
28. $749 \div 60$
29. $197 \div 20$
30. $753 \div 40$

31. $423 \div 60$
32. $866 \div 70$
33. $373 \div 50$
34. $591 \div 30$
35. $891 \div 90$

Two-Digit Quotients

Step 1
Divide.
Write 9 in the tens place of the quotient.
Multiply. Subtract. Bring down ones.

$$
\begin{array}{r}
9 \\
40\overline{)3816} \\
-\ 360 \\
\hline
216 \\
\end{array}
$$

Step 2
Divide.
Write 5 in the ones place of the quotient.
Multiply. Subtract. Write the remainder.

$$
\begin{array}{r}
95\ \text{r}16 \\
40\overline{)3816} \\
-\ 360 \\
\hline
216 \\
-\ 200 \\
\hline
16 \\
\end{array}
$$

Divide.

1. $30\overline{)2786}$ 92 r26

2. $80\overline{)4348}$

3. $20\overline{)1564}$

4. $80\overline{)6122}$

5. $40\overline{)2519}$

6. $60\overline{)1715}$

7. $50\overline{)3186}$

8. $70\overline{)6213}$

9. $30\overline{)2301}$

10. $20\overline{)1337}$

11. $30\overline{)2125}$

12. $30\overline{)1478}$

13. $60\overline{)5931}$

14. $40\overline{)3381}$

15. $80\overline{)7364}$

16. $50\overline{)4269}$

17. $90\overline{)8992}$

18. $20\overline{)1388}$

19. $70\overline{)6103}$

20. $30\overline{)2897}$

21. The Post Office sells books of stamps. There are 40 stamps in each book. If the Post Office sold 3240 stamps last week, how many books of stamps did it sell?

Division Code

Crack the code to answer the riddle.

What does Cinderella Shark wear?

Code	
p	2 r 18
f	8 r 5
r	5 r 19
l	13 r 42
s	14 r 11
e	34 r 15
i	132 r 25
g	142 r 48
a	214 r 8

Divide.

142 r48, g

1. 50)7148

2. 70)952

3. 40)8568

4. 50)711

5. 60)851

6. 30)245

7. 60)822

8. 70)9265

9. 40)98

10. 30)78

11. 80)2735

12. 60)319

13. 40)571

14. The answer is: ___ ___ ___ ___ ___ ___ ___ ___ ___ ___ ___ ___ ___
  1.   2.   3.   4.   5.   6.   7.   8.   9.   10.   11.   12.   13.

Review (pp. 265–271)

Divide.

1. 20)53

2. 40)726

3. 30)4261

4. 60)574

5. 30)2865

Rounding the Divisor

Step 1
Round the divisor.
Guess the first digit of
the quotient.

$$\overset{\displaystyle 2}{36\overline{)89}}$$

36 rounds to 40.
40$\overline{)89}$ is about 2.
Try 2.

Step 2
Multiply. Subtract.
Write the remainder.

$$\begin{array}{r} 2\ \text{r}17 \\ 36\overline{)89} \\ -72 \\ \hline 17 \end{array}$$

Check
Multiply the divisor
by the quotient. Then
add the remainder.

$$\begin{array}{r} 36 \\ \times\ 2 \\ \hline 72 \\ +17 \\ \hline 89 \end{array}$$

Divide. Check the first row.

1. $\overset{\displaystyle 2\ \text{r}14}{41\overline{)96}}$

2. $18\overline{)61}$

3. $59\overline{)72}$

4. $37\overline{)95}$

5. $22\overline{)74}$

6. $33\overline{)81}$

7. $47\overline{)63}$

8. $29\overline{)84}$

9. $17\overline{)42}$

10. $36\overline{)78}$

11. $23\overline{)99}$

12. $36\overline{)81}$

13. $19\overline{)64}$

14. $21\overline{)45}$

15. $79\overline{)97}$

16. $79 \div 22$

17. $84 \div 39$

18. $49 \div 26$

19. $85 \div 31$

20. $91 \div 42$

21. $67 \div 59$

22. $99 \div 24$

23. $73 \div 66$

24. $83 \div 19$

25. $94 \div 29$

26. Dr. Gonzales sees about 25 patients
a day. About how many days does
it take her to see 75 patients?

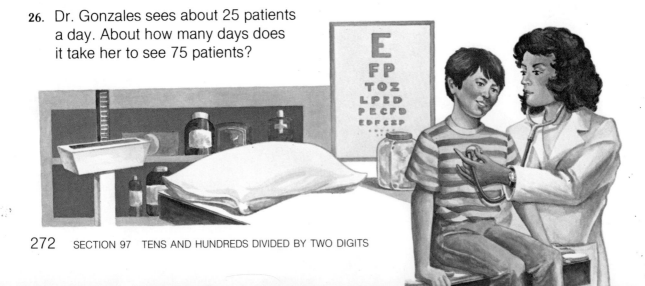

Dividing by Two Digits

Step 1
Round the divisor.
Guess the first digit
of the quotient.

$$\begin{array}{r} 3 \\ 28\overline{)913} \end{array}$$

28 rounds to 30.
$30\overline{)91}$ is about 3.

Step 2
Multiply. Subtract.
Bring down ones.
Guess the second digit
of the quotient.

$$\begin{array}{r} 32 \\ 28\overline{)913} \\ -\ 84 \\ \hline 73 \end{array}$$

$30\overline{)73}$ is about 2.

Step 3
Multiply. Subtract.
Write the remainder.

$$\begin{array}{r} 32 \text{ r}17 \\ 28\overline{)913} \\ -\ 84 \\ \hline 73 \\ -\ 56 \\ \hline 17 \end{array}$$

Divide.

1. $\begin{array}{r} 31 \text{ r}8 \\ 27\overline{)845} \end{array}$
2. $33\overline{)689}$
3. $28\overline{)939}$
4. $39\overline{)863}$
5. $32\overline{)679}$

6. $18\overline{)447}$
7. $43\overline{)518}$
8. $19\overline{)816}$
9. $52\overline{)613}$
10. $22\overline{)932}$

Now do these.

11. $21\overline{)514}$
12. $48\overline{)62}$
13. $62\overline{)706}$
14. $31\overline{)995}$
15. $43\overline{)91}$

16. $57\overline{)73}$
17. $38\overline{)842}$
18. $22\overline{)98}$
19. $29\overline{)969}$
20. $19\overline{)72}$

21. $23\overline{)59}$
22. $34\overline{)627}$
23. $67\overline{)711}$
24. $41\overline{)96}$
25. $57\overline{)794}$

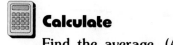 **Calculate**

Find the average. (Add. Then divide by 13.)

26. $61 + 84 + 69 + 28 + 79 + 25 + 76 + 23 + 25 + 22 + 61 + 13 + 71$

Correcting Your Guess

Sometimes you need to guess more than once to find the first digit of the quotient. If your guess is too large or too small, guess again.

$$\begin{array}{r} 3 \\ 23\overline{)61} \\ -69 \end{array}$$

$20\overline{)61}$ is about 3, but 3 is **too large** because the product, 69, is larger than 61. Your guess is too large. Try 2.

$$\begin{array}{r} 4 \\ 17\overline{)87} \\ -68 \\ \hline 19 \end{array}$$

$20\overline{)87}$ is about 4, but 4 is **too small** because the difference, 19, is larger than 17. Your guess is too small. Try 5.

Find the first digit of the quotient. If your guess is too large, try a smaller number. Then divide.

1. $13\overline{)68}$ 5 r3

2. $23\overline{)629}$

3. $32\overline{)63}$

4. $42\overline{)834}$

5. $34\overline{)96}$

Find the first digit of the quotient. If your guess is too small, try a larger number. Then divide.

6. $19\overline{)78}$

7. $27\overline{)245}$

8. $18\overline{)99}$

9. $25\overline{)77}$

10. $38\overline{)349}$

Divide.

11. $23\overline{)129}$

12. $37\overline{)345}$

13. $26\overline{)859}$

14. $52\overline{)413}$

15. $22\overline{)840}$

16. $15\overline{)681}$

17. $43\overline{)842}$

18. $19\overline{)98}$

19. $52\overline{)358}$

20. $48\overline{)437}$

Dividing Thousands

Step 1
Round the divisor.
Find the first digit.
Multiply. Subtract.
Bring down tens.

$$
\begin{array}{r}
4 \\
21\overline{)8649} \\
-\;84 \\
\hline
24
\end{array}
$$

21 rounds to 20.
20)86 is about 4.

Step 2
Find the second digit.
Multiply. Subtract.
Bring down ones.

$$
\begin{array}{r}
41 \\
21\overline{)8649} \\
-\;84 \\
\hline
24 \\
-\;21 \\
\hline
39
\end{array}
$$

Step 3
Find the third digit.
Multiply. Subtract.
Write the remainder.

$$
\begin{array}{r}
411\ \text{r}18 \\
21\overline{)8649} \\
-\;84 \\
\hline
24 \\
-\;21 \\
\hline
39 \\
-\;21 \\
\hline
18
\end{array}
$$

Divide. Check the first row.

310 r31

1. 32)9951

2. 19)2461

3. 21)4344

4. 38)5269

5. 13)3852

6. 43)9856

7. 65)7412

8. 16)4785

9. 22)8973

10. 29)7523

11. 55)6437

12. 26)9446

13. 46)6595

14. 13)5064

15. 45)7682

16. $9743 \div 64$

17. $7492 \div 35$

18. $8961 \div 23$

19. $6846 \div 66$

20. $2561 \div 14$

21. A baker made 1800 muffins. He put
12 muffins in each package to sell.
How many packages did he fill?

Flower Problems

Philip and Barbara Norris own a flower shop. Each morning they buy fresh flowers at the flower market. Solve each problem.

1. One morning they bought 609 daisies. Barbara put 21 daisies in a bunch. How many bunches did she make? 29

2. The Norris's bought 476 daffodils. They put 14 daffodils in each bunch. How many bunches of daffodils did they make?

3. One morning the Norris's bought 378 tulips. Barbara made 63 arrangements with the tulips. How many tulips in each arrangement?

4. The Norris's bought 108 roses. They made bouquets with 12 roses in each one. How many bouquets did they make?

5. One morning they bought 675 carnations. Philip put 45 carnations in each bucket. How many buckets did he fill with carnations?

6. They bought 1377 mums. Philip made 81 bouquets. How many mums did he put in each bouquet?

Rounding the Divisor and the Dividend

Step 1
Round both the divisor and the dividend
to the nearest ten. Guess the first
digit of the quotient.

$$\overset{7}{38\overline{)286}}$$

$38\overline{)286}$ rounds to $40\overline{)290}$.
Try 7.

Step 2
Multiply. Subtract.
Write the remainder.

$$\begin{array}{r} 7\ \text{r}20 \\ 38\overline{)286} \\ -266 \\ \hline 20 \end{array}$$

Divide.

1. $\overset{8\ \text{r}10}{41\overline{)338}}$ 2. $82\overline{)663}$ 3. $58\overline{)438}$ 4. $29\overline{)192}$ 5. $73\overline{)298}$

6. $94\overline{)486}$ 7. $62\overline{)191}$ 8. $18\overline{)177}$ 9. $86\overline{)314}$ 10. $52\overline{)272}$

Divide.

11. $23\overline{)744}$ 12. $46\overline{)379}$ 13. $19\overline{)462}$ 14. $68\overline{)648}$ 15. $31\overline{)696}$

16. $262 \div 58$ 17. $914 \div 72$ 18. $741 \div 33$ 19. $640 \div 27$ 20. $345 \div 83$

21. $439 \div 71$ 22. $653 \div 67$ 23. $277 \div 23$ 24. $983 \div 84$ 25. $716 \div 15$

26. Anne saved 32 pennies a day until
she had 288 pennies. How many
days did she save?

27. Ben wants to buy a $112 bicycle.
If he saves $14 a month, how many
months will it be until he has $112?

Dividing Thousands

Step 1
Round both the divisor and the dividend.
Find the first digit of the quotient.
Multiply. Subtract. Bring down ones.

$$
\begin{array}{r}
6 \\
27\overline{)1798} \\
-\ 162 \\
\hline
178
\end{array}
$$

$27\overline{)179}$ rounds to $30\overline{)180}$.
Try 6.

Step 2
Find the second digit of the quotient.
Multiply. Subtract.
Write the remainder.

$$
\begin{array}{r}
66\ \text{r}16 \\
27\overline{)1798} \\
-\ 162 \\
\hline
178 \\
-\ 162 \\
\hline
16
\end{array}
$$

Divide.

1. $42\overline{)2370}$ 56 r18
2. $58\overline{)4613}$
3. $27\overline{)1345}$
4. $36\overline{)3264}$
5. $69\overline{)4973}$

6. $83\overline{)4246}$
7. $91\overline{)5923}$
8. $49\overline{)1678}$
9. $23\overline{)1983}$
10. $64\overline{)1858}$

11. $54\overline{)3636}$
12. $18\overline{)1373}$
13. $88\overline{)3193}$
14. $32\overline{)1518}$
15. $75\overline{)3985}$

16. $25\overline{)1037}$
17. $73\overline{)6963}$
18. $46\overline{)2728}$
19. $32\overline{)2145}$
20. $28\overline{)1783}$

⭐ Challenge
Copy and complete each puzzle. Each X stands for a digit.

21.
$$
\begin{array}{r}
35 \\
58\overline{)20X0} \\
-XXX \\
\hline
29X \\
-XXX
\end{array}
$$

22.
$$
\begin{array}{r}
X9 \\
67\overline{)XXX3} \\
-268 \\
\hline
60X \\
-XXX
\end{array}
$$

23.
$$
\begin{array}{r}
3X \\
8X\overline{)2X8X} \\
-249 \\
\hline
4X8 \\
-XXX
\end{array}
$$

Gift Shop Problems

Scott Douglas is opening a gift shop. He spent three days arranging the gifts in the store. Solve each problem.

1. Scott had 1503 glasses. He put 28 glasses in each set. How many sets did he make? How many glasses left over? 53, 19

2. Scott had 233 potholders. He hung 8 potholders on each hook. How many hooks did he use? How many potholders left over?

3. He had 1305 candles. He arranged 45 candles on each shelf. How many shelves of candles in Scott's shop?

4. Scott bought 387 vases. He put 43 vases on each shelf. How many shelves of vases in his store?

5. He had 1240 greeting cards. He put 35 cards in each box. How many boxes of greeting cards did Scott fill? How many cards left over?

6. Scott had 1125 calendars. He arranged them in 25 equal stacks. How many calendars did he put in each stack?

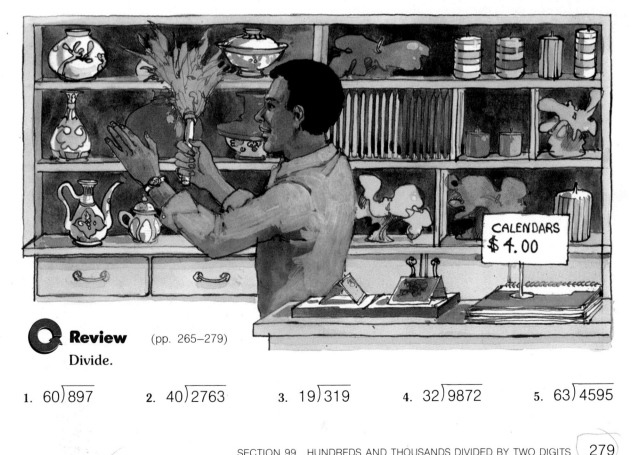

Review (pp. 265–279)

Divide.

1. $60\overline{)897}$ 2. $40\overline{)2763}$ 3. $19\overline{)319}$ 4. $32\overline{)9872}$ 5. $63\overline{)4595}$

Dividing Money

Divide money the same way you divide whole numbers.

```
        $1.45
32) $46.40
   − 32
     144
   − 128
     160
   − 160
       0
```

Divide. Remember to use $ and . in your answers.

1. 24) $69.84 $2.91

2. 15) $18.45

3. 72) $32.40

4. 43) $11.61

5. 32) $65.28

6. 53) $82.68

7. 39) $79.56

8. 77) $66.22

9. 62) $89.90

10. 14) $89.46

11. 43) $15.91

12. 26) $81.12

13. 35) $14.35

14. 17) $55.93

15. 86) $27.52

16. Sam Lee earns $13,520 in 52 weeks. How much does he earn each week?

17. Rita Paoli earns $18,720 in 52 weeks. How much does she earn each week?

⭐ **Challenge**

Add and then divide to find each average cost.

18a. Three toys cost $17.82, $20.19, and $9.78.

b. Four model cars cost $8.96, $4.58, $10.87, and $9.23.

Practice with Two-Digit Divisors

Practice the kinds of division you have learned.

```
      9 r16          99 r8           253 r2
37) 349        22) 2186        31) 7845
  - 333          - 198           - 62
     16             206             164
                  - 198           - 155
                       8              95
                                   - 93
                                      2
```

Divide.

        3 r24

1. 68) 228   2. 46) 1434   3. 33) 8165   4. 82) 511   5. 28) 1210

6. 18) 7439   7. 78) 737   8. 43) 1217   9. 23) 870   10. 17) 9541

11. 99) 837   12. 45) 993   13. 31) 4866   14. 63) 356   15. 24) 903

16. 32) 9661   17. 58) 383   18. 16) 7432   19. 38) 830   20. 92) 441

⭐ Challenge

21. There are 12 cans of juice in a box.
    A box costs $4.68. There are
    24 cans of juice in a carton. A carton
    costs $8.64. Which is the better buy?
    How much less is the cost of each can?

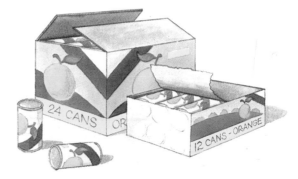

Chapter Review

Divide. (ex. 1-5: p. 265), (ex. 6-10: p. 266), (ex. 11-15: p. 267)

1. $20\overline{)79}$ 2. $30\overline{)87}$ 3. $40\overline{)92}$ 4. $10\overline{)39}$ 5. $20\overline{)47}$

6. $50\overline{)514}$ 7. $70\overline{)811}$ 8. $40\overline{)998}$ 9. $40\overline{)616}$ 10. $40\overline{)713}$

11. $50\overline{)5471}$ 12. $30\overline{)9165}$ 13. $40\overline{)7319}$ 14. $20\overline{)7112}$ 15. $60\overline{)6841}$

Divide. (ex. 16-20: p. 269), (ex. 21-25: p. 270)

16. $70\overline{)651}$ 17. $20\overline{)199}$ 18. $30\overline{)168}$ 19. $60\overline{)523}$ 20. $60\overline{)324}$

21. $30\overline{)1337}$ 22. $50\overline{)3186}$ 23. $20\overline{)1447}$ 24. $60\overline{)1615}$ 25. $40\overline{)2539}$

Divide. (ex. 26-30: p. 272), (ex. 31-35: p. 273), (ex. 36-40: p. 275)

26. $24\overline{)98}$ 27. $66\overline{)73}$ 28. $21\overline{)45}$ 29. $22\overline{)74}$ 30. $18\overline{)61}$

31. $21\overline{)933}$ 32. $17\overline{)716}$ 33. $16\overline{)447}$ 34. $31\overline{)679}$ 35. $27\overline{)939}$

36. $13\overline{)3852}$ 37. $22\overline{)8973}$ 38. $14\overline{)4785}$ 39. $62\overline{)7426}$ 40. $55\overline{)6347}$

Divide. (ex. 41-42: p. 277), (ex. 43-47: p. 278), (ex. 48-50: p. 280)

41. $72\overline{)663}$ 42. $51\overline{)274}$ 43. $27\overline{)1345}$ 44. $75\overline{)3986}$ 45. $64\overline{)1859}$

46. $33\overline{)7845}$ 47. $23\overline{)1938}$ 48. $43\overline{)\$15.91}$ 49. $28\overline{)\$11.76}$ 50. $53\overline{)\$82.68}$

Chapter Test

Divide.

1. $10\overline{)29}$
2. $30\overline{)84}$
3. $50\overline{)621}$
4. $30\overline{)7186}$
5. $50\overline{)8389}$

Divide.

6. $40\overline{)759}$
7. $30\overline{)452}$
8. $70\overline{)863}$
9. $60\overline{)4148}$
10. $30\overline{)2378}$

Divide.

11. $27\overline{)93}$
12. $55\overline{)69}$
13. $29\overline{)745}$
14. $61\overline{)7239}$
15. $43\overline{)7183}$

Divide.

16. $53\overline{)185}$
17. $72\overline{)714}$
18. $48\overline{)4306}$
19. $19\overline{)1324}$
20. $81\overline{)8043}$

Brush Up

Write two equal fractions for each.

1. $\frac{1}{8}$ 2. $\frac{3}{4}$ 3. $\frac{2}{5}$ 4. $\frac{5}{6}$ 5. $\frac{4}{9}$ 6. $\frac{1}{3}$

7. $\frac{2}{3}$ 8. $\frac{1}{4}$ 9. $\frac{4}{5}$ 10. $\frac{1}{6}$ 11. $\frac{3}{8}$ 12. $\frac{3}{10}$

Write each fraction in simplest form.

13. $\frac{4}{12}$ 14. $\frac{4}{14}$ 15. $\frac{20}{30}$ 16. $\frac{8}{10}$ 17. $\frac{5}{15}$ 18. $\frac{5}{25}$

19. $\frac{6}{8}$ 20. $\frac{4}{16}$ 21. $\frac{20}{40}$ 22. $\frac{2}{4}$ 23. $\frac{2}{22}$ 24. $\frac{5}{10}$

Write a fraction for each mixed number.

25. $8\frac{3}{7}$ 26. $4\frac{5}{9}$ 27. $3\frac{6}{7}$ 28. $5\frac{8}{9}$ 29. $1\frac{3}{4}$ 30. $4\frac{1}{3}$

31. $3\frac{5}{6}$ 32. $6\frac{1}{2}$ 33. $9\frac{4}{5}$ 34. $2\frac{2}{3}$ 35. $1\frac{5}{8}$ 36. $5\frac{6}{7}$

Write a decimal for each.

37. $2\frac{1}{10}$ 38. $\frac{65}{100}$ 39. $\frac{90}{1000}$ 40. $\frac{3}{10}$ 41. $\frac{51}{100}$

42. $\frac{4}{100}$ 43. $6\frac{20}{1000}$ 44. $\frac{98}{1000}$ 45. $\frac{37}{100}$ 46. $1\frac{9}{10}$

Write a fraction or mixed number for each.

47. 0.90 48. 0.3 49. 2.46 50. 0.119 51. 0.09

52. 0.73 53. 1.34 54. 0.216 55. 0.568 56. 0.342

CHAPTER 11

Fractions and Decimals

Using Decimals at Work

Ted Randall is a travel agent. He is helping the Cliftons plan their vacation. Their hotel room will cost $87.50 per day. They will be staying there 5 days. Ted multiplies $87.50 × 5 to find the cost of their hotel room for 5 days. The hotel room will cost $437.50.

Adding Fractions

Like fractions have the same denominator.

$\frac{1}{5}$ and $\frac{3}{5}$ are like fractions.

To add like fractions, add numerators.

$\frac{1}{5} + \frac{3}{5} = \frac{4}{5}$ or

$$\begin{array}{r} \frac{1}{5} \\ + \frac{3}{5} \\ \hline \frac{4}{5} \end{array}$$

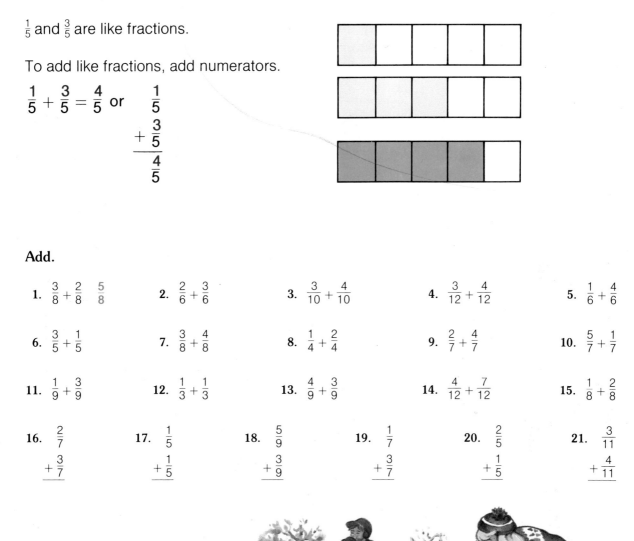

Add.

1. $\frac{3}{8} + \frac{2}{8}$ $\frac{5}{8}$

2. $\frac{2}{6} + \frac{3}{6}$

3. $\frac{3}{10} + \frac{4}{10}$

4. $\frac{3}{12} + \frac{4}{12}$

5. $\frac{1}{6} + \frac{4}{6}$

6. $\frac{3}{5} + \frac{1}{5}$

7. $\frac{3}{8} + \frac{4}{8}$

8. $\frac{1}{4} + \frac{2}{4}$

9. $\frac{2}{7} + \frac{4}{7}$

10. $\frac{5}{7} + \frac{1}{7}$

11. $\frac{1}{9} + \frac{3}{9}$

12. $\frac{1}{3} + \frac{1}{3}$

13. $\frac{4}{9} + \frac{3}{9}$

14. $\frac{4}{12} + \frac{7}{12}$

15. $\frac{1}{8} + \frac{2}{8}$

16. $\begin{array}{r} \frac{2}{7} \\ + \frac{3}{7} \\ \hline \end{array}$

17. $\begin{array}{r} \frac{1}{5} \\ + \frac{1}{5} \\ \hline \end{array}$

18. $\begin{array}{r} \frac{5}{9} \\ + \frac{3}{9} \\ \hline \end{array}$

19. $\begin{array}{r} \frac{1}{7} \\ + \frac{3}{7} \\ \hline \end{array}$

20. $\begin{array}{r} \frac{2}{5} \\ + \frac{1}{5} \\ \hline \end{array}$

21. $\begin{array}{r} \frac{3}{11} \\ + \frac{4}{11} \\ \hline \end{array}$

Challenge

22. Kenneth shoveled snow for $\frac{1}{4}$ of an hour. Then Margarette shoveled snow for $\frac{3}{4}$ of an hour. How long did they shovel snow in all?

Sums Greater Than One

Sometimes when you add like fractions, the sum is greater than one. When this happens, change the fraction to a whole number or a mixed number.

$$\frac{7}{8}$$
$$+\frac{4}{8}$$
$$\frac{11}{8} \text{ or } 1\frac{3}{8}$$

Change each fraction to a whole number or a mixed number.

1. $\frac{10}{9}$ $1\frac{1}{9}$

2. $\frac{11}{7}$

3. $\frac{8}{8}$

4. $\frac{12}{11}$

5. $\frac{6}{3}$

6. $\frac{9}{4}$

7. $\frac{16}{4}$

8. $\frac{13}{6}$

9. $\frac{8}{4}$

10. $\frac{7}{2}$

11. $\frac{11}{9}$

12. $\frac{4}{3}$

Add. Write the answers as whole or mixed numbers.

13. $\frac{5}{6}$
$+\frac{2}{6}$
$1\frac{1}{6}$

14. $\frac{7}{10}$
$+\frac{6}{10}$

15. $\frac{7}{9}$
$+\frac{6}{9}$

16. $\frac{9}{12}$
$+\frac{4}{12}$

17. $\frac{4}{5}$
$+\frac{3}{5}$

18. $\frac{5}{8}$
$+\frac{4}{8}$

19. $\frac{4}{7}$
$+\frac{6}{7}$

20. $\frac{3}{4}$
$+\frac{2}{4}$

21. $\frac{7}{11}$
$+\frac{5}{11}$

22. $\frac{4}{9}$
$+\frac{7}{9}$

23. $\frac{5}{10}$
$+\frac{8}{10}$

24. $\frac{6}{8}$
$+\frac{7}{8}$

25. $\frac{1}{6}$
$\frac{3}{6}$
$+\frac{2}{6}$

26. $\frac{2}{7}$
$\frac{3}{7}$
$+\frac{2}{7}$

27. $\frac{3}{4}$
$\frac{3}{4}$
$+\frac{1}{4}$

28. $\frac{4}{5}$
$\frac{3}{5}$
$+\frac{2}{5}$

29. $\frac{3}{9}$
$\frac{3}{9}$
$+\frac{4}{9}$

30. $\frac{3}{8}$
$\frac{3}{8}$
$+\frac{3}{8}$

Adding Mixed Numbers

Follow these steps to add mixed numbers that have the same denominator.

Step 1
Add the fractions.

$$3\frac{2}{3}$$
$$+\,2\frac{2}{3}$$
$$\overline{\frac{4}{3}}$$

Step 2
Add the whole numbers.

$$3\frac{2}{3}$$
$$+\,2\frac{2}{3}$$
$$\overline{5\frac{4}{3}}$$

Step 3
Change the fraction to a mixed number.

$$3\frac{2}{3}$$
$$+\,2\frac{2}{3}$$
$$\overline{5\frac{4}{3}}$$

$$\frac{4}{3} = 1\frac{1}{3}$$

Step 4
Add the mixed number to the whole number.

$$3\frac{2}{3}$$
$$+\,2\frac{2}{3}$$
$$\overline{5\frac{4}{3}} \text{ or } 6\frac{1}{3}$$

$$5 + 1\frac{1}{3} = 6\frac{1}{3}$$

Add.

1. $6\frac{5}{7}$ $+\,4\frac{6}{7}$ $\overline{11\frac{4}{7}}$

2. $8\frac{3}{6}$ $+\,5\frac{4}{6}$

3. $14\frac{5}{8}$ $+\,6\frac{6}{8}$

4. $17\frac{6}{10}$ $+\,8\frac{5}{10}$

5. $30\frac{10}{12}$ $+\,17\frac{3}{12}$

6. $15\frac{7}{9}$ $+\,4\frac{4}{9}$

7. $12\frac{7}{8}$ $+\,8\frac{4}{8}$

8. $7\frac{9}{11}$ $+\,9\frac{3}{11}$

9. $13\frac{5}{9}$ $+\,6\frac{8}{9}$

10. $23\frac{3}{5}$ $+\,9\frac{4}{5}$

11. $32\frac{7}{15}$ $+\,8\frac{10}{15}$

12. $11\frac{4}{6}$ $+\,7\frac{3}{6}$

Now add these.

13. $1\frac{3}{8}$ $2\frac{7}{8}$ $+\,7\frac{3}{8}$

14. $2\frac{5}{7}$ $3\frac{2}{7}$ $+\,6\frac{1}{7}$

15. $4\frac{8}{9}$ $6\frac{1}{9}$ $+\,3\frac{1}{9}$

16. $6\frac{2}{3}$ $4\frac{1}{3}$ $+\,5\frac{2}{3}$

17. $7\frac{8}{12}$ $3\frac{2}{12}$ $+\,8\frac{1}{12}$

18. $3\frac{4}{6}$ $5\frac{5}{6}$ $+\,2\frac{2}{6}$

Subtracting Fractions

To subtract like fractions, subtract numerators.

$$\frac{5}{6} - \frac{4}{6} = \frac{1}{6} \quad \text{or} \quad \begin{array}{r} \frac{5}{6} \\ -\frac{4}{6} \\ \hline \frac{1}{6} \end{array}$$

Subtract.

1. $\frac{7}{8} - \frac{6}{8} \quad \frac{1}{8}$

2. $\frac{5}{7} - \frac{3}{7}$

3. $\frac{9}{10} - \frac{6}{10}$

4. $\frac{3}{4} - \frac{2}{4}$

5. $\frac{8}{10} - \frac{5}{10}$

6. $\frac{5}{8} - \frac{4}{8}$

7. $\frac{10}{12} - \frac{9}{12}$

8. $\frac{5}{8} - \frac{2}{8}$

9. $\frac{4}{5} - \frac{2}{5}$

10. $\frac{7}{8} - \frac{2}{8}$

11. $\frac{6}{7} - \frac{2}{7}$

12. $\frac{7}{9} - \frac{5}{9}$

13. $\frac{7}{8} - \frac{4}{8}$

14. $\frac{9}{10} - \frac{2}{10}$

15. $\frac{3}{7} - \frac{2}{7}$

16. $\frac{6}{11} - \frac{4}{11}$

17. $\frac{11}{12} - \frac{6}{12}$

18. $\frac{11}{15} - \frac{7}{15}$

19. $\frac{5}{6} - \frac{4}{6}$

20. $\frac{5}{7} - \frac{2}{7}$

21. $\begin{array}{r} \frac{9}{7} \\ -\frac{4}{7} \\ \hline \end{array}$

22. $\begin{array}{r} \frac{3}{5} \\ -\frac{2}{5} \\ \hline \end{array}$

23. $\begin{array}{r} \frac{11}{14} \\ -\frac{8}{14} \\ \hline \end{array}$

24. $\begin{array}{r} \frac{7}{12} \\ -\frac{2}{12} \\ \hline \end{array}$

25. $\begin{array}{r} \frac{11}{13} \\ -\frac{6}{13} \\ \hline \end{array}$

26. $\begin{array}{r} \frac{5}{9} \\ -\frac{3}{9} \\ \hline \end{array}$

27. Judy spends $\frac{3}{4}$ of an hour getting to work. Ron spends $\frac{2}{4}$ of an hour getting to work. How much longer does it take Judy to get to work?

Subtracting Mixed Numbers

Follow these steps to subtract mixed numbers that have the same denominator.

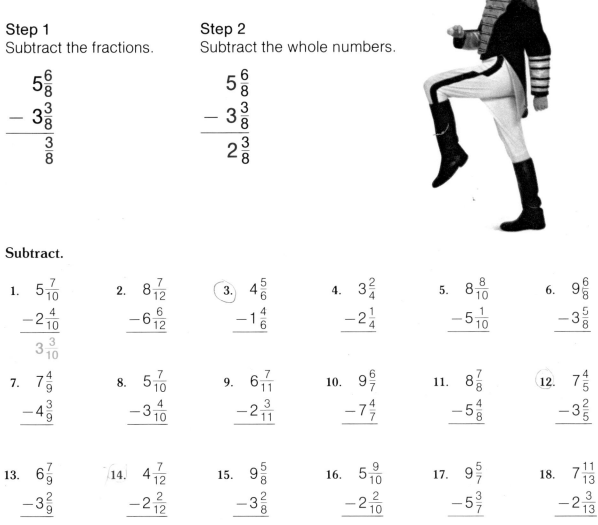

Step 1
Subtract the fractions.

$$5\frac{6}{8}$$
$$-3\frac{3}{8}$$
$$\overline{\quad\ \frac{3}{8}}$$

Step 2
Subtract the whole numbers.

$$5\frac{6}{8}$$
$$-3\frac{3}{8}$$
$$\overline{2\frac{3}{8}}$$

Subtract.

1. $5\frac{7}{10}$
$-2\frac{4}{10}$
$\overline{3\frac{3}{10}}$

2. $8\frac{7}{12}$
$-6\frac{6}{12}$

3. $4\frac{5}{6}$
$-1\frac{4}{6}$

4. $3\frac{2}{4}$
$-2\frac{1}{4}$

5. $8\frac{8}{10}$
$-5\frac{1}{10}$

6. $9\frac{6}{8}$
$-3\frac{5}{8}$

7. $7\frac{4}{9}$
$-4\frac{3}{9}$

8. $5\frac{7}{10}$
$-3\frac{4}{10}$

9. $6\frac{7}{11}$
$-2\frac{3}{11}$

10. $9\frac{6}{7}$
$-7\frac{4}{7}$

11. $8\frac{7}{8}$
$-5\frac{4}{8}$

12. $7\frac{4}{5}$
$-3\frac{2}{5}$

13. $6\frac{7}{9}$
$-3\frac{2}{9}$

14. $4\frac{7}{12}$
$-2\frac{2}{12}$

15. $9\frac{5}{8}$
$-3\frac{2}{8}$

16. $5\frac{9}{10}$
$-2\frac{2}{10}$

17. $9\frac{5}{7}$
$-5\frac{3}{7}$

18. $7\frac{11}{13}$
$-2\frac{3}{13}$

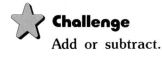

Challenge
Add or subtract.

19. $45\frac{8}{9}+66\frac{6}{9}$

20. $38\frac{8}{10}-29\frac{1}{10}$

21. $37\frac{4}{6}+53\frac{3}{6}$

22. $76\frac{8}{9}-39\frac{1}{9}$

Trading in Subtraction

Sometimes you need to trade a whole number for a fraction
before you can subtract. Here are two examples.

$$3 = 2\frac{5}{5}$$
$$-1\frac{2}{5} = -1\frac{2}{5}$$
$$1\frac{3}{5}$$

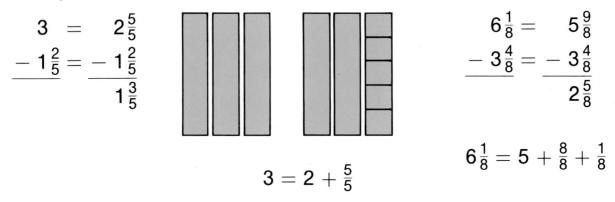

$$3 = 2 + \frac{5}{5}$$

$$6\frac{1}{8} = 5\frac{9}{8}$$
$$-3\frac{4}{8} = -3\frac{4}{8}$$
$$2\frac{5}{8}$$

$$6\frac{1}{8} = 5 + \frac{8}{8} + \frac{1}{8}$$

Copy and complete.

1. $3 = ?\frac{8}{8}$ $3 = 2\frac{8}{8}$ 2. $7 = ?\frac{6}{6}$ 3. $6 = 5\frac{?}{4}$ 4. $4 = 3\frac{?}{10}$ 5. $5 = ?\frac{7}{7}$

6. $3\frac{2}{5} = ?\frac{7}{5}$ 7. $4\frac{3}{4} = 3\frac{?}{4}$ 8. $9\frac{2}{9} = 8\frac{?}{9}$ 9. $7\frac{1}{6} = 6\frac{?}{6}$ 10. $6\frac{2}{3} = 5\frac{?}{3}$

Subtract.

11. $\begin{array}{r} 7 \\ -2\frac{4}{7} \\ \hline \end{array}$

12. $\begin{array}{r} 9 \\ -5\frac{3}{4} \\ \hline \end{array}$

13. $\begin{array}{r} 12 \\ -3\frac{5}{8} \\ \hline \end{array}$

14. $\begin{array}{r} 6 \\ -2\frac{1}{6} \\ \hline \end{array}$

15. $\begin{array}{r} 8 \\ -1\frac{1}{4} \\ \hline \end{array}$

16. $\begin{array}{r} 9 \\ -4\frac{2}{9} \\ \hline \end{array}$

17. $\begin{array}{r} 8\frac{2}{7} \\ -1\frac{4}{7} \\ \hline \end{array}$

18. $\begin{array}{r} 9\frac{1}{5} \\ -3\frac{4}{5} \\ \hline \end{array}$

19. $\begin{array}{r} 6\frac{2}{9} \\ -4\frac{7}{9} \\ \hline \end{array}$

20. $\begin{array}{r} 8 \\ -3\frac{1}{12} \\ \hline \end{array}$

21. $\begin{array}{r} 5\frac{4}{7} \\ -2\frac{5}{7} \\ \hline \end{array}$

22. $\begin{array}{r} 6 \\ -3\frac{6}{11} \\ \hline \end{array}$

23. $\begin{array}{r} 6\frac{2}{5} \\ -2\frac{3}{5} \\ \hline \end{array}$

24. $\begin{array}{r} 5\frac{1}{3} \\ -2\frac{2}{3} \\ \hline \end{array}$

25. $\begin{array}{r} 4 \\ -1\frac{1}{2} \\ \hline \end{array}$

26. $\begin{array}{r} 7\frac{3}{11} \\ -5\frac{8}{11} \\ \hline \end{array}$

27. $\begin{array}{r} 8 \\ -4\frac{2}{3} \\ \hline \end{array}$

28. $\begin{array}{r} 5 \\ -3\frac{3}{7} \\ \hline \end{array}$

Writing Answers in Simplest Form

When you add or subtract mixed numbers, you often need to change your answer to simplest form.

$$3\frac{7}{10}$$
$$+\ 4\frac{9}{10}$$
$$7\frac{16}{10} = 8\frac{6}{10} \text{ or } 8\frac{3}{5}$$

$8\frac{3}{5}$ is the simplest form of $7\frac{16}{10}$.

$$4\frac{5}{6}$$
$$-\ 2\frac{1}{6}$$
$$2\frac{4}{6} = 2\frac{2}{3}$$

$2\frac{2}{3}$ is the simplest form of $2\frac{4}{6}$.

Add or subtract. Write each answer in simplest form.

1. $2\frac{3}{4}$
$+\ 1\frac{3}{4}$
$4\frac{1}{2}$

2. $6\frac{7}{8}$
$-\ 2\frac{3}{8}$

3. $1\frac{11}{12}$
$+\ 3\frac{7}{12}$

4. $3\frac{5}{6}$
$-\ 1\frac{1}{6}$

5. $2\frac{5}{9}$
$+\ 9\frac{7}{9}$

6. $3\frac{9}{10}$
$-\ 1\frac{3}{10}$

7. $3\frac{1}{2}$
$+\ 2\frac{1}{2}$

8. $4\frac{7}{9}$
$-\ 2\frac{4}{9}$

9. $6\frac{3}{8}$
$+\ 1\frac{7}{8}$

10. $2\frac{11}{12}$
$-\ 1\frac{7}{12}$

11. $5\frac{3}{8}$
$+\ 3\frac{3}{8}$

12. $9\frac{5}{8}$
$-\ 4\frac{3}{8}$

13. Rosemary and Howard are volunteers at a hospital. Rosemary spent $1\frac{3}{4}$ hours reading to a patient and $1\frac{3}{4}$ hours delivering flowers. How many hours was that?

14. Howard spent $1\frac{3}{4}$ hours delivering mail and $2\frac{3}{4}$ hours visiting with patients. How many hours was that?

A Magic Square

Find these sums. Write each sum in simplest form.

1. $1\frac{1}{2} + \frac{1}{2}$ **2**

2. $\frac{3}{4} + \frac{3}{4}$

3. $1\frac{2}{3} + 1\frac{2}{3} + \frac{2}{3}$

4. $3\frac{11}{16} + \frac{13}{16}$

5. $1\frac{7}{12} + \frac{11}{12}$

6. $\frac{1}{4} + \frac{1}{4}$

7. $\frac{5}{6} + \frac{1}{6}$

8. $2\frac{7}{8} + \frac{5}{8}$

9. $1\frac{1}{2} + 1\frac{1}{2}$

Copy this magic square. Write the nine sums in the boxes.

1.	2.	3.
4.	5.	6.
7.	8.	9.

10. In the magic square, find the sum of each column, row, and diagonal. You should get the same number for each of the eight sums. What is the number?

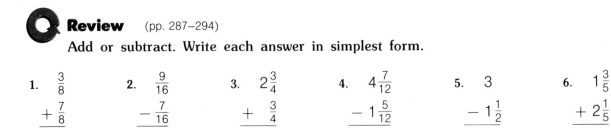

Review   (pp. 287–294)

Add or subtract. Write each answer in simplest form.

1. $\begin{array}{r} \frac{3}{8} \\ + \frac{7}{8} \end{array}$

2. $\begin{array}{r} \frac{9}{16} \\ - \frac{7}{16} \end{array}$

3. $\begin{array}{r} 2\frac{3}{4} \\ + \frac{3}{4} \end{array}$

4. $\begin{array}{r} 4\frac{7}{12} \\ - 1\frac{5}{12} \end{array}$

5. $\begin{array}{r} 3 \\ - 1\frac{1}{2} \end{array}$

6. $\begin{array}{r} 1\frac{3}{5} \\ + 2\frac{1}{5} \end{array}$

Adding and Subtracting Like Fractions

Review what you have learned about
adding and subtracting fractions.

Add or subtract. Write each answer in simplest form.

1. $\frac{3}{5}$
    $+\frac{1}{5}$
    $\frac{4}{5}$

2. $\frac{7}{9}$
    $-\frac{5}{9}$

3. $\frac{9}{10}$
    $-\frac{7}{10}$

4. $\frac{5}{6}$
    $+\frac{5}{6}$

5. $\frac{9}{10}$
    $+\frac{3}{10}$

6. $\frac{3}{4}$
    $-\frac{1}{4}$

7. $1\frac{1}{2}$
    $+2\frac{1}{2}$

8. $7\frac{3}{4}$
    $-1\frac{1}{4}$

9. 8
    $-4\frac{1}{2}$

10. $7\frac{3}{4}$
    $+1\frac{1}{4}$

11. $1\frac{4}{7}$
    $+3\frac{3}{7}$

12. $9\frac{7}{8}$
    $-8\frac{3}{8}$

13. $1\frac{1}{4}$
    $+4\frac{1}{4}$

14. $10\frac{9}{10}$
    $-6\frac{3}{10}$

15. $\frac{11}{15}$
    $-\frac{7}{15}$

16. $3\frac{5}{8}$
    $+2\frac{5}{8}$

17. $6\frac{6}{7}$
    $-1\frac{3}{7}$

18. $3\frac{5}{12}$
    $+7\frac{1}{12}$

19. $9\frac{4}{5}$
    $-3\frac{2}{5}$

20. 7
    $-2\frac{1}{4}$

21. $6\frac{3}{8}$
    $+4\frac{1}{8}$

22. $\frac{1}{6}$
    $+\frac{5}{6}$

23. $1\frac{7}{8}$
    $-\frac{1}{8}$

24. 4
    $-1\frac{5}{12}$

 **Challenge**

25. $46\frac{1}{3}$
    $32\frac{2}{3}$
    $+18\frac{2}{3}$

26. $89\frac{1}{6}$
    $36\frac{5}{6}$
    $+65\frac{5}{6}$

27. $12\frac{9}{10}$
    $41\frac{7}{10}$
    $+76\frac{3}{10}$

28. $88\frac{3}{4}$
    $-49\frac{3}{4}$

29. $65\frac{7}{12}$
    $-38\frac{11}{12}$

Walking Problems

Add or subtract to solve each problem.

1. Susan hiked $3\frac{1}{5}$ kilometers to the waterfall. Then she hiked $3\frac{1}{5}$ kilometers back to camp. How far did she hike in all?   **$6\frac{2}{5}$ kilometers**

2. One day Joe hiked $7\frac{1}{2}$ kilometers around the lake. He hiked $1\frac{1}{2}$ kilometers in the morning. How far did he hike during the rest of the day?

3. Anita walked $\frac{1}{2}$ kilometer to the bus stop. Then she rode 8 kilometers on the bus. How much farther did she ride than walk?

4. Whitney walked $2\frac{3}{5}$ kilometers to the library. Then he walked $2\frac{3}{5}$ kilometers home. How far did he walk in all?

5. Louise walked $1\frac{3}{10}$ kilometers to the swimming pool. Then she walked $2\frac{7}{10}$ kilometers to the park. How far did she walk in all?

6. Dave walked $3\frac{2}{5}$ kilometers from his home to the grocery store. He walked $2\frac{4}{5}$ kilometers to return home. How much longer was his first route?

Equal Fractions

You can multiply or divide both the numerator and the denominator of a fraction by the same number to find an equal fraction.

$$\frac{3}{8} = \frac{3 \times 2}{8 \times 2} \text{ or } \frac{6}{16}$$

$$\frac{12}{16} = \frac{12 \div 4}{16 \div 4} \text{ or } \frac{3}{4}$$

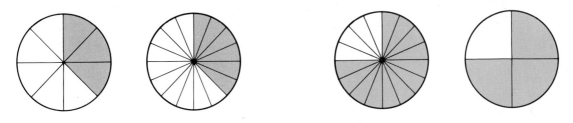

Copy and complete to find equal fractions.

1. $\frac{3}{18} = \frac{?}{6}$ $\frac{3}{18} = \frac{1}{6}$

2. $\frac{7}{14} = \frac{?}{2}$

3. $\frac{3}{9} = \frac{?}{3}$

4. $\frac{6}{10} = \frac{?}{5}$

5. $\frac{3}{7} = \frac{?}{14}$

6. $\frac{5}{9} = \frac{?}{36}$

7. $\frac{9}{24} = \frac{?}{8}$

8. $\frac{15}{25} = \frac{?}{5}$

9. $\frac{3}{8} = \frac{?}{40}$

10. $\frac{8}{20} = \frac{?}{5}$

Find any two equal fractions for each.

11. $\frac{1}{4}$

12. $\frac{9}{12}$

13. $\frac{3}{6}$

14. $\frac{9}{15}$

15. $\frac{15}{21}$

16. $\frac{18}{24}$

17. $\frac{30}{36}$

18. $\frac{1}{3}$

19. $\frac{4}{5}$

20. $\frac{6}{12}$

21. $\frac{40}{50}$

22. $\frac{1}{7}$

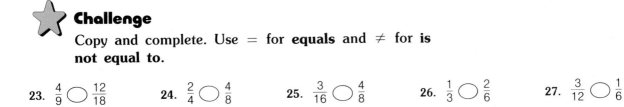

Challenge

Copy and complete. Use = for **equals** and ≠ for **is not equal to.**

23. $\frac{4}{9} \bigcirc \frac{12}{18}$

24. $\frac{2}{4} \bigcirc \frac{4}{8}$

25. $\frac{3}{16} \bigcirc \frac{4}{8}$

26. $\frac{1}{3} \bigcirc \frac{2}{6}$

27. $\frac{3}{12} \bigcirc \frac{1}{6}$

Finding a Common Denominator

Before you can add or subtract two
fractions with unlike denominators,
you need to find a common denominator.

$\frac{5}{8}$ and $\frac{3}{4}$ are **unlike fractions.** 8 is a
common denominator because 4 divides
into 8 with a remainder of zero.

Choose one of the denominators as the common denominator.

1. $\frac{2}{9}$ and $\frac{2}{3}$ 9

2. $\frac{3}{8}$ and $\frac{1}{4}$

3. $\frac{3}{16}$ and $\frac{3}{8}$

4. $\frac{1}{4}$ and $\frac{3}{8}$

5. $\frac{3}{10}$ and $\frac{3}{5}$

6. $\frac{7}{12}$ and $\frac{5}{6}$

7. $\frac{3}{4}$ and $\frac{5}{12}$

8. $\frac{11}{15}$ and $\frac{3}{5}$

9. $\frac{5}{24}$ and $\frac{7}{12}$

10. $\frac{1}{4}$ and $\frac{3}{16}$

Choose a common denominator for each pair of fractions.

11. $\frac{2}{5}$ and $\frac{1}{3}$
(5, 10, or 15)

12. $\frac{2}{7}$ and $\frac{1}{4}$
(7, 28, or 35)

13. $\frac{3}{4}$ and $\frac{1}{3}$
(3, 8, or 12)

14. $\frac{1}{9}$ and $\frac{1}{4}$
(9, 20, or 36)

15. $\frac{1}{4}$ and $\frac{1}{5}$
(4, 20, or 24)

16. $\frac{3}{7}$ and $\frac{4}{5}$
(5, 35, or 45)

17. $\frac{1}{6}$ and $\frac{2}{7}$
(7, 42, or 48)

18. $\frac{1}{3}$ and $\frac{5}{7}$
(7, 12, or 21)

⭐ Challenge
Choose the lowest common denominator for each pair.

19. $\frac{2}{9}$ and $\frac{1}{12}$
(12, 36, or 108)

20. $\frac{1}{6}$ and $\frac{3}{4}$
(12, 18, or 24)

21. $\frac{3}{8}$ and $\frac{5}{6}$
(8, 24, or 48)

22. $\frac{1}{9}$ and $\frac{5}{6}$
(9, 36, or 54)

Multiplying to Find a Common Denominator

You can multiply to find a common denominator.

Step 1
Multiply the denominators of the fractions to find a common denominator.

$$\frac{3}{5} = \frac{?}{40}$$

$$5 \times 8 = 40$$

$$\frac{1}{8} = \frac{?}{40}$$

Step 2
Find equal fractions.

$$\frac{3}{5} = \frac{24}{40}$$

$$\frac{1}{8} = \frac{5}{40}$$

Multiply to find a common denominator for these fractions.

1. $\frac{1}{4}$ and $\frac{1}{3}$ 12

2. $\frac{1}{5}$ and $\frac{1}{3}$

3. $\frac{7}{9}$ and $\frac{1}{5}$

4. $\frac{1}{8}$ and $\frac{2}{3}$

5. $\frac{1}{7}$ and $\frac{3}{4}$

6. $\frac{1}{4}$ and $\frac{2}{9}$

7. $\frac{1}{3}$ and $\frac{1}{8}$

8. $\frac{2}{5}$ and $\frac{8}{9}$

9. $\frac{5}{6}$ and $\frac{1}{7}$

10. $\frac{4}{5}$ and $\frac{1}{2}$

Copy and complete.

11. $\frac{1}{5} = \frac{?}{15}$
    $\frac{1}{3} = \frac{?}{15}$

12. $\frac{6}{7} = \frac{?}{?}$
    $\frac{1}{5} = \frac{?}{35}$

13. $\frac{5}{9} = \frac{?}{36}$
    $\frac{1}{4} = \frac{?}{?}$

14. $\frac{1}{4} = \frac{?}{28}$
    $\frac{1}{7} = \frac{?}{?}$

15. $\frac{2}{7} = \frac{?}{21}$
    $\frac{1}{3} = \frac{?}{?}$

16. $\frac{4}{5} = \frac{?}{?}$
    $\frac{1}{4} = \frac{?}{20}$

17. $\frac{3}{4} = \frac{?}{12}$
    $\frac{1}{3} = \frac{?}{?}$

18. $\frac{7}{8} = \frac{?}{?}$
    $\frac{2}{3} = \frac{?}{?}$

19. $\frac{1}{9} = \frac{?}{?}$
    $\frac{1}{2} = \frac{?}{?}$

20. $\frac{2}{5} = \frac{?}{?}$
    $\frac{1}{3} = \frac{?}{?}$

Calculate

Add. Write each answer in simplest form.

21. $\frac{13}{50} + \frac{23}{50} + \frac{7}{50} + \frac{11}{50} + \frac{37}{50} + \frac{41}{50}$

22. $\frac{11}{20} + \frac{17}{20} + \frac{19}{20} + \frac{9}{20} + \frac{7}{20} + \frac{13}{20} + \frac{3}{20}$

Adding Unlike Fractions

To add $\frac{1}{4}$ and $\frac{5}{12}$, you can use 12 as a common denominator because 4 divides into 12 with a remainder of zero.

Step 1
Find a common denominator.

Step 2
Find an equal fraction. Add. Write the answer in simplest form.

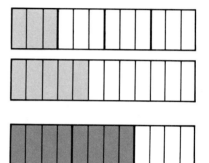

$$\frac{1}{4} = \frac{?}{12}$$
$$+\frac{5}{12} = +\frac{5}{12}$$

$$\frac{1}{4} = \frac{3}{12}$$
$$+\frac{5}{12} = +\frac{5}{12}$$
$$\frac{8}{12} \text{ or } \frac{2}{3}$$

Choose one of the denominators as a common denominator. Add. Write each answer in simplest form.

1. $\frac{7}{12}$ $+\frac{1}{6}$ $\frac{3}{4}$

2. $\frac{5}{16}$ $+\frac{1}{8}$

3. $\frac{1}{2}$ $+\frac{3}{10}$

4. $\frac{5}{12}$ $+\frac{1}{3}$

5. $\frac{7}{24}$ $+\frac{5}{12}$

6. $\frac{5}{18}$ $+\frac{4}{9}$

7. $\frac{1}{6}$ $+\frac{7}{12}$

8. $\frac{2}{15}$ $+\frac{1}{5}$

9. $\frac{4}{7}$ $+\frac{3}{14}$

10. $\frac{4}{27}$ $+\frac{4}{9}$

11. $\frac{4}{7}$ $+\frac{5}{21}$

12. $\frac{5}{6}$ $+\frac{1}{18}$

Multiply to find a common denominator. Add. Write each answer in simplest form.

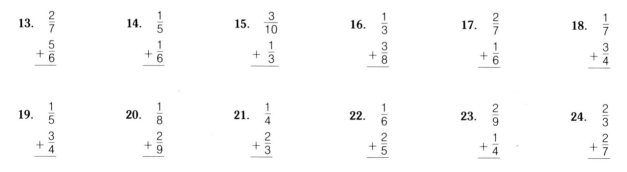

13. $\frac{2}{7}$ $+\frac{5}{6}$

14. $\frac{1}{5}$ $+\frac{1}{6}$

15. $\frac{3}{10}$ $+\frac{1}{3}$

16. $\frac{1}{3}$ $+\frac{3}{8}$

17. $\frac{2}{7}$ $+\frac{1}{6}$

18. $\frac{1}{7}$ $+\frac{3}{4}$

19. $\frac{1}{5}$ $+\frac{3}{4}$

20. $\frac{1}{8}$ $+\frac{2}{9}$

21. $\frac{1}{4}$ $+\frac{2}{3}$

22. $\frac{1}{6}$ $+\frac{2}{5}$

23. $\frac{2}{9}$ $+\frac{1}{4}$

24. $\frac{2}{3}$ $+\frac{2}{7}$

Adding Mixed Numbers with Unlike Denominators

Follow these steps to add mixed numbers with unlike denominators.

Step 1
Find a common denominator and equal fractions.

$$2\tfrac{1}{3} = \quad 2\tfrac{4}{12}$$
$$+\,3\tfrac{3}{4} = +\,3\tfrac{9}{12}$$

Step 2
Add the fractions.

$$2\tfrac{1}{3} = \quad 2\tfrac{4}{12}$$
$$+\,3\tfrac{3}{4} = +\,3\tfrac{9}{12}$$
$$\tfrac{13}{12}$$

Step 3
Add the whole numbers. Write the answer in simplest form.

$$2\tfrac{1}{3} = \quad 2\tfrac{4}{12}$$
$$+\,3\tfrac{3}{4} = +\,3\tfrac{9}{12}$$
$$5\tfrac{13}{12} \text{ or } 6\tfrac{1}{12}$$

Find a common denominator. Add. Write each answer in simplest form.

1. $5\tfrac{1}{5}$
$+3\tfrac{3}{10}$
$8\tfrac{1}{2}$

2. $3\tfrac{1}{6}$
$+2\tfrac{5}{7}$

3. $4\tfrac{1}{3}$
$+7\tfrac{1}{2}$

4. $2\tfrac{3}{5}$
$+5\tfrac{5}{6}$

5. $9\tfrac{7}{20}$
$+4\tfrac{1}{5}$

6. $8\tfrac{1}{5}$
$+3\tfrac{1}{4}$

7. $2\tfrac{1}{4}$
$+3\tfrac{5}{8}$

8. $1\tfrac{3}{4}$
$+8\tfrac{1}{7}$

9. $11\tfrac{5}{8}$
$+\ 8\tfrac{1}{3}$

10. $2\tfrac{1}{4}$
$+6\tfrac{5}{12}$

11. $9\tfrac{5}{9}$
$+6\tfrac{1}{3}$

12. $4\tfrac{3}{8}$
$+2\tfrac{1}{2}$

13. $11\tfrac{5}{9}$
$+\ 4\tfrac{1}{2}$

14. $14\tfrac{9}{10}$
$+\ 6\tfrac{3}{5}$

15. $1\tfrac{1}{6}$
$+10\tfrac{5}{12}$

16. $3\tfrac{3}{10}$
$+4\tfrac{3}{5}$

17. $4\tfrac{1}{10}$
$+13\tfrac{1}{5}$

18. $5\tfrac{1}{9}$
$+9\tfrac{3}{4}$

 **Challenge**
Copy and complete. Then add.

19. $2\tfrac{3}{16} = \quad 2\tfrac{?}{48}$
$+1\tfrac{5}{12} = +1\tfrac{?}{48}$

20. $1\tfrac{5}{9} = \quad 1\tfrac{?}{18}$
$+3\tfrac{5}{6} = +3\tfrac{?}{18}$

21. $4\tfrac{7}{8} = \quad 4\tfrac{?}{24}$
$+4\tfrac{5}{6} = +4\tfrac{?}{24}$

22. $10\tfrac{3}{10} = \quad 10\tfrac{?}{30}$
$+\ 4\tfrac{1}{6} = +\ 4\tfrac{?}{30}$

Subtracting Unlike Fractions

To subtract $\frac{1}{3}$ from $\frac{7}{12}$, you need to find a common denominator.

Step 1
Find a common denominator.

$$\frac{7}{12} = \frac{7}{12}$$
$$-\frac{1}{3} = -\frac{?}{12}$$

Step 2
Find an equal fraction. Subtract. Write the answer in simplest form.

$$\frac{7}{12} = \frac{7}{12}$$
$$-\frac{1}{3} = -\frac{4}{12}$$
$$\frac{3}{12} \text{ or } \frac{1}{4}$$

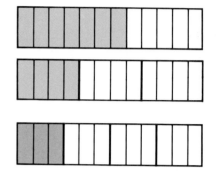

Choose one of the denominators as a common denominator. Subtract. Write each answer in simplest form.

1. $\frac{7}{10}$
$-\frac{2}{5}$
$\overline{\frac{3}{10}}$

2. $\frac{5}{8}$
$-\frac{1}{4}$

3. $\frac{8}{15}$
$-\frac{2}{5}$

4. $\frac{7}{12}$
$-\frac{1}{6}$

5. $\frac{5}{6}$
$-\frac{1}{3}$

6. $\frac{5}{6}$
$-\frac{1}{2}$

7. $\frac{5}{8}$
$-\frac{1}{2}$

8. $\frac{2}{3}$
$-\frac{4}{9}$

9. $\frac{7}{10}$
$-\frac{1}{5}$

10. $\frac{13}{16}$
$-\frac{3}{4}$

11. $\frac{7}{12}$
$-\frac{1}{3}$

12. $\frac{5}{9}$
$-\frac{1}{3}$

Multiply to find a common denominator. Subtract. Write each answer in simplest form.

13. $\frac{2}{3}$
$-\frac{3}{10}$

14. $\frac{3}{5}$
$-\frac{1}{4}$

15. $\frac{5}{8}$
$-\frac{1}{3}$

16. $\frac{5}{6}$
$-\frac{1}{4}$

17. $\frac{5}{8}$
$-\frac{1}{5}$

18. $\frac{5}{6}$
$-\frac{3}{5}$

19. $\frac{7}{8}$
$-\frac{2}{3}$

20. $\frac{2}{3}$
$-\frac{3}{8}$

21. $\frac{5}{9}$
$-\frac{1}{4}$

22. $\frac{4}{5}$
$-\frac{2}{3}$

23. $\frac{1}{3}$
$-\frac{1}{5}$

24. $\frac{5}{6}$
$-\frac{2}{7}$

Subtracting Mixed Numbers with Unlike Denominators

Follow these steps to subtract mixed numbers with unlike denominators.

Step 1
Find a common denominator and equal fractions.

$$8\frac{5}{6} = \quad 8\frac{5}{6}$$
$$-5\frac{1}{3} = -5\frac{2}{6}$$

Step 2
Subtract the fractions.

$$8\frac{5}{6} = \quad 8\frac{5}{6}$$
$$-5\frac{1}{3} = -5\frac{2}{6}$$
$$\frac{3}{6}$$

Step 3
Subtract the whole number. Write the answer in simplest form.

$$8\frac{5}{6} = \quad 8\frac{5}{6}$$
$$-5\frac{1}{3} = -5\frac{2}{6}$$
$$3\frac{3}{6} \text{ or } 3\frac{1}{2}$$

Find a common denominator. Subtract. Write each answer in simplest form.

1. $9\frac{7}{12}$
   $-4\frac{1}{4}$
   $5\frac{1}{3}$

2. $3\frac{2}{3}$
   $-1\frac{1}{4}$

3. $7\frac{7}{12}$
   $-2\frac{1}{6}$

4. $6\frac{4}{5}$
   $-3\frac{3}{10}$

5. $7\frac{1}{4}$
   $-3\frac{1}{8}$

6. $8\frac{5}{6}$
   $-1\frac{1}{2}$

7. $8\frac{7}{10}$
   $-5\frac{2}{5}$

8. $10\frac{11}{12}$
   $-6\frac{3}{4}$

9. $4\frac{1}{2}$
   $-2\frac{1}{8}$

10. $7\frac{1}{2}$
    $-4\frac{1}{6}$

11. $2\frac{1}{2}$
    $-1\frac{1}{5}$

12. $3\frac{3}{5}$
    $-1\frac{1}{6}$

13. $7\frac{1}{4}$
    $-3\frac{1}{9}$

14. $9\frac{9}{10}$
    $-6\frac{2}{5}$

15. $8\frac{2}{3}$
    $-4\frac{1}{2}$

16. There are $2\frac{1}{2}$ liters of orange juice in a pitcher. Miyako pours $1\frac{2}{5}$ liters into glasses. How much orange juice is left in the pitcher?

Using Pictures to Multiply Fractions

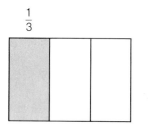

$\frac{1}{3}$

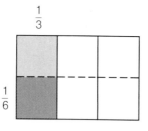

$\frac{1}{3}$

$\frac{1}{6}$

$\frac{1}{3}$ of the area is shaded blue.

$\frac{1}{2}$ of $\frac{1}{3}$ of the area, or $\frac{1}{6}$ of the total area, is dark blue.

$\frac{1}{2}$ of $\frac{1}{3}$ means $\frac{1}{2} \times \frac{1}{3}$.

Use the pictures to help you multiply.

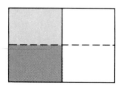

1. $\frac{1}{2} \times \frac{1}{2} = \frac{?}{?}$ $\frac{1}{2} \times \frac{1}{2} = \frac{1}{4}$

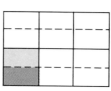

2. $\frac{1}{2} \times \frac{1}{6} = \frac{?}{?}$

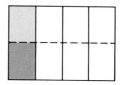

3. $\frac{1}{2} \times \frac{1}{4} = \frac{?}{?}$

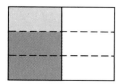

4. $\frac{2}{3} \times \frac{1}{2} = \frac{?}{?}$

5. $\frac{2}{3} \times \frac{1}{3} = \frac{?}{?}$

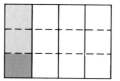

6. $\frac{1}{3} \times \frac{1}{4} = \frac{?}{?}$

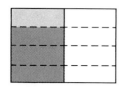

7. $\frac{3}{4} \times \frac{1}{2} = \frac{?}{?}$

8. $\frac{2}{3} \times \frac{2}{3} = \frac{?}{?}$

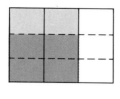

9. $\frac{2}{4} \times \frac{1}{2} = \frac{?}{?}$

Multiplying Fractions

Follow these steps to multiply a fraction by a fraction.

Step 1
Multiply the numerators.

$$\frac{5}{8} \times \frac{3}{5} = \frac{15}{}$$

Step 2
Multiply the denominators.

$$\frac{5}{8} \times \frac{3}{5} = \frac{15}{40}$$

Step 3
Write the answer in simplest form.

$$\frac{15}{40} = \frac{3}{8}$$

Multiply. Write each answer in simplest form.

1. $\frac{1}{2} \times \frac{2}{3}$ $\frac{1}{3}$

2. $\frac{2}{7} \times \frac{1}{6}$

3. $\frac{1}{3} \times \frac{3}{7}$

4. $\frac{2}{3} \times \frac{3}{4}$

5. $\frac{2}{5} \times \frac{1}{2}$

6. $\frac{1}{5} \times \frac{7}{10}$

7. $\frac{4}{9} \times \frac{1}{4}$

8. $\frac{1}{5} \times \frac{3}{10}$

9. $\frac{3}{4} \times \frac{1}{2}$

10. $\frac{3}{8} \times \frac{1}{4}$

11. $\frac{5}{6} \times \frac{1}{3}$

12. $\frac{1}{10} \times \frac{5}{6}$

13. $\frac{3}{5} \times \frac{2}{3}$

14. $\frac{5}{6} \times \frac{3}{4}$

15. $\frac{4}{9} \times \frac{1}{2}$

16. $\frac{3}{4} \times \frac{1}{9}$

17. $\frac{6}{7} \times \frac{1}{2}$

18. $\frac{4}{5} \times \frac{7}{10}$

19. $\frac{1}{2} \times \frac{4}{9}$

20. $\frac{2}{3} \times \frac{1}{6}$

21. $\frac{3}{4} \times \frac{5}{8}$

22. $\frac{2}{3} \times \frac{1}{4}$

23. $\frac{1}{2} \times \frac{5}{8}$

24. $\frac{2}{5} \times \frac{5}{6}$

25. $\frac{1}{6} \times \frac{5}{6}$

26. $\frac{1}{7} \times \frac{2}{6}$

27. $\frac{5}{8} \times \frac{3}{8}$

28. $\frac{5}{6} \times \frac{1}{4}$

29. $\frac{2}{9} \times \frac{1}{4}$

30. $\frac{1}{3} \times \frac{5}{6}$

⭐ Challenge
**Multiply. First change the mixed number to a fraction.
Write each answer in simplest form.**

31. $\frac{2}{3} \times 1\frac{1}{4}$

32. $2\frac{1}{3} \times \frac{6}{7}$

33. $\frac{6}{11} \times 3\frac{1}{2}$

34. $\frac{3}{4} \times 1\frac{5}{7}$

35. $\frac{1}{4} \times 3\frac{1}{2}$

36. $2\frac{1}{3} \times \frac{3}{4}$

37. $6\frac{5}{6} \times \frac{1}{6}$

38. $4\frac{1}{2} \times \frac{1}{2}$

39. $8\frac{2}{3} \times \frac{1}{4}$

40. $\frac{1}{6} \times 2\frac{5}{6}$

Multiplying a Whole Number and a Fraction

Follow these steps to multiply a whole number by a fraction.

Step 1
Write the whole number as a fraction with a denominator of one.

$$8 \times \frac{3}{5} = \frac{8}{1} \times \frac{3}{5}$$

Step 2
Multiply.

$$\frac{8}{1} \times \frac{3}{5} = \frac{24}{5}$$

Step 3
Write the answer in simplest form.

$$\frac{24}{5} = 4\frac{4}{5}$$

Multiply. Write each answer in simplest form.

1. $6 \times \frac{3}{4}$ $4\frac{1}{2}$ 2. $5 \times \frac{1}{2}$ 3. $\frac{5}{6} \times 18$ 4. $\frac{3}{7} \times 28$ 5. $35 \times \frac{5}{7}$

6. $56 \times \frac{1}{2}$ 7. $9 \times \frac{5}{6}$ 8. $24 \times \frac{3}{4}$ 9. $8 \times \frac{2}{3}$ 10. $\frac{3}{5} \times 9$

11. $4 \times \frac{5}{6}$ 12. $\frac{2}{3} \times 21$ 13. $9 \times \frac{1}{4}$ 14. $\frac{3}{5} \times 6$ 15. $\frac{5}{6} \times 8$

Multiply. Try to do these in just one step.

16. $\frac{1}{6} \times 36$ 17. $\frac{1}{8} \times 24$ 18. $\frac{1}{6} \times 42$ 19. $\frac{1}{2} \times 18$ 20. $\frac{1}{5} \times 40$

21. $\frac{1}{8} \times 16$ 22. $\frac{1}{7} \times 21$ 23. $\frac{1}{3} \times 18$ 24. $\frac{1}{4} \times 16$ 25. $\frac{1}{5} \times 20$

26. 700 people went to a concert. $\frac{3}{7}$ of them sat in the balcony. How many people sat in the balcony?

27. There are 81 musicians in the orchestra. $\frac{2}{9}$ of them play violins. How many play violins?

Multiplication Code

Crack the code to answer the riddle.

What never asks questions yet often has to be answered?

Code	p	t	l	o	e	h	n
	15	16	2	5	10	8	12

Multiply.

1. $\frac{8}{9} \times 18$ 16,t

2. $\frac{1}{3} \times 24$

3. $\frac{5}{8} \times 16$

4. $\frac{4}{5} \times 20$

5. $\frac{5}{12} \times 24$

6. $\frac{1}{4} \times 8$

7. $\frac{5}{6} \times 12$

8. $\frac{5}{11} \times 33$

9. $\frac{2}{3} \times 12$

10. $\frac{1}{4} \times 20$

11. $\frac{4}{5} \times 15$

12. $\frac{2}{7} \times 35$

13. The answer is: ___ ___ ___   ___ ___ ___ ___ ___ ___ ___ ___ ___

    1.   2.   3.   4.   5.   6.   7.   8.   9.   10.   11.   12.

Adding with Decimals

Add decimals the same way you add whole numbers.
Remember to put a decimal point in the sum.

Step 1
Line up the
decimal points.
Add the hundredths.

$$\begin{array}{r} 6.38 \\ +\ 2.94 \\ \hline 2 \end{array}$$

Step 2
Add the
tenths.

$$\begin{array}{r} 6.38 \\ +\ 2.94 \\ \hline 32 \end{array}$$

Step 3
Add the ones.
Write the decimal
point in the answer.

$$\begin{array}{r} 6.38 \\ +\ 2.94 \\ \hline 9.32 \end{array}$$

Add.

1. $\begin{array}{r} 7.43 \\ +2.58 \\ \hline 10.01 \end{array}$

2. $\begin{array}{r} 12.6 \\ +\ 3.5 \\ \hline \end{array}$

3. $\begin{array}{r} 21.16 \\ +35.59 \\ \hline \end{array}$

4. $\begin{array}{r} 2.78 \\ +5.94 \\ \hline \end{array}$

5. $\begin{array}{r} 12.4 \\ +37.9 \\ \hline \end{array}$

6. $\begin{array}{r} 8.49 \\ +3.92 \\ \hline \end{array}$

7. $\begin{array}{r} 3.24 \\ +2.57 \\ \hline \end{array}$

8. $\begin{array}{r} 6.09 \\ +2.68 \\ \hline \end{array}$

9. Sadie used 8.2 meters of rope
   to make a swing. Joey used 8.5
   meters of rope. How much rope
   did they use in all?

⭐ Challenge

Write in a column. Add.

10. $3.81 + 14.07 + 6.95$

11. $14.28 + 9.73 + 1.65$

12. $0.76 + 1.8 + 8.09$

13. $5.65 + 2.85 + 3.9$

14. $4.87 + 10.8 + 6.42$

15. $0.6 + 9.87 + 5.43$

More Adding with Decimals

Fill in missing zeros before you add.

Step 1
Write a zero in
the thousandths place.

$$18.65 = 18.650$$

18.65	18.650
+ 41.598	+ 41.598

Step 2
Add.

18.650
+ 41.598
60.248

Add.

1. 12.47
   +19.465
   31.935

2. 0.127
   +0.74

3. 4.564
   +0.19

4. 9.37
   +8.557

5. 68.50
   + 3.286

6. 9.425
   +7.788

7. 16.874
   +18.888

8. 46.3
   +95.68

9. 10.59
   +32.516

10. 7.46
    +5.789

Now do these.

11. 62.312+47.252

12. 12.986+8.347

13. 72.689+6.789

14. 4.605+3.729

15. 1.824+6.286

16. 3.659+2.863

17. Adam and Betty hike 15.1
    kilometers one day and 13.552
    kilometers the next day. How many
    kilometers do they hike in all?

Subtracting with Decimals

Subtract decimals the same way you subtract whole numbers. Remember to put a decimal point in the difference.

Step 1
Line up the
decimal points.
Subtract the hundredths.

$$\begin{array}{r} 9.13 \\ \leftarrow 4.57 \\ \hline 6 \end{array}$$

Step 2
Subtract
the tenths.

$$\begin{array}{r} 9.13 \\ -\ 4.57 \\ \hline .56 \end{array}$$

Step 3
Subtract the ones.
Write the decimal
point in the answer.

$$\begin{array}{r} 9.13 \\ -\ 4.57 \\ \hline 4.56 \end{array}$$

Subtract.

1. $\begin{array}{r} 6.81 \\ -4.96 \\ \hline 1.85 \end{array}$
2. $\begin{array}{r} 7.27 \\ -1.58 \\ \hline \end{array}$
3. $\begin{array}{r} 6.7 \\ -4.9 \\ \hline \end{array}$
4. $\begin{array}{r} 2.73 \\ -1.38 \\ \hline \end{array}$
5. $\begin{array}{r} 1.2 \\ -0.6 \\ \hline \end{array}$

6. $\begin{array}{r} 5.1 \\ -2.7 \\ \hline \end{array}$
7. $\begin{array}{r} 3.44 \\ -1.28 \\ \hline \end{array}$
8. $\begin{array}{r} 6.27 \\ -3.92 \\ \hline \end{array}$
9. $\begin{array}{r} 12.4 \\ -\ 9.6 \\ \hline \end{array}$
10. $\begin{array}{r} 52.6 \\ -23.8 \\ \hline \end{array}$

11. $\begin{array}{r} 8.21 \\ -3.75 \\ \hline \end{array}$
12. $\begin{array}{r} 9.40 \\ -5.31 \\ \hline \end{array}$
13. $\begin{array}{r} 15.33 \\ -\ 7.84 \\ \hline \end{array}$
14. $\begin{array}{r} 31.95 \\ -16.40 \\ \hline \end{array}$
15. $\begin{array}{r} 26.84 \\ -\ 9.32 \\ \hline \end{array}$

16. $23.7 - 4.9$
17. $7.38 - 1.86$
18. $8.72 - 3.46$
19. $6.41 - 2.79$

20. $6.8 - 2.9$
21. $7.38 - 5.18$

22. $8.4 - 6.9$
23. $4.32 - 1.65$

24. Arthur is painting his house. He
started with 37.85 liters of paint and
has used 16.43 liters. How much
paint does he have left?

Estimating with Decimals

You can round to the nearest whole number to estimate a sum or a difference. Look at the tenths place to round each number to the nearest whole number. Then add or subtract the rounded numbers.

8.367	8		6.743	7
+ 4.295	+ 4		− 3.463	− 3
	12			4

The sum is about 12.   The difference is about 4.

Estimate each answer. Then find the exact answer.

1. 6.471
    +1.624
    8, 8.095

2. 6.419
    −3.282

3. 4.269
    +8.403

4. 9.965
    −4.807

5. 7.709
    −3.562

6. 4.859
    +3.265

7. 9.967
    +9.062

8. 6.375
    +1.446

9. 7.165
    −4.586

10. 9.127
    −2.653

11. 3.602
    −1.589

12. 8.174
    +8.967

13. 2.486
    +1.907

14. 8.443
    −6.162

15. 7.265
    −3.528

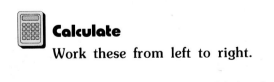 **Calculate**

Work these from left to right.

16. $32,733 - 23,485 + 0.374 - 26.9 + 1.1$

17. $347 - 23 + 1.302 + 11.07 - 6.53$

18. $89 + 102 - 12.871 + 62.05 - 8.931$

Hardware Store Problems

Jiffy Hardware Store is always busy on Saturday mornings.
Add or subtract to solve each problem.

1. Julia buys a hammer for $3.89 and nails for $0.99. How much does she spend? $4.88

2. Pamela buys a mirror for $9.79 and cleaning supplies for $3.59. How much does she spend?

3. Douglas buys house paint for $22.39 and brushes for $5.49. How much does he spend?

4. Christopher buys lumber for $40.70 and wire for $8.65. How much does he spend?

5. Ricardo buys grass seed for $4.79, flower seeds for $1.25, and a rake for $8.99. How much does he spend?

6. Ruth buys wallpaper for $22.50, paste for $4.19, and brushes for $7.89. How much does she spend?

7. Sandi buys a small rug for $10.25. She gives the clerk $20.00. What is her change?

8. Donald buys baking pans for $5.79. He gives the clerk $10.00. What is his change?

Multiplying Whole Numbers and Tenths

When you multiply whole numbers and tenths, the product has one decimal place.

Step 1
Multiply the same way you multiply whole numbers.

$$\begin{array}{r} 1.8 \\ \times\ \ 4 \\ \hline 72 \end{array}$$

Step 2
Start at the right and count over one decimal place. Put in the decimal point.

$$\begin{array}{r} 1.8 \\ \times\ \ 4 \\ \hline 7.2 \end{array}$$

Multiply. Remember to put the decimal point in the product.

1. $\begin{array}{r} 2.7 \\ \times\ 3 \\ \hline 8.1 \end{array}$

2. $\begin{array}{r} 0.6 \\ \times\ 5 \\ \hline \end{array}$

3. $\begin{array}{r} 6.1 \\ \times\ 5 \\ \hline \end{array}$

4. $\begin{array}{r} 4.7 \\ \times\ 7 \\ \hline \end{array}$

5. $\begin{array}{r} 0.4 \\ \times\ 9 \\ \hline \end{array}$

6. $\begin{array}{r} 9.6 \\ \times\ 5 \\ \hline \end{array}$

7. $\begin{array}{r} 0.7 \\ \times\ 5 \\ \hline \end{array}$

8. $\begin{array}{r} 1.6 \\ \times\ 6 \\ \hline \end{array}$

9. $\begin{array}{r} 0.3 \\ \times\ 4 \\ \hline \end{array}$

10. $\begin{array}{r} 0.9 \\ \times\ 8 \\ \hline \end{array}$

11. $\begin{array}{r} 4.3 \\ \times\ 7 \\ \hline \end{array}$

12. $\begin{array}{r} 0.8 \\ \times\ 8 \\ \hline \end{array}$

 **Challenge**

13. James is taking care of 4 cats. Each cat eats 0.3 kilograms of cat food each day.
    a. How much cat food does James need for each day?
    b. How much food do the cats eat in 7 days?
    c. How much food do the cats eat in 30 days?

Multiplying Whole Numbers and Hundredths

When you multiply whole numbers and hundredths, the product has two decimal places.

Step 1
Multiply the same way you multiply whole numbers.

$$\begin{array}{r} 3.63 \\ \times\ \ \ \ 8 \\ \hline 2904 \end{array}$$

Step 2
Start at the right and count over two decimal places. Put in the decimal point.

$$\begin{array}{r} 3.63 \\ \times\ \ \ \ 8 \\ \hline 29.04 \end{array}$$

Multiply.

1. $\begin{array}{r}1.32\\ \times\ \ 6\\ \hline 7.92\end{array}$	2. $\begin{array}{r}0.08\\ \times\ \ 9\\ \hline\end{array}$	3. $\begin{array}{r}6.51\\ \times\ \ 9\\ \hline\end{array}$	4. $\begin{array}{r}0.09\\ \times\ \ 4\\ \hline\end{array}$	5. $\begin{array}{r}0.14\\ \times\ \ 7\\ \hline\end{array}$
6. $\begin{array}{r}0.56\\ \times\ \ 8\\ \hline\end{array}$	7. $\begin{array}{r}3.47\\ \times\ \ 4\\ \hline\end{array}$	8. $\begin{array}{r}1.19\\ \times\ \ 9\\ \hline\end{array}$	9. $\begin{array}{r}0.99\\ \times\ \ 2\\ \hline\end{array}$	10. $\begin{array}{r}0.05\\ \times\ \ 7\\ \hline\end{array}$

Now do these.

11. $\begin{array}{r}0.39\\ \times\ 29\\ \hline\end{array}$	12. $\begin{array}{r}0.06\\ \times\ 15\\ \hline\end{array}$	13. $\begin{array}{r}1.43\\ \times\ 56\\ \hline\end{array}$	14. $\begin{array}{r}0.25\\ \times\ 55\\ \hline\end{array}$	15. $\begin{array}{r}3.06\\ \times\ 42\\ \hline\end{array}$
16. $\begin{array}{r}0.21\\ \times\ 61\\ \hline\end{array}$	17. $\begin{array}{r}4.12\\ \times\ 75\\ \hline\end{array}$	18. $\begin{array}{r}0.73\\ \times\ 49\\ \hline\end{array}$	19. $\begin{array}{r}6.65\\ \times\ 15\\ \hline\end{array}$	20. $\begin{array}{r}8.09\\ \times\ 22\\ \hline\end{array}$

21. 0.35×14 22. 28×6.52 23. 14×6.09 24. 1.04×12

25. 55×0.15 26. 0.29×62 27. 92×1.63 28. 2.74×89

Multiplying Money

Multiply money the same way
you multiply whole numbers.

$$\begin{array}{r} \$33.89 \\ \times \qquad 3 \\ \hline \$101.67 \end{array}$$

Multiply. Remember to use $ and . in the answer.

1. $11.51
   × 7
   $80.57

2. $4.65
   × 8

3. $27.91
   × 5

4. $32.41
   × 6

5. $18.65
   × 9

6. $3.47
   × 6

7. $67.41
   × 8

8. $4.99
   × 6

9. $18.77
   × 5

10. $14.86
    × 3

11. $20.69
    × 18

12. $6.52
    × 21

13. $31.46
    × 15

14. $9.06
    × 48

15. $16.52
    × 12

16. Lynne and Fred spent one Saturday
    doing chores to earn money.
    a. Lynne washed 7 cars at $1.25
       each. How much money did
       she earn?
    b. Fred washed 22 windows at
       $0.50 each. How much money
       did he earn?
    c. Who earned more money? How
       much more?

Chapter Review

Add. (ex. 1-3: p. 288), (ex. 4-6: p. 289)

1. $\dfrac{4}{9}$
$+\dfrac{7}{9}$

2. $\dfrac{6}{8}$
$+\dfrac{7}{8}$

3. $\dfrac{4}{7}$
$+\dfrac{6}{7}$

4. $5\dfrac{7}{8}$
$+8\dfrac{4}{8}$

5. $5\dfrac{5}{7}$
$+3\dfrac{6}{7}$

6. $1\dfrac{4}{6}$
$+3\dfrac{3}{6}$

Subtract. (ex. 7-9: p. 291), (ex. 10-12: p. 292)

7. $6\dfrac{9}{10}$
$-3\dfrac{2}{10}$

8. $4\dfrac{7}{11}$
$-1\dfrac{3}{11}$

9. $8\dfrac{6}{8}$
$-4\dfrac{5}{8}$

10. 5
$-2\dfrac{1}{6}$

11. 9
$-4\dfrac{2}{9}$

12. $5\dfrac{1}{3}$
$-2\dfrac{2}{3}$

Add, subtract, or multiply. Write each answer in simplest form. (ex. 13-18: pp. 300–301), (ex. 19-24: pp. 302–303), (ex. 25-27: p. 305), (ex. 28-29: p. 306)

13. $\dfrac{5}{12}$
$+\dfrac{1}{6}$

14. $\dfrac{1}{3}$
$+\dfrac{1}{8}$

15. $\dfrac{2}{15}$
$+\dfrac{1}{5}$

16. $3\dfrac{3}{8}$
$+6\dfrac{1}{2}$

17. $5\dfrac{1}{2}$
$+4\dfrac{1}{8}$

18. $11\dfrac{5}{9}$
$+\ 9\dfrac{1}{2}$

19. $\dfrac{7}{12}$
$-\dfrac{1}{6}$

20. $\dfrac{3}{8}$
$-\dfrac{1}{5}$

21. $\dfrac{2}{3}$
$-\dfrac{4}{9}$

22. $3\dfrac{2}{3}$
$-1\dfrac{1}{4}$

23. $8\dfrac{2}{3}$
$-3\dfrac{1}{2}$

24. $9\dfrac{7}{10}$
$-6\dfrac{2}{5}$

25. $\dfrac{3}{4} \times \dfrac{1}{9}$

26. $\dfrac{1}{3} \times \dfrac{5}{6}$

27. $\dfrac{1}{2} \times \dfrac{4}{9}$

28. $\dfrac{2}{3} \times 18$

29. $6 \times \dfrac{4}{8}$

Add, subtract, or multiply. (ex. 30: p. 308), (ex. 31-32: p. 310), (ex. 33-34: p. 315)

30. 3.78
$+6.94$

31. 2.78
-1.39

32. 46.5
-12.7

33. 1.9
$\times\ 8$

34. 0.6
$\times\ 5$

Chapter Test

Add.

1. $\dfrac{1}{7}$
    $+\dfrac{3}{7}$

2. $\dfrac{7}{11}$
    $+\dfrac{2}{11}$

3. $\dfrac{1}{8}$
    $+\dfrac{2}{8}$

4. $3\dfrac{2}{3}$
    $+2\dfrac{2}{3}$

5. $9\dfrac{5}{9}$
    $+5\dfrac{8}{9}$

6. $\dfrac{5}{6}$
    $+\dfrac{2}{6}$

Subtract.

7. $\dfrac{8}{10}$
    $-\dfrac{5}{10}$

8. 9
    $-4\dfrac{2}{5}$

9. $5\dfrac{7}{11}$
    $-1\dfrac{3}{11}$

10. $\dfrac{11}{13}$
    $-\dfrac{6}{13}$

11. $8\dfrac{4}{9}$
    $-3\dfrac{2}{9}$

12. 4
    $-2\dfrac{1}{6}$

Add, subtract, or multiply. Write each answer in simplest form.

13. $\dfrac{5}{16}$
    $+\dfrac{3}{8}$

14. $\dfrac{8}{9}$
    $-\dfrac{3}{4}$

15. $9\dfrac{5}{9}$
    $+3\dfrac{1}{2}$

16. $7\dfrac{3}{7}$
    $-2\dfrac{1}{6}$

17. $\dfrac{11}{12}$
    $-\dfrac{5}{6}$

18. $2\dfrac{1}{4}$
    $+6\dfrac{5}{8}$

19. $\dfrac{2}{3} \times \dfrac{1}{4}$

20. $\dfrac{1}{4} \times 24$

21. $\dfrac{2}{5} \times \dfrac{5}{6}$

22. $18 \times \dfrac{2}{3}$

23. $\dfrac{1}{2} \times \dfrac{4}{9}$

Add, subtract, or multiply.

24. 5.59
    $+4.08$

25. 12.43
    $-\ 3.45$

26. 12.65
    $+\ 4.89$

27. 2.3
    $\times\ 4$

28. 0.6
    $\times\ 5$

Brush Up

Add or subtract.

1. 2475
  −1668

2. 67,280
  − 3981

3. 8619
  + 527

4. 3009
  +8193

5. 9987
  −3664

6. 48,953
  +21,235

7. 298
  +563

8. 9645
  −8609

9. 6008
  − 564

10. 7689
  +4021

Multiply or divide.

11. 860
  × 5

12. 460
  × 30

13. 39
  ×15

14. 204
  × 52

15. 94
  ×61

16. 23
  ×14

17. 530
  × 44

18. $2.14
  × 4

19. $8.23
  × 16

20. $1.98
  × 20

21. $30\overline{)982}$

22. $60\overline{)663}$

23. $40\overline{)4397}$

24. $20\overline{)9135}$

25. $10\overline{)469}$

26. $26\overline{)9761}$

27. $55\overline{)84,987}$

28. $31\overline{)473}$

29. $41\overline{)6309}$

30. $18\overline{)2149}$

Add or subtract.

31. $\frac{3}{8} + \frac{2}{8}$

32. $\frac{3}{4} + \frac{1}{8}$

33. $\frac{8}{9} - \frac{3}{9}$

34. $\frac{5}{6} - \frac{1}{3}$

35. $\frac{4}{10} + \frac{1}{5}$

36. $\frac{7}{11} - \frac{4}{11}$

37. $\frac{7}{5} - \frac{3}{5}$

38. $\frac{1}{3} + \frac{4}{9}$

39. $\frac{6}{8} - \frac{3}{8}$

40. $\frac{2}{5} + \frac{2}{5}$

41. 0.6
  +0.8

42. 2.9
  −1.7

43. 4.3
  +9.1

44. 2.70
  −0.17

45. 8.13
  +2.05

46. 4.543
  +0.355

47. 9.987
  −0.954

48. 8.621
  −5.693

49. 47.10
  + 6.31

50. 8.70
  +1.09

CHAPTER 12

Graphing and Probability

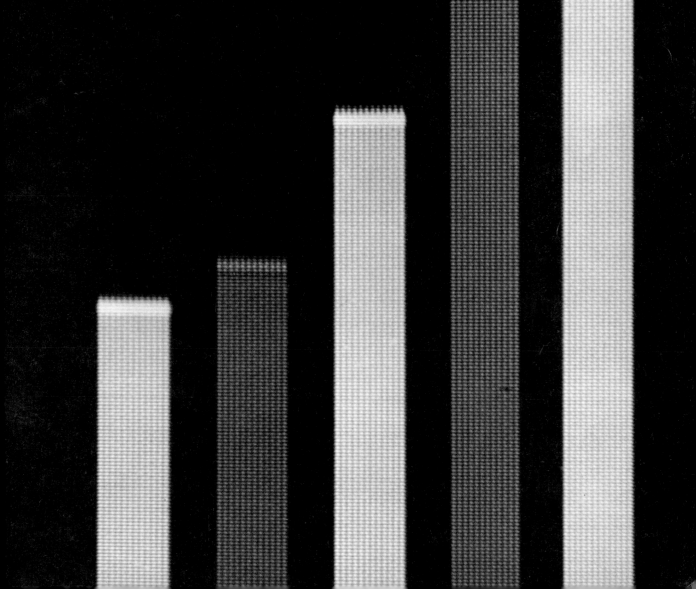

Using Graphing at Work

Helen Lin is a brain specialist. She uses a machine that records a patient's brain waves on a graph. Helen analyzes the graph to see how well the patient is recovering. If there are no unusual patterns on the graph, the patient will be healthy soon.

Reading a Horizontal Bar Graph

Ellen Bauer took a survey of some people's favorite fruits.
This horizontal **bar graph** shows the results of her survey.
Bar graphs make information easy to see and compare.

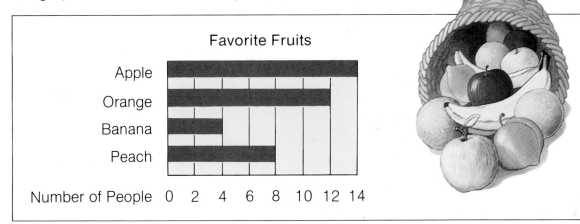

Use the horizontal bar graph to answer these questions.

1. How many people like apples
   best?   14

2. How many people like oranges
   best?

3. How many people like bananas
   best?

4. How many people like peaches
   best?

5. How many more people like apples
   than oranges?

6. How many more people like oranges
   than bananas?

7. How many more people like apples
   than bananas?

8. How many more people like peaches
   than bananas?

Calculate

9. Ellen kept track of the price of peaches for 12 months.
   Her results were 95¢, 92¢, 93¢, 79¢, 64¢, 30¢, 32¢, 33¢,
   39¢, 58¢, 80¢, and 85¢. What was the average price?

Choosing a Scale

This is a vertical bar graph. The information on a graph is measured along two **scales**—the **horizontal scale** and the **vertical scale**. Before you can make a graph, you need to choose a scale.

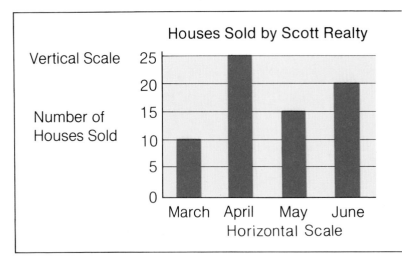

Houses Sold by Scott Realty

Vertical Scale

Number of Houses Sold

Horizontal Scale

Which vertical scale would you use to graph the numbers in each table?

100	400	100
90	390	98
80	380	96
70	370	94
60	360	92
50	350	90
Scale A	Scale B	Scale C

1. Attendance at Jones School

Month	Number Absent
September	80
October	60
November	90

Scale A

2. Library Book Survey

Kind of Book	Numbers
Music	400
Art	360
Poetry	380

3. Miguel's Test Scores

Day	Score
Monday	96
Tuesday	94
Thursday	98

Making a Bar Graph from a Table

You can make a bar graph to show
the information on this table.

Pets Owned by Children

Pets	Fish	Cat	Dog
Number	10	15	20

Step 1
Choose a scale to show the number of pets owned. Then label it.

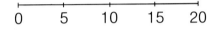

0   5   10   15   20

Step 2
Make a scale for the different pets.

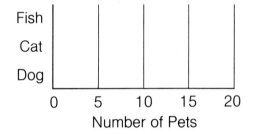

Number of Pets

Step 3
Draw a bar for each pet. Give the graph
a title.

Children's Pets

Number of Pets

Make a horizontal bar graph using the information in each table.

1. Number of Children Who Bought Lunch

Day	Mon.	Wed.	Fri.
Number	8	12	6

2. Number of Books Read in One Year

Child	Suzy	Leda	Marian
Number	22	28	20

3. Number of Tickets Sold for a Play

Grade	3	4	5	6
Number	15	25	20	30

4. Number of Cars Sold

Day	Tues.	Thurs.	Fri.	Sat.
Number	6	9	4	8

Reading a Picture Graph

Picture graphs have pictures instead of bars.

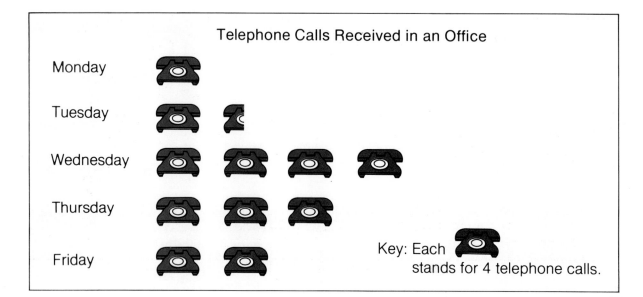

Telephone Calls Received in an Office

Monday

Tuesday

Wednesday

Thursday

Friday

Key: Each ☎ stands for 4 telephone calls.

Use the picture graph to answer the questions.

1. What does  stand for?
   2 telephone calls

2. How many telephone calls were received on Wednesday?

3. How many telephone calls were received on Friday?

4. How many telephone calls were received during the week?

5. How many more calls were received on Thursday than on Tuesday?

6. How many fewer calls were received on Monday than on Wednesday?

⭐ **Challenge**

7. Make a picture graph from the information on this table. Use a symbol that stands for 6 books.

Number of Books Sold

Day	Mon.	Tues.	Wed.	Thurs.	Fri.
Number	60	45	54	42	30

Reading a Line Graph

Line graphs are used to show change.

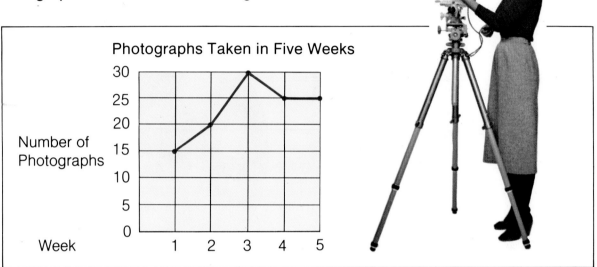

Photographs Taken in Five Weeks

Number of Photographs / Week

Use the line graph to answer the questions.

1. How many photographs were taken in the first week? 15

2. How many photographs were taken altogether?

3. How many more photographs were taken in the third week than in the second week?

4. How many fewer photographs were taken in the first week than in the fifth week?

5. Were more photographs taken in the first two weeks or the second two weeks? How many more?

6. During which two-week period were the greatest number of photographs taken? How many photographs was that?

 **Challenge**

7. Make a line graph from the information on this table. Choose 5, 10, or 20 for the vertical scale.

Bottles Recycled in Four Weeks

Week	1	2	3	4
Number	60	70	50	40

Circle Graphs

The **circle graph** shows how 100 children at Jefferson School get to school.

How Some Children Get to School

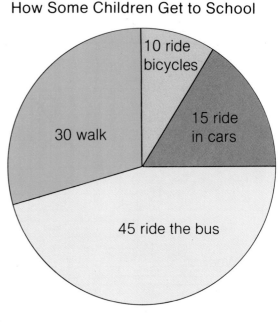

10 ride bicycles

30 walk

15 ride in cars

45 ride the bus

Use the circle graph to answer these questions.

1. How do most of the children get to school?   ride the bus

2. How do the fewest number of children get to school?

3. How many children ride the bus or ride in cars?

4. How many children ride bicycles or walk to school?

5. How many more children ride the bus than ride bicycles?

6. How many more children walk than ride in cars?

7. How many fewer children ride bicycles than ride the bus?

8. How many fewer children ride in cars than walk?

 **Challenge**

9. Make a circle graph to show that Linda goes to school 6 hours a day, sleeps 9 hours a day, eats 3 hours a day, and plays 6 hours a day.

Ordered Pairs

The points on the graph below are named with **ordered pairs**.
To find the ordered pair for point A, go from 0 to 2 on the
horizontal scale, then move up 3 on the vertical scale.
The ordered pair for point A is (2,3).

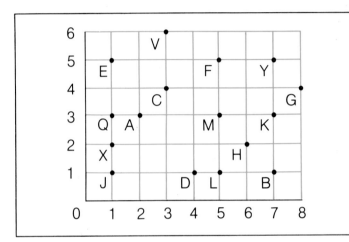

Find the ordered pair that names each point.

1. C   (3,4)   2. B   3. G   4. H   5. E   6. J

7. F   8. K   9. L   10. M   11. X   12. V

Find each ordered pair on the graph. Then write the point that it names.

13. (7,1)   14. (4,1)   15. (7,5)   16. (3,6)   17. (5,5)

 Review   (pp. 323–329)

Make a horizontal bar graph using the information in this table.

1. Baseball Games Won

Team	Tigers	Lions	Hawks	Eagles
Score	8	12	6	4

Probability

Christopher and Suzette toss a penny to see who will do the dishes. Each possible result is called an **outcome**. The two possible outcomes are heads up or tails up.

The **probability** that an outcome will happen is written as a fraction. The denominator is the total number of outcomes.

Christopher has 1 chance out of 2 of getting heads, so the probability is 1 out of 2, or $\frac{1}{2}$.

Use the pictures to find the answers.

1a. What are the two possible outcomes if you spin the arrow?   blue, green

b. What is the probability of the arrow pointing to green?

c. What is the probability of the arrow pointing to blue?

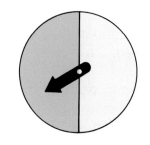

2a. How many possible outcomes are there if you pick one ball without looking?

b. What is the probability of picking a red ball?

c. What is the probability of picking a ball that is not red?

3a. How many possible outcomes are there if you pick one marble without looking?

b. What is the probability of picking a blue marble?

c. What is the probability of picking a yellow marble?

d. What is the probability of picking a marble that is not blue?

More Probability

What is the probability of the arrow pointing to brown?

1. 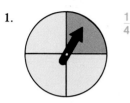 $\frac{1}{4}$

2.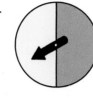

3.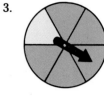

4.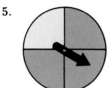

5.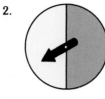

6.

There are 12 buttons in a jar. 4 of them are green, 3 are blue, 4 are white, and 1 is red. Find the probability of picking each of these.

7. a green button

8. a red button

9. a blue button

10. a white button

11. a blue or a red button

12. a button that is not white

13. a green or a white button

14. a button that is not green

Review (pp. 323–331)

Make a horizontal bar graph using the information in the table.

1. Television Sales at Jean's Television Shop

Day	Mon.	Tues.	Wed.	Thurs.	Fri.
Number	16	18	10	26	8

Chapter Review

Answer the questions.   (ex. 1: p. 323),   (ex. 2: p. 327),
                               (ex. 3: p. 329),   (ex. 4: p. 330)

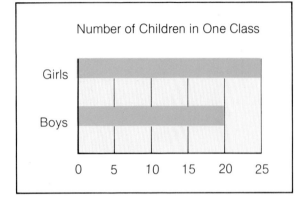

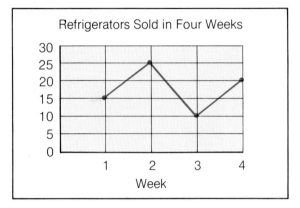

1a. How many girls in the class?
 b. How many boys in the class?
 c. How many more girls than boys in the class?
 d. What is the vertical scale of this graph?

2a. How many refrigerators were sold in the first week?
 b. How many refrigerators were sold in the last two weeks?
 c. How many refrigerators were sold in all?

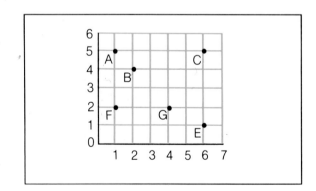

3a. Which ordered pair names point C?
 b. Which ordered pair names point F?
 c. Which ordered pair names point A?
 d. Which ordered pair names point G?
 e. Which ordered pair names point E?
 f. Which ordered pair names point B?

4. What is the probability of picking each of these?
 a. a red button
 b. a white button
 c. a green or a red button
 d. a button that is not white

Chapter Test

Answer the questions.

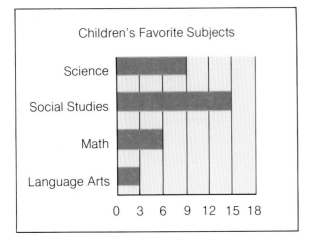

1a. How many children like math best?
 b. How many children like science best?
 c. How many children like social studies best?
 d. How many children like language arts best?

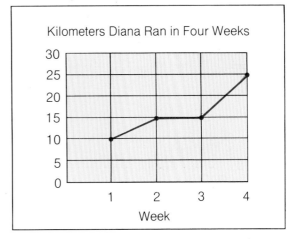

2a. How many kilometers did Diana run during the first week?
 b. How many kilometers did she run during the fourth week?
 c. How many kilometers did she run in all?

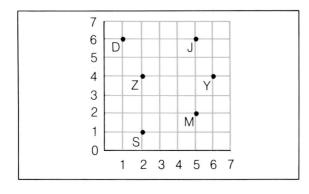

3a. Which ordered pair names point D?
 b. Which ordered pair names point J?
 c. Which ordered pair names point Z?
 d. Which ordered pair names point Y?
 e. Which ordered pair names point M?
 f. Which ordered pair names point S?

4. What is the probability of picking each of these?
 a. a red marble
 b. a yellow marble
 c. a blue or a red marble
 d. a marble that is not red

Brush Up

Add, subtract, multiply, or divide.

1. $3\overline{)465}$
2. $10\overline{)979}$
3. $29\overline{)805}$
4. $31\overline{)2109}$
5. $20\overline{)500}$

6. $\frac{2}{6}$ $+\frac{3}{6}$
7. $\frac{12}{16}$ $-\frac{8}{16}$
8. $\frac{4}{7}$ $+\frac{3}{7}$
9. $13\frac{4}{7}$ $-4\frac{2}{8}$
10. $8\frac{2}{7}$ $+3\frac{3}{7}$

11. 8 $-4\frac{2}{3}$
12. $\frac{8}{9}$ $+\frac{7}{9}$
13. $24\frac{7}{20}$ $+9\frac{3}{5}$
14. $16\frac{5}{9}$ $-5\frac{1}{3}$
15. $2\frac{3}{5}$ $+9\frac{4}{5}$

16. $\frac{1}{3} \times 24$
17. $\frac{2}{9} \times \frac{1}{3}$
18. $\frac{1}{2} \times \frac{1}{2}$
19. $\frac{1}{4} \times 16$
20. $\frac{3}{8} \times \frac{1}{3}$

21. 6.9 $+1.3$
22. 15.49 -5.08
23. 7.0 -3.6
24. 88.8 $+6.5$
25. 34.40 $+23.60$

26. 35 $\times 0.9$
27. 354 $\times 0.16$
28. 129 $\times 0.4$
29. 13 $\times 0.03$
30. 811 $\times 0.34$

Rosa took a short trip to the country. Use the information in this table to make a bar graph. Answer the questions about her trip.

31. How many kilometers did Rosa drive?

32. What is the average number of kilometers Rosa drove per hour?

Kilometers Driven in Five Hours

Hour	1	2	3	4	5
Number	45	30	20	35	40

33. Rosa stopped twice for gas and spent a total of $7.91. The first time she stopped she spent $5.49. How much did she spend the second time?

34. Rosa took a ferry across a bay. The distance around the bay is 102 kilometers. How many hours would it have taken Rosa to drive the distance at her average rate of speed?

Extra Practice

Set 1 For use after pages 3–9.
Add or subtract.

1. $\begin{array}{r} 5 \\ +2 \end{array}$	**2.** $\begin{array}{r} 8 \\ +1 \end{array}$	**3.** $\begin{array}{r} 10 \\ -\ 3 \end{array}$	**4.** $\begin{array}{r} 14 \\ -\ 9 \end{array}$	**5.** $\begin{array}{r} 6 \\ +6 \end{array}$	**6.** $\begin{array}{r} 5 \\ +0 \end{array}$
7. $\begin{array}{r} 11 \\ -\ 6 \end{array}$	**8.** $\begin{array}{r} 9 \\ +0 \end{array}$	**9.** $\begin{array}{r} 15 \\ -\ 7 \end{array}$	**10.** $\begin{array}{r} 7 \\ +3 \end{array}$	**11.** $\begin{array}{r} 3 \\ -1 \end{array}$	**12.** $\begin{array}{r} 8 \\ +6 \end{array}$

13. $5+1$ **14.** $7-0$ **15.** $8+9$ **16.** $2+6$ **17.** $11-3$ **18.** $10-5$

19. $6+7$ **20.** $9-8$ **21.** $4+0$ **22.** $7-2$ **23.** $14-7$ **24.** $3+9$

25. $7+3$ **26.** $18-9$ **27.** $5+6$ **28.** $4-0$ **29.** $9-4$ **30.** $8+8$

31. $5+5$ **32.** $8+0$ **33.** $4+7$ **34.** $16-8$ **35.** $10-4$ **36.** $8+5$

Set 2 For use after pages 10–14.
Add or subtract.

1. $4+1+7$ **2.** $6+2+3$ **3.** $8+2+9$ **4.** $9+0+5$

5. $2+5+6+1$ **6.** $4+6+1+9$ **7.** $9+8+1+5$ **8.** $6+8+3+2$

9. $\begin{array}{r} 46 \\ +21 \end{array}$	**10.** $\begin{array}{r} 53 \\ +25 \end{array}$	**11.** $\begin{array}{r} 67 \\ -30 \end{array}$	**12.** $\begin{array}{r} 99 \\ -45 \end{array}$	**13.** $\begin{array}{r} 126 \\ +\ 43 \end{array}$
14. $\begin{array}{r} 345 \\ +321 \end{array}$	**15.** $\begin{array}{r} 495 \\ -123 \end{array}$	**16.** $\begin{array}{r} 674 \\ -413 \end{array}$	**17.** $\begin{array}{r} 8723 \\ +1144 \end{array}$	**18.** $\begin{array}{r} 6342 \\ -3122 \end{array}$

Set 3 For use after pages 15–25.
Multiply or divide.

1. 2×3 **2.** 6×5 **3.** 10×8 **4.** 1×6 **5.** 4×7

6. 3×0 **7.** 7×7 **8.** $16\div2$ **9.** $15\div3$ **10.** $30\div6$

11. $24\div4$ **12.** $32\div8$ **13.** $35\div5$ **14.** $27\div3$ **15.** $18\div9$

16. $(4\times3)\div2$ **17.** $(10\div2)\times3$ **18.** $(20\div4)\times7$ **19.** $(24\div4)\times8$

20. $(5\times2)\div2$ **21.** $(6\times3)\div9$ **22.** $(18\div3)\times4$ **23.** $(4\times6)\div8$

Set 4   For use after pages 34–36.
Write the numbers.

1. seven thousand one hundred twenty   2. two hundred million

3. one million, three hundred forty-six thousand, four hundred seventeen

Write the words.

4. 37,500   5. 180,000   6. 347,000,000   7. 12,000,000

Write > or < to order the numbers.

8. 4000 ◯ 4500   9. 31,263 ◯ 31,927   10. 729,835 ◯ 729,419

11. 6034 ◯ 6043   12. 11,151 ◯ 11,511   13. 904,627 ◯ 940,672

14. 5983 ◯ 5893   15. 12,441 ◯ 12,440   16. 665,656 ◯ 664,645

Set 5   For use after pages 37–40.
Round to the nearest ten.

1. 31   2. 45   3. 59   4. 94   5. 86   6. 73

Round to the nearest hundred.

7. 901   8. 799   9. 835   10. 747   11. 666   12. 384

Round to the nearest thousand.

13. 4320   14. 6703   15. 1927   16. 5403   17. 8240   18. 6748

Set 6   For use after pages 45–47.
Write the numbers.

1. three and seven-hundredths   2. ten and three-tenths

Write the words.

3. 7.8   4. 19.6   5. 12.05   6. 6.24   7. 92.137

8. 1.324   9. 6.5   10. 11.91   11. 8.3   12. 14.65

Set 7 For use after pages 55–59.
Add.

1. 48 + 7	2. 63 + 8	3. 24 +19	4. 37 +37	5. 29 +13	6. 76 +38
7. 56 +73	8. 89 +42	9. 65 +75	10. 44 +36	11. 18 +23	12. 71 +36
13. 643 +291	14. 775 +132	15. 462 +297	16. 358 +171	17. 723 +184	18. 591 +385
19. 43 28 + 7	20. 35 29 + 8	21. 43 25 +18	22. 81 143 +232	23. 42 133 +291	24. 361 33 + 42
25. 25 13 9 +31	26. 37 8 23 +17	27. 10 15 45 +22	28. 142 20 31 +253	29. 83 351 12 +102	30. 151 52 345 + 61

Set 8 For use after pages 60–66.
Add.

1. 148 + 63	2. 247 + 95	3. 456 +179	4. 538 +199	5. 645 +387	6. 738 +153
7. 4673 +3849	8. 6245 +2872	9. 3827 +4385	10. 2195 +1843	11. 3147 +2351	12. 2165 +1999
13. 38 143 + 75	14. 173 48 + 54	15. 318 45 +163	16. 148 256 +193	17. 527 183 +234	18. 97 145 +368
19. 345 13 +631	20. 413 151 + 97	21. 63 248 + 84	22. 1243 45 + 612	23. 238 14 +1973	24. 2649 483 + 21
25. 67 176 +2348	26. 4617 381 + 45	27. 6325 163 +2478	28. 97 3418 + 132	29. 416 2385 +3147	30. 267 1591 +3285

Set 9   For use after pages 67–71.
Subtract.

1. 35 − 8	2. 42 − 7	3. 53 −27	4. 96 −48	5. 85 −39	6. 67 −48
7. 45 −18	8. 22 − 6	9. 67 −32	10. 84 −68	11. 34 −25	12. 94 −55
13. 437 − 62	14. 928 − 43	15. 465 −181	16. 357 −163	17. 265 −193	18. 837 −585
19. 425 −138	20. 613 −346	21. 938 −517	22. 737 −483	23. 324 −186	24. 731 −399

Set 10   For use after pages 72–77.
Subtract.

1. 300 −167	2. 420 −243	3. 703 −548	4. 800 −361	5. 530 −279	6. 900 −531
7. 650 −325	8. 801 −433	9. 210 −178	10. 3765 −1598	11. 9241 −3615	12. 5613 −2579
13. 6923 −4565	14. 4317 −1869	15. 5000 −2893	16. 6800 −3497	17. 7060 −2593	18. 8000 −2999

Set 11   For use after pages 78–83.
Add or subtract.

1. 129 + 38	2. 435 − 57	3. 561 −293	4. 418 +329	5. 700 −238	6. 406 −137
7. 294 +147	8. 6217 + 485	9. 9007 −4318	10. 4315 −1967	11. 2937 +4386	12. 1000 − 378
13. $6.92 + 1.35	14. $4.95 + 2.63	15. $3.47 − 1.35	16. $4.00 − 2.63	17. $7.29 + 3.45	18. $3.75 + 4.92
19. $7.85 − 4.87	20. $8.19 − 5.95	21. $1.25 + 7.99	22. $2.19 + 4.35	23. $4.49 − 2.75	24. $9.37 − 5.48

Set 12 For use after pages 89–93.
Multiply.

1. 32
   × 2

2. 21
   × 4

3. 24
   × 2

4. 61
   × 5

5. 92
   × 3

6. 31
   × 6

7. 43
   × 5

8. 62
   × 6

9. 94
   × 3

10. 35
    × 7

11. 63
    × 4

12. 44
    × 8

13. $2 \times 3 \times 7$
14. $4 \times 8 \times 2$
15. $5 \times 4 \times 3$
16. $9 \times 1 \times 7$
17. $2 \times 8 \times 3$

18. $4 \times 6 \times 3$
19. $7 \times 2 \times 3$
20. $8 \times 7 \times 1$
21. $4 \times 4 \times 4$
22. $7 \times 6 \times 5$

23. $6 \times 2 \times 5$
24. $4 \times 1 \times 8$
25. $5 \times 5 \times 2$
26. $3 \times 2 \times 1$
27. $6 \times 4 \times 2$

Set 13 For use after pages 94–97.
Multiply.

1. 402
   × 3

2. 612
   × 2

3. 322
   × 4

4. 503
   × 2

5. 611
   × 7

6. 823
   × 3

7. 324
   × 3

8. 435
   × 6

9. 718
   × 2

10. 539
    × 4

11. 647
    × 8

12. 423
    × 4

13. 562
    × 3

14. 861
    × 9

15. 735
    × 2

16. 943
    × 5

17. 627
    × 4

18. 398
    × 7

19. 479×3
20. 724×5
21. 598×2
22. 387×7
23. 643×8

24. 323×6
25. 489×2
26. 669×2
27. 282×9
28. 416×5

Set 14 For use after pages 98–101.
Multiply.

1. 2413
   × 2

2. 3245
   × 6

3. 4176
   × 9

4. 5008
   × 7

5. 7041
   × 3

6. $3.17
   × 2

7. $5.24
   × 7

8. $6.08
   × 3

9. $13.27
   × 4

10. $23.18
    × 6

11. 3124
    × 2

12. 2122
    × 4

13. 2675
    × 9

14. 5148
    × 2

15. 3819
    × 5

Set 15 For use after pages 102–104.
Multiply.

1. 30 × 6	2. 4000 × 9	3. 600 × 6	4. 3000 × 8	5. 50 × 7	6. 900 × 4
7. 400 × 30	8. 70 ×70	9. 80 ×20	10. 900 × 60	11. 400 × 80	12. 60 ×90
13. 12 ×60	14. 53 ×200	15. 82 ×40	16. 65 ×3000	17. 76 ×900	18. 43 ×7000

Set 16 For use after pages 105–111.
Multiply.

1. 43 ×15	2. 68 ×12	3. 49 ×17	4. 37 ×18	5. 51 ×19	6. 27 ×16
7. 92 ×43	8. 45 ×27	9. 52 ×38	10. 84 ×46	11. 41 ×35	12. 38 ×29
13. 30 ×19	14. 400 × 7	15. 2000 × 73	16. 30 ×41	17. 500 × 57	18. 3000 × 34

19. 26×26 20. 49×49 21. 11×11 22. 13×13 23. 32×32

24. 47×23 25. 72×19 26. 87×42 27. 53×32 28. 94×85

29. 65×13 30. 41×83 31. 12×33 32. 48×12 33. 51×61

Set 17 For use after pages 112–115.
Multiply.

1. 123 × 41	2. 625 × 13	3. 908 × 27	4. 320 × 46	5. 713 × 52	6. 238 × 19
7. 826 × 37	8. 418 × 72	9. 609 × 23	10. 267 × 93	11. 580 × 64	12. 307 × 43
13. 461 × 92	14. 173 × 47	15. 368 × 56	16. 257 × 83	17. 729 × 27	18. 296 × 74

Set 18   For use after pages 121–123.
Divide.

1. $3\overline{)17}$ 2. $4\overline{)37}$ 3. $2\overline{)17}$ 4. $4\overline{)21}$ 5. $3\overline{)28}$ 6. $9\overline{)47}$

7. $4\overline{)22}$ 8. $8\overline{)19}$ 9. $2\overline{)13}$ 10. $7\overline{)19}$ 11. $5\overline{)42}$ 12. $3\overline{)13}$

13. $6\overline{)40}$ 14. $8\overline{)35}$ 15. $7\overline{)50}$ 16. $9\overline{)39}$ 17. $5\overline{)38}$ 18. $6\overline{)27}$

19. $5\overline{)49}$ 20. $9\overline{)13}$ 21. $6\overline{)15}$ 22. $7\overline{)25}$ 23. $4\overline{)38}$ 24. $8\overline{)67}$

25. $7\overline{)53}$ 26. $8\overline{)65}$ 27. $4\overline{)25}$ 28. $6\overline{)37}$ 29. $9\overline{)80}$ 30. $8\overline{)71}$

Set 19   For use after pages 124–128.
Divide.

1. $2\overline{)54}$ 2. $3\overline{)72}$ 3. $7\overline{)91}$ 4. $6\overline{)66}$ 5. $5\overline{)75}$ 6. $4\overline{)68}$

7. $6\overline{)72}$ 8. $5\overline{)95}$ 9. $8\overline{)96}$ 10. $7\overline{)84}$ 11. $3\overline{)93}$ 12. $2\overline{)78}$

13. $3\overline{)88}$ 14. $5\overline{)64}$ 15. $7\overline{)88}$ 16. $6\overline{)94}$ 17. $4\overline{)93}$ 18. $2\overline{)43}$

19. $8\overline{)64}$ 20. $3\overline{)19}$ 21. $4\overline{)88}$ 22. $9\overline{)95}$ 23. $6\overline{)79}$ 24. $5\overline{)63}$

25. $48 \div 4$ 26. $69 \div 3$ 27. $98 \div 7$ 28. $85 \div 5$ 29. $78 \div 6$

30. $83 \div 6$ 31. $97 \div 7$ 32. $25 \div 2$ 33. $47 \div 3$ 34. $77 \div 5$

Set 20   For use after pages 129–135.
Divide.

1. $2\overline{)364}$ 2. $3\overline{)933}$ 3. $4\overline{)848}$ 4. $2\overline{)682}$ 5. $3\overline{)693}$ 6. $5\overline{)765}$

7. $5\overline{)724}$ 8. $4\overline{)741}$ 9. $3\overline{)533}$ 10. $7\overline{)924}$ 11. $8\overline{)946}$ 12. $6\overline{)863}$

13. $7\overline{)365}$ 14. $9\overline{)843}$ 15. $6\overline{)437}$ 16. $4\overline{)225}$ 17. $5\overline{)413}$ 18. $8\overline{)517}$

19. $3\overline{)644}$ 20. $7\overline{)729}$ 21. $6\overline{)969}$ 22. $4\overline{)851}$ 23. $5\overline{)567}$ 24. $3\overline{)929}$

25. $5\overline{)136}$ 26. $3\overline{)217}$ 27. $4\overline{)239}$ 28. $9\overline{)875}$ 29. $7\overline{)538}$ 30. $6\overline{)473}$

Set 21 For use after pages 136–139.
Divide.

1. $3\overline{)7327}$ 2. $4\overline{)9318}$ 3. $2\overline{)6245}$ 4. $5\overline{)8723}$ 5. $6\overline{)9649}$

6. $7\overline{)3621}$ 7. $4\overline{)1947}$ 8. $6\overline{)3842}$ 9. $8\overline{)5625}$ 10. $5\overline{)2673}$

11. $4\overline{)\$5.48}$ 12. $3\overline{)\$9.63}$ 13. $5\overline{)\$15.75}$ 14. $8\overline{)\$26.48}$ 15. $6\overline{)\$55.26}$

16. $4318 \div 3$ 17. $9731 \div 5$ 18. $6248 \div 4$ 19. $8453 \div 2$ 20. $7925 \div 6$

21. $6215 \div 8$ 22. $2951 \div 7$ 23. $4987 \div 9$ 24. $1743 \div 5$ 25. $3811 \div 6$

26. $6348 \div 5$ 27. $8471 \div 7$ 28. $3945 \div 2$ 29. $2546 \div 3$ 30. $9406 \div 6$

31. $4859 \div 3$ 32. $6432 \div 8$ 33. $2823 \div 3$ 34. $9162 \div 9$ 35. $7767 \div 6$

Set 22 For use after pages 140–141.
Find the averages.

1. 27, 33, 45, 54, 31

2. 11, 32, 73, 55, 64

3. 147, 200, 353, 425, 680

4. 361, 280, 432, 303, 294

5. 126, 720, 96, 87, 111, 210

6. 304, 200, 186, 324, 500, 202

7. 38, 19, 67, 45, 33, 26, 17

8. 101, 97, 245, 83, 91, 238, 223

Set 23 For use after pages 142–145.
Divide. Use short division.

1. $3\overline{)28}$ 2. $2\overline{)47}$ 3. $4\overline{)53}$ 4. $6\overline{)86}$ 5. $5\overline{)67}$

6. $4\overline{)725}$ 7. $7\overline{)923}$ 8. $5\overline{)846}$ 9. $3\overline{)674}$ 10. $8\overline{)972}$

11. $6\overline{)857}$ 12. $2\overline{)539}$ 13. $3\overline{)751}$ 14. $4\overline{)973}$ 15. $5\overline{)738}$

16. $3\overline{)629}$ 17. $7\overline{)721}$ 18. $4\overline{)6413}$ 19. $2\overline{)4037}$ 20. $8\overline{)9609}$

21. $45 \div 2$ 22. $68 \div 3$ 23. $93 \div 8$ 24. $57 \div 4$ 25. $86 \div 3$

26. $446 \div 3$ 27. $928 \div 5$ 28. $673 \div 4$ 29. $875 \div 6$ 30. $749 \div 4$

31. $4978 \div 3$ 32. $4827 \div 4$ 33. $9328 \div 3$ 34. $8875 \div 7$ 35. $8563 \div 6$

Set 24 For use after pages 151–157.

Answer the questions about each problem.

1. There are 127 cars and 48 bicycles in the parking lot. How many more cars are there?
   a. What are the important facts?
   b. Will you add, subtract, multiply, or divide?
   c. Solve the problem.

2. 392 people ride to school in carpools. There are 4 people in each car. How many cars are there?
   a. What are the important facts?
   b. Will you add, subtract, multiply, or divide?
   c. Solve the problem.

3. A grocery store sells whole wheat bread for $0.83 a loaf and raisin bread for $0.91 a loaf. How much do 3 loaves of whole wheat bread cost?
   a. What information is not needed?
   b. Solve the problem.

4. Jerry buys 6 more bottles of orange juice than Louis buys. How many bottles of orange juice does Louis buy?
   a. What do you need to know before you can solve the problem?

Set 25 For use after pages 158–165.

Use two steps to solve each problem.

1. Maria buys 3 records for $4.95 each and gives the clerk $20. What is her change?

2. Janice buys 2 records for $3.95 each and an album for $10.95. How much does she spend in all?

3. Randy buys 4 magazines for $0.75 each and gives the clerk $5. What is his change?

4. Anne buys 3 books for $2.95 each and a magazine for $1.25. How much does she spend in all?

5. Jill and Rick earn $2.75 an hour for washing cars. One day they spend 4 hours washing cars. If they divide their earnings equally, how much does each earn?

6. A family of 5 people picks about 2 kilograms of tomatoes from each of their 10 tomato plants. If they divide the tomatoes equally, how many kilograms does each get?

Make a diagram to help solve each problem.

7. Two trains leave a station going in opposite directions. After one train has gone 20 kilometers and the other has gone 18 kilometers, how far apart are the trains?

8. An elevator leaves the 19th floor and goes up 10 floors, down 3 floors, up 5 floors, and then down 12 floors. On what floor does it stop?

Set 26 For use after pages 171–178.

Use the quadrilateral to find the answers.

1. Name each angle.

2. Tell whether each angle is **right,**
   acute, or **obtuse.**

3. Name a pair of parallel line segments.

4. Name a pair of perpendicular line segments.

5. Write a name for the quadrilateral.

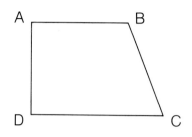

Set 27 For use after pages 179–183.

Use this circle to find the answers.

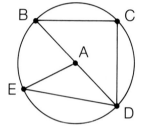

1. Name the center.   2. Name three radii.

3. Name two chords.   4. Name a diameter.

Tell whether each pair of shapes is similar, congruent, or both.

5.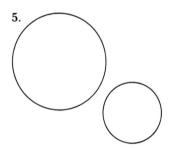

6.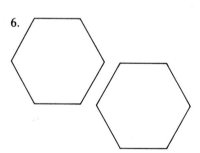

7.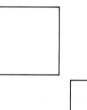

Set 28 For use after pages 186–187.

Use this solid shape to find the answers.

1. How many edges does it have?

2. How many faces does it have?

3. How many vertices does it have?

4. Write a name for the shape.

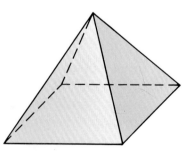

Set 29   For use after pages 193–194.
Write a fraction for each.

1. one-third   2. two-fifths   3. three-eighths   4. seven-tenths

Set 30   For use after pages 197–204.
Copy and complete.

1. $\frac{1}{2} = \frac{?}{10}$ 2. $\frac{3}{5} = \frac{?}{15}$ 3. $\frac{7}{10} = \frac{?}{100}$ 4. $\frac{5}{8} = \frac{?}{32}$ 5. $\frac{1}{6} = \frac{?}{18}$

6. $\frac{3}{21} = \frac{?}{7}$ 7. $\frac{12}{18} = \frac{?}{3}$ 8. $\frac{20}{36} = \frac{?}{9}$ 9. $\frac{7}{28} = \frac{?}{4}$ 10. $\frac{20}{25} = \frac{?}{5}$

Write each fraction in simplest form.

11. $\frac{8}{24}$ 12. $\frac{3}{15}$ 13. $\frac{4}{2}$ 14. $\frac{70}{90}$ 15. $\frac{9}{9}$ 16. $\frac{10}{25}$

17. $\frac{48}{8}$ 18. $\frac{7}{21}$ 19. $\frac{9}{15}$ 20. $\frac{12}{28}$ 21. $\frac{24}{6}$ 22. $\frac{60}{80}$

Write > or < to order the fractions.

23. $\frac{1}{3} \bigcirc \frac{2}{3}$ 24. $\frac{7}{12} \bigcirc \frac{5}{12}$ 25. $\frac{1}{4} \bigcirc \frac{1}{2}$ 26. $\frac{2}{5} \bigcirc \frac{2}{9}$

Set 31   For use after pages 205–209.
Change each fraction to a whole number or a mixed number.

1. $\frac{7}{3}$ 2. $\frac{5}{2}$ 3. $\frac{8}{5}$ 4. $\frac{10}{3}$ 5. $\frac{8}{2}$ 6. $\frac{10}{5}$

7. $\frac{12}{7}$ 8. $\frac{9}{4}$ 9. $\frac{10}{10}$ 10. $\frac{15}{3}$ 11. $\frac{16}{11}$ 12. $\frac{12}{5}$

Change each mixed number to a fraction.

13. $2\frac{1}{3}$ 14. $4\frac{1}{5}$ 15. $3\frac{2}{3}$ 16. $1\frac{3}{4}$ 17. $2\frac{3}{10}$ 18. $3\frac{5}{8}$

19. $6\frac{1}{7}$ 20. $2\frac{1}{2}$ 21. $1\frac{5}{6}$ 22. $2\frac{5}{12}$ 23. $3\frac{2}{7}$ 24. $4\frac{9}{10}$

Set 32 For use after pages 212–214.
Write each ratio as a fraction.

1. 3 cats to 5 kittens
2. 6 robins to 10 sparrows
3. 4 tigers to 1 lion

Complete the equal ratios to write a proportion.

4. $\frac{4}{9} = \frac{?}{27}$
5. $\frac{3}{10} = \frac{?}{100}$
6. $\frac{3}{5} = \frac{?}{20}$
7. $\frac{7}{8} = \frac{?}{16}$
8. $\frac{5}{6} = \frac{?}{18}$

9. $\frac{1}{2} = \frac{?}{10}$
10. $\frac{2}{25} = \frac{?}{100}$
11. $\frac{1}{8} = \frac{?}{24}$
12. $\frac{2}{9} = \frac{?}{18}$
13. $\frac{1}{4} = \frac{?}{16}$

Set 33 For use after pages 217–218.
Write a decimal for each.

1. $\frac{3}{10}$
2. $\frac{9}{10}$
3. $\frac{13}{100}$
4. $\frac{27}{100}$
5. $\frac{125}{1000}$
6. $\frac{8}{1000}$

7. $1\frac{1}{10}$
8. $3\frac{7}{10}$
9. $2\frac{17}{100}$
10. $5\frac{95}{100}$
11. $4\frac{297}{1000}$
12. $3\frac{17}{1000}$

Write a fraction or mixed number for each.

13. 0.4
14. 0.7
15. 0.03
16. 0.11
17. 0.238
18. 0.009
19. 2.6
20. 1.8
21. 1.21
22. 1.09
23. 2.475
24. 2.031
25. 6.3
26. 4.2
27. 6.38
28. 0.31
29. 5.624
30. 0.038

Set 34 For use after pages 219–223.
Write > or < to order the decimals.

1. 2.8 ◯ 2.7
2. 4.23 ◯ 4.27
3. 0.571 ◯ 0.576
4. 6.1 ◯ 6.7
5. 1.1 ◯ 1.0
6. 2.65 ◯ 2.56
7. 0.314 ◯ 0.431
8. 5.8 ◯ 5.9

Round to the nearest tenth.

9. 1.78
10. 2.13
11. 4.24
12. 6.37
13. 4.55

Round to the nearest hundredth.

14. 1.329
15. 2.041
16. 0.975
17. 1.626
18. 3.142

Set 35   For use after pages 229–233.

Copy and complete.

1. 5 m = ⬚ cm
2. 600 cm = ⬚ m
3. 11 m = ⬚ cm
4. 1700 cm = ⬚ m
5. 7 dm = ⬚ cm
6. 40 cm = ⬚ dm
7. 50 mm = ⬚ cm
8. 1 cm = ⬚ mm
9. 9 cm = ⬚ mm
10. 40 mm = ⬚ cm
11. 2 km = ⬚ m
12. 1000 m = ⬚ km
13. 2 cm = ⬚ mm
14. 9 m = ⬚ cm
15. 3 dm = ⬚ cm

Set 36   For use after pages 234–242.

Find the perimeter and area of each shape.

1.
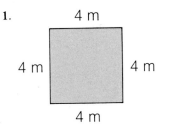
4 m
4 m
4 m
4 m

2.
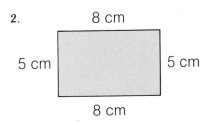
8 cm
5 cm
5 cm
8 cm

3. A rectangle with a length of 40 centimeters and a width of 15 centimeters.

4. A rectangle with a length of 16 millimeters and a width of 12 millimeters.

Find the volume of each box.

5. A box with a length of 4 meters, a width of 2 meters, and a height of 1 meter.

6. A box with a length of 10 meters, a width of 5 meters, and a height of 4 meters.

Set 37   For use after pages 243–247.

Copy and complete.

1. 7 ℓ = ⬚ ml
2. 1 ℓ = ⬚ ml
3. 9 ℓ = ⬚ ml
4. 2000 ml = ⬚ ℓ
5. 6000 ml = ⬚ ℓ
6. 4000 ml = ⬚ ℓ
7. 4 kg = ⬚ g
8. 7 kg = ⬚ g
9. 9 kg = ⬚ g
10. 5000 g = ⬚ kg
11. 1000 g = ⬚ kg
12. 6000 g = ⬚ kg
13. 3000 g = ⬚ kg
14. 7000 g = ⬚ kg
15. 4000 g = ⬚ kg

Set 38 For use after pages 248–251.
Copy and complete.

1. 3 ft = ⬚ in.
2. 5 ft = ⬚ in.
3. 2 yd = ⬚ ft
4. 10 yd = ⬚ ft
5. 1 yd = ⬚ in.
6. 4 yd = ⬚ in.
7. 3 yd = ⬚ ft
8. 6 ft = ⬚ in.
9. 4 ft = ⬚ in.
10. 7 ft = ⬚ in.
11. 9 ft = ⬚ yd
12. 2 ft = ⬚ in.

Solve the problems.

13. A playground is 50 yards long and 25 yards wide. What is the area of the playground?

14. A box is 4 feet long, 3 feet wide, and 2 feet high. What is the volume of the box?

Set 39 For use after pages 252–255.
Copy and complete.

1. 6 pt = ⬚ cups
2. 15 pt = ⬚ cups
3. 5 qt = ⬚ pt
4. 19 qt = ⬚ pt
5. 4 qt = ⬚ cups
6. 10 qt = ⬚ cups
7. 32 cups = ⬚ gal
8. 8 qt = ⬚ gal
9. 16 pt = ⬚ gal
10. 6 lb = ⬚ oz
11. 20 lb = ⬚ oz
12. 3 T = ⬚ lb

Set 40 For use after pages 256–257.
Copy and complete.

1. 4 h = ⬚ min
2. 3 min = ⬚ s
3. 3 wk = ⬚ d
4. 5 yr = ⬚ wk
5. 240 min = ⬚ h
6. 600 s = ⬚ min
7. 2 min = ⬚ s
8. 3 yr = ⬚ wk
9. 7 hr = ⬚ min
10. 4 wk = ⬚ d
11. 120 min = ⬚ h
12. 7 yr = ⬚ wk

Solve the problems.

13. Kelly leaves home at 8:05 A.M. and arrives at school at 8:23 A.M. How long does it take her to get to school?

14. Marvin leaves school at 3:51 P.M. and arrives at home at 4:26 P.M. How long does it take him to get home?

Set 41 For use after pages 265–268.
Divide.

1. $30\overline{)97}$ 2. $20\overline{)71}$ 3. $10\overline{)38}$ 4. $50\overline{)85}$ 5. $40\overline{)92}$

6. $60\overline{)827}$ 7. $30\overline{)735}$ 8. $10\overline{)153}$ 9. $40\overline{)861}$ 10. $50\overline{)945}$

11. $70\overline{)8271}$ 12. $20\overline{)3729}$ 13. $60\overline{)8126}$ 14. $50\overline{)7583}$ 15. $40\overline{)3362}$

Set 42 For use after pages 269–271.
Divide.

1. $20\overline{)136}$ 2. $60\overline{)437}$ 3. $80\overline{)645}$ 4. $30\overline{)158}$ 5. $40\overline{)259}$

6. $50\overline{)3291}$ 7. $20\overline{)1372}$ 8. $90\overline{)4618}$ 9. $70\overline{)6485}$ 10. $80\overline{)7468}$

11. $798 \div 90$ 12. $387 \div 50$ 13. $2743 \div 30$ 14. $4896 \div 60$ 15. $1734 \div 20$

16. $273 \div 80$ 17. $461 \div 90$ 18. $6103 \div 70$ 19. $2897 \div 30$ 20. $2519 \div 40$

Set 43 For use after pages 272–276.
Divide.

1. $23\overline{)97}$ 2. $19\overline{)62}$ 3. $35\overline{)86}$ 4. $29\overline{)91}$ 5. $43\overline{)89}$

6. $14\overline{)457}$ 7. $21\overline{)653}$ 8. $38\overline{)419}$ 9. $27\overline{)948}$ 10. $41\overline{)635}$

11. $23\overline{)812}$ 12. $43\overline{)845}$ 13. $13\overline{)678}$ 14. $32\overline{)951}$ 15. $25\overline{)672}$

16. $8291 \div 34$ 17. $6372 \div 51$ 18. $4318 \div 29$ 19. $8765 \div 19$ 20. $4344 \div 21$

Set 44 For use after pages 277–281.
Divide.

1. $18\overline{)167}$ 2. $21\overline{)193}$ 3. $47\overline{)331}$ 4. $36\overline{)276}$ 5. $42\overline{)289}$

6. $33\overline{)2179}$ 7. $45\overline{)3827}$ 8. $62\overline{)2388}$ 9. $23\overline{)1875}$ 10. $92\overline{)8437}$

11. $12\overline{)\$16.92}$ 12. $23\overline{)\$93.38}$ 13. $41\overline{)\$16.81}$ 14. $37\overline{)\$11.47}$ 15. $72\overline{)\$32.40}$

Set 45 For use after pages 293–296.

Add or subtract. Write each answer in simplest form.

1. $\frac{1}{7} + \frac{3}{7}$ 2. $\frac{7}{9} - \frac{4}{9}$ 3. $\frac{4}{11} + \frac{5}{11}$ 4. $\frac{11}{12} - \frac{6}{12}$ 5. $\frac{3}{10} + \frac{6}{10}$

6. $\frac{9}{10} - \frac{8}{10}$ 7. $\frac{1}{4} + \frac{1}{4}$ 8. $\frac{7}{8} - \frac{3}{8}$ 9. $\frac{5}{8} + \frac{3}{8}$ 10. $\frac{8}{15} - \frac{2}{15}$

11. $1\frac{1}{7}$ 12. $4\frac{5}{9}$ 13. $6\frac{1}{3}$ 14. $5\frac{9}{10}$ 15. $3\frac{1}{6}$ 16. $4\frac{2}{3}$
$+2\frac{3}{7}$ $-1\frac{1}{9}$ $+4\frac{1}{3}$ $-2\frac{6}{10}$ $+1\frac{1}{6}$ $+2\frac{1}{3}$

17. $8\frac{7}{12}$ 18. $2\frac{3}{4}$ 19. $3\frac{1}{3}$ 20. $3\frac{1}{8}$ 21. 7 22. 9
$-3\frac{5}{12}$ $+2\frac{1}{4}$ $-1\frac{2}{3}$ $+2\frac{5}{8}$ $-3\frac{5}{6}$ $-3\frac{1}{5}$

Set 46 For use after pages 297–299.

Find a common denominator for each pair of fractions.

1. $\frac{1}{4}$ and $\frac{1}{2}$ 2. $\frac{3}{8}$ and $\frac{1}{4}$ 3. $\frac{1}{5}$ and $\frac{4}{15}$ 4. $\frac{6}{7}$ and $\frac{11}{14}$ 5. $\frac{3}{5}$ and $\frac{1}{10}$

6. $\frac{5}{6}$ and $\frac{7}{12}$ 7. $\frac{3}{10}$ and $\frac{11}{100}$ 8. $\frac{4}{9}$ and $\frac{1}{3}$ 9. $\frac{1}{6}$ and $\frac{1}{5}$ 10. $\frac{1}{3}$ and $\frac{1}{2}$

11. $\frac{2}{5}$ and $\frac{1}{4}$ 12. $\frac{3}{5}$ and $\frac{2}{3}$ 13. $\frac{7}{10}$ and $\frac{2}{7}$ 14. $\frac{2}{3}$ and $\frac{7}{8}$ 15. $\frac{2}{5}$ and $\frac{3}{7}$

Set 47 For use after pages 300–303.

Add or subtract. Write each answer in simplest form.

1. $\frac{5}{8} + \frac{1}{4}$ 2. $\frac{7}{9} - \frac{1}{3}$ 3. $\frac{3}{10} + \frac{3}{5}$ 4. $\frac{7}{12} - \frac{1}{6}$ 5. $\frac{8}{15} + \frac{1}{3}$

6. $\frac{5}{6} - \frac{1}{5}$ 7. $\frac{1}{2} + \frac{2}{3}$ 8. $\frac{7}{8} - \frac{1}{5}$ 9. $\frac{6}{7} + \frac{1}{4}$ 10. $\frac{9}{10} - \frac{3}{4}$

11. $1\frac{1}{2}$ 12. $3\frac{2}{3}$ 13. $4\frac{1}{8}$ 14. $5\frac{9}{10}$ 15. $3\frac{8}{15}$ 16. $4\frac{1}{12}$
$+2\frac{1}{4}$ $-1\frac{1}{6}$ $+2\frac{1}{4}$ $-2\frac{2}{5}$ $+1\frac{1}{5}$ $+2\frac{5}{6}$

Set 48 For use after pages 304–307.
Multiply. Write each answer in simplest form.

1. $\frac{2}{3} \times \frac{4}{5}$ 2. $\frac{6}{7} \times \frac{1}{5}$ 3. $\frac{5}{8} \times \frac{1}{2}$ 4. $\frac{1}{7} \times \frac{2}{3}$ 5. $\frac{1}{10} \times \frac{1}{2}$

6. $\frac{3}{4} \times \frac{2}{3}$ 7. $\frac{5}{6} \times \frac{3}{4}$ 8. $\frac{7}{8} \times \frac{2}{7}$ 9. $\frac{3}{10} \times \frac{2}{3}$ 10. $\frac{4}{9} \times \frac{3}{5}$

11. $\frac{3}{5} \times \frac{5}{6}$ 12. $\frac{5}{7} \times \frac{3}{10}$ 13. $\frac{2}{9} \times \frac{4}{5}$ 14. $\frac{1}{6} \times \frac{3}{4}$ 15. $\frac{7}{9} \times \frac{3}{4}$

16. $4 \times \frac{5}{6}$ 17. $2 \times \frac{7}{8}$ 18. $\frac{5}{6} \times 8$ 19. $\frac{3}{8} \times 12$ 20. $\frac{7}{10} \times 5$

21. $\frac{1}{2} \times 10$ 22. $\frac{1}{6} \times 12$ 23. $\frac{1}{9} \times 18$ 24. $\frac{1}{5} \times 25$ 25. $\frac{1}{3} \times 15$

Set 49 For use after pages 308–314.
Add or subtract.

1. $\begin{array}{r} 1.27 \\ +2.41 \\ \hline \end{array}$ 2. $\begin{array}{r} 3.68 \\ -1.35 \\ \hline \end{array}$ 3. $\begin{array}{r} 6.24 \\ +2.95 \\ \hline \end{array}$ 4. $\begin{array}{r} 8.75 \\ -3.89 \\ \hline \end{array}$ 5. $\begin{array}{r} 4.22 \\ +3.75 \\ \hline \end{array}$ 6. $\begin{array}{r} 5.91 \\ +2.48 \\ \hline \end{array}$

7. $\begin{array}{r} 4.71 \\ -2.6 \\ \hline \end{array}$ 8. $\begin{array}{r} 5.63 \\ +2.795 \\ \hline \end{array}$ 9. $\begin{array}{r} 7.8 \\ -3.69 \\ \hline \end{array}$ 10. $\begin{array}{r} 3.751 \\ +9.83 \\ \hline \end{array}$ 11. $\begin{array}{r} 8.327 \\ -5.49 \\ \hline \end{array}$ 12. $\begin{array}{r} 2.6 \\ -0.975 \\ \hline \end{array}$

13. $\begin{array}{r} \$7.25 \\ +\ 1.31 \\ \hline \end{array}$ 14. $\begin{array}{r} \$9.03 \\ -\ 4.32 \\ \hline \end{array}$ 15. $\begin{array}{r} \$6.75 \\ +\ 1.38 \\ \hline \end{array}$ 16. $\begin{array}{r} \$8.34 \\ -\ 2.25 \\ \hline \end{array}$ 17. $\begin{array}{r} \$6.29 \\ +\ 2.91 \\ \hline \end{array}$ 18. $\begin{array}{r} \$9.51 \\ -\ 4.63 \\ \hline \end{array}$

Set 50 For use after pages 315–317.
Multiply.

1. $\begin{array}{r} 2.8 \\ \times\ 9 \\ \hline \end{array}$ 2. $\begin{array}{r} 1.5 \\ \times\ 7 \\ \hline \end{array}$ 3. $\begin{array}{r} 0.6 \\ \times\ 4 \\ \hline \end{array}$ 4. $\begin{array}{r} 3.1 \\ \times\ 5 \\ \hline \end{array}$ 5. $\begin{array}{r} 0.7 \\ \times\ 8 \\ \hline \end{array}$ 6. $\begin{array}{r} 9.3 \\ \times\ 2 \\ \hline \end{array}$

7. $\begin{array}{r} 1.25 \\ \times\ 3 \\ \hline \end{array}$ 8. $\begin{array}{r} 2.08 \\ \times\ 4 \\ \hline \end{array}$ 9. $\begin{array}{r} 8.71 \\ \times\ 9 \\ \hline \end{array}$ 10. $\begin{array}{r} 0.37 \\ \times\ 6 \\ \hline \end{array}$ 11. $\begin{array}{r} 0.41 \\ \times\ 2 \\ \hline \end{array}$ 12. $\begin{array}{r} 2.73 \\ \times\ 8 \\ \hline \end{array}$

13. $\begin{array}{r} \$1.75 \\ \times\ 3 \\ \hline \end{array}$ 14. $\begin{array}{r} \$4.68 \\ \times\ 7 \\ \hline \end{array}$ 15. $\begin{array}{r} \$3.01 \\ \times\ 5 \\ \hline \end{array}$ 16. $\begin{array}{r} \$7.29 \\ \times\ 6 \\ \hline \end{array}$ 17. $\begin{array}{r} \$5.23 \\ \times\ 6 \\ \hline \end{array}$ 18. $\begin{array}{r} \$9.27 \\ \times\ 8 \\ \hline \end{array}$

Set 51   For use after pages 323–325.

Make a horizontal bar graph using the information in each table.

1. Number of Bicycles Sold

Day	Mon.	Tues.	Wed.	Thurs.	Fri.
Number	3	1	4	7	9

2. Number of Field Trips in One Year

Grade	3	4	5	6
Number	5	3	6	7

Set 52   For use after pages 326–329.

Use the graph to answer the questions.   **Find the ordered pair that names each point.**

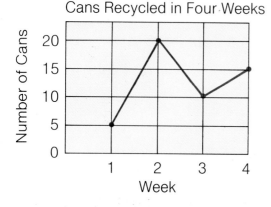

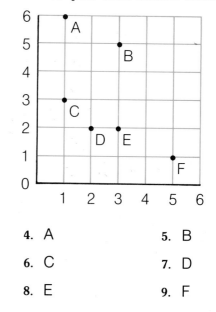

1. How many cans were recycled in the first week?

2. How many cans were recycled in the fourth week?

3. How many cans were recycled in all?

4. A   5. B

6. C   7. D

8. E   9. F

Set 53   For use after pages 330–331.

There are 10 apples in a bag. 5 are red, 3 are green, and 2 are yellow. Use this information to find the answers.

1. How many outcomes are possible if you pick an apple without looking?

2. What is the probability of picking a red apple?

3. What is the probability of picking a green apple?

4. What is the probability of picking an apple that is not yellow?

5. What is the probability of picking an apple that is red or green?

6. What is the probability of picking an apple that is green or yellow?

Enrichment

Set 1 For use after page 14.

The ⬚ in each problem stands for the same digit. Find the digit.

1.
```
  4⬚56
 −⬚01⬚
 ─────
  1⬚4⬚
```

2.
```
  34⬚⬚
 +⬚⬚00
 ─────
  78⬚⬚
```

3.
```
  80⬚2
 +1⬚44
 ─────
  9⬚96
```

4.
```
  899⬚
 −⬚340
 ─────
  2⬚5⬚
```

5.
```
  9⬚⬚5
 −⬚1⬚2
 ─────
  1703
```

Set 2 For use after page 22.

Solve each problem. What do you find?

1a. $(6+4)\div 2$
 b. $(6\div 2)+(4\div 2)$

2a. $2\times(8-4)$
 b. $(2\times 8)-(2\times 4)$

3a. $2\times(3+4)$
 b. $(2\times 3)+(2\times 4)$

4a. $(10-6)\div 2$
 b. $(10\div 2)-(6\div 2)$

5a. $3\times(3+5)$
 b. $(3\times 3)+(3\times 5)$

6a. $(15-6)\div 3$
 b. $(15\div 3)-(6\div 3)$

Set 3 For use after page 33.

1. Write the number that is 6000 less than 56,434.

2. Write the number that is 20,000 less than 751,782.

3. Write the number that is 3000 greater than 435,861.

4. Write the number that is 300,000 less than 552,689.

5. Write the number that is 500 less than 641,608.

6. Write the number that is 200,000 greater than 79,347.

7. Write the number that is 40,000 greater than 200,042.

8. Write the number that is 600,000 less than 963,444.

Set 4 For use after page 36.

1. When you are counting by ten thousands, what number comes next after 1,260,000?

2. When you are counting by hundred thousands, what number comes next after 900,000?

3. When you are counting by ten thousands, what number comes before 2,470,000?

4. When you are counting by hundred thousands, what number comes before 1,900,000?

Set 5   For use after page 40.

In a magic square, the sum of each row, column, and diagonal is the same. In this magic square, all the sums are 15.

2	7	6
9	5	1
4	3	8

1. Round each number to the nearest ten. Is the result a magic square?

423	657	629
784	572	355
511	479	718

2. Round each number to the nearest hundred. Is the result a magic square?

4389	7867	9289
11,648	7468	1972
4761	5986	10,439

Set 6   For use after page 59.
Write in a column. Add.

1. $327 + 211 + 36 + 112 + 7 + 512$

2. $20 + 631 + 162 + 370 + 421 + 3$

3. $504 + 301 + 26 + 102 + 9 + 217$

4. $42 + 63 + 420 + 111 + 1 + 230$

Set 7   For use after page 63.
Write in a column. Add.

1. $476,928 + 231,987 + 726,142 + 7624$

2. $9060 + 421 + 86 + 83,954 + 408,103$

3. $238,761 + 81,932 + 3672 + 10,768$

4. $340,019 + 76 + 8 + 93,677 + 2625$

5. $29 + 37,762 + 1738 + 129,376 + 2077$

6. $163 + 70,829 + 4326 + 6 + 1955$

Set 8   For use after page 68.
Copy and complete these magic squares.

1.

52	72	
80		
60		

2.

		83
	78	
73		86

3.

	41	52
		31
		49

Set 9 For use after page 71.

Find the pattern. Write the next two numbers.

1. 834, 646, 458

2. 813, 716, 619

3. 942, 853, 764

4. 637, 534, 431

5. 759, 625, 491

6. 957, 744, 531

Set 10 For use after page 77.

In one week a new bookstore bought and sold the number of books shown in the table. Estimate how many books were left at the end of the week. Then find the exact amount.

1.

	Mon.	Tues.	Wed.	Thurs.	Fri.
Bought	5340			7729	
Sold	572	1625	1750	1228	1153

Set 11 For use after page 83.

Estimate each answer. Then find the exact sum or difference.

1. $159.60
   213.40
   + 302.81

2. $2130.27
   − 1470.32

3. $6.75
   5.05
   + 3.71

4. $567.80
   − 328.40

5. $3124.50
   2378.49
   531.44
   + 246.57

Set 12 For use after page 91.

First estimate the product. Then find the exact product.

1. 49
   × 4

2. 84
   × 6

3. 87
   × 8

4. 21
   × 7

5. 39
   × 9

6. 62
   × 5

7. 26
   × 5

8. 92
   × 7

9. 67
   × 3

10. 56
    × 2

11. 71
    × 8

12. 13
    × 6

Set 13 For use after page 97.

1. Barbara earns $3.50 an hour. She works for 6 hours. She spends $2.85 for lunch. How much does she have left?

2. Juan has $10.00. He buys 4 pairs of socks for $1.29 each. How much does he have left?

Set 14   For use after page 101.

The □ in each problem stands for the same digit.
Find the digit.

1.	4□9	2.	5□1	3.	2□2□	4.	□63	5.	10□□
	× 6		× □		× 7		× 2		× □
	28□4		159□		14,14□		5□6		□27□

6.	3□□□	7.	□561	8.	81□	9.	□□□	10.	4□□
	× 3		× □		× 3		× □		× □
	9□□□		39,3□□		2□□2		8□□1		279□

Set 15   For use after page 109.

1. Study these multiplication facts. Make a rule for multiplying by 10.

$10 \times 4 = 40$
$10 \times 15 = 150$
$10 \times 24 = 240$

2. Make rules for multiplying by 20, 30, or 40.

3. Make a rule for multiplying by 100.

Set 16   For use after page 123.

The □ in each problem stands for the same digit.
Find the digit.

	6r5		□r2		□r2		□r□		8r2
1.	□)4□	2.	7)5□	3.	4)2□	4.	9)□0	5.	□)3□

	7r2		4r2		□r2		5r4		□r4
6.	□)5□	7.	□)2□	8.	3)1□	9.	□)4□	10.	□)6□

Set 17   For use after page 126.

1. Maria and Carl have 85 grapes. They share them equally. How many grapes does each one get? How many are left over?

2. Alice, Bill, and Kim pick 47 plums. They share them equally. How many plums does each one get? How many are left over?

3. John has 57 pencils. He shares them equally with four friends. How many pencils does each one get? How many are left over?

4. Jane has 62 flowers. She divides them equally among 5 vases. How many flowers are in each vase? How many are left over?

Set 18 For use after page 132.

For each problem, answer these questions:
How many digits are in the quotient?
Where will you write the first digit of the quotient?
Then solve the problem.

1. $7\overline{)574}$ 2. $6\overline{)275}$ 3. $7\overline{)876}$ 4. $8\overline{)265}$ 5. $7\overline{)534}$

Set 19 For use after page 139.

1. Mark has $7.25. Juan has $10.95. They share their money equally. How much does each one get?

2. Four girls share the costs of a trip. They pay $24.20 for bus tickets and $16.60 for food. How much does each girl pay?

Set 20 For use after page 145.

Divide. Use short division.

1. $69,643 \div 3$ 2. $98,745 \div 5$ 3. $12,648 \div 4$ 4. $59,703 \div 7$

5. $47,921 \div 6$ 6. $52,477 \div 3$ 7. $79,422 \div 2$ 8. $23,079 \div 8$

Set 21 For use after page 154.

Write a word problem for each number problem.

1. $96 \div 4 = 24 2. $23 \times 5 = 115$ 3. $496 + 531 = 1027$ 4. $64 - $13 = 51

Set 22 For use after page 160.

1. Suzy has $10.00. She spends $9.12 for two records. She shares her change equally with her brother. How much money does she have left?

2. Josie works after school 5 days. She earns $8.50 a day. She then buys 4 books for $6.95 each. How much money does she have left?

3. Tom works after school 3 days. He earns $3.30 on Monday, $2.80 on Tuesday, and $3.50 on Friday. He puts $5.50 in the bank and spends $2.20 at the movies. How much money does he have left?

4. Bill collects 250 kilograms of newspapers. He sells them for $0.10 a kilogram. Then he buys 3 baseballs for $3.98 each. How much money does he have left?

Set 23 For use after page 165.

Remember, to find the area of a rectangle, multiply its length by its width. Area is measured in square units.

Make a diagram to help solve each problem.

1. Tina wants to wallpaper a wall of her room that has one window. The wall is 4 meters long and 3 meters high. The window is 2 meters long and 1 meter high. How many square meters of wallpaper does Tina need to cover the wall?

2. Miguel has a rug in his room. The floor is 5 meters long and 4 meters wide. 6 square meters of the floor are not covered by the rug. How many square meters in the rug?

Set 24 For use after page 173.

1. Draw two angles that have the same vertex but no common sides. Label the angles. Name each angle.

2. Draw two angles that have the same vertex and one common side. Label the angles. Name each angle.

Set 25 For use after page 183.

1. Why is a rectangle also a quadrilateral and a parallelogram?

2. Why is a square also a rectangle and a rhombus?

3. Is a square also a quadrilateral and a parallelogram? Why or why not?

4. Is a trapezoid also a quadrilateral and a parallelogram? Why or why not?

5. Are all squares similar? Why or why not?

6. Are all squares congruent? Why or why not?

Set 26 For use after page 186.

1. Find the surface area of a cube that measures 4 centimeters on each edge.

2. A rectangular prism is 9 meters long, 3 meters wide, and 2 meters high. What is its surface area?

3. A rectangular prism is 14 meters long, 12 meters wide, and 3 meters high. What is its surface area?

4. Find the surface area of a cube that measures 9 centimeters on each edge.

Set 27 For use after page 199.

Find equal fractions.

1. $\frac{1}{5} = \frac{?}{15} = \frac{?}{20} = \frac{?}{30}$

2. $\frac{1}{4} = \frac{?}{12} = \frac{?}{16} = \frac{?}{20}$

3. $\frac{1}{2} = \frac{?}{8} = \frac{?}{16} = \frac{?}{32}$

4. $\frac{1}{3} = \frac{?}{12} = \frac{?}{15} = \frac{?}{21}$

5. $\frac{1}{8} = \frac{?}{16} = \frac{?}{24} = \frac{?}{64}$

6. $\frac{1}{7} = \frac{?}{14} = \frac{?}{42} = \frac{?}{63}$

Set 28 For use after page 204.

1. Tom and Jane each buy the same size bottle of milk. Jane drinks $\frac{2}{3}$ of her bottle. Tom drinks $\frac{3}{4}$ of his. Who has more milk left?

2. Marie and Hector plant tomatoes in equal rows. Marie plants $\frac{5}{8}$ of a row. Hector plants $\frac{3}{4}$ of a row. Who plants more?

Set 29 For use after page 209.

1. Mark needs 3 kilograms of dried apricots. How many $\frac{1}{2}$-kilogram bags should he buy?

2. Carla needs $4\frac{2}{5}$ kilograms of nails. How many $\frac{1}{5}$-kilogram bags should she buy?

Set 30 For use after page 216.

1. What part of a dollar is $0.36? Write the name for 0.36.

2. Do 0.30 and 0.3 name the same number? Explain.

Set 31 For use after page 233.

Copy and complete.

1. $1\text{ m} - 13\text{ cm} = \square\text{ cm}$

2. $1\text{ km} + 69\text{ m} = \square\text{ m}$

3. $78\text{ cm} + 4\text{ m} = \square\text{ cm}$

4. $60\text{ cm} \times 2 = \square\text{ m} + \square\text{ cm}$

5. $1\text{ km} - 30\text{ m} = \square\text{ m}$

6. $14\text{ mm} \times 4 = \square\text{ cm} + \square\text{ mm}$

Set 32 For use after page 238.

1. A rectangle has a perimeter of 36 centimeters. One side is 4 centimeters long. What is the area of the rectangle?

2. A square has a perimeter of 32 meters. What is the area of the square?

Set 33 For use after page 244.

1. A tub is 60 centimeters long, 35 centimeters wide, and 20 centimeters high. How many 2-liter buckets of water can it hold?

2. How many 5-liter containers of water can be filled from a tank 80 centimeters long, 80 centimeters wide, and 100 centimeters high?

Set 34 For use after page 250.

1. A bedroom floor is 15 feet long and 12 feet wide. How many square yards of carpet are needed to cover the floor?

2. A patio is 14 feet long and 10 feet wide. How many 8-inch square tiles are needed to cover the patio exactly?

3. A wall in a restaurant is 42 feet long and 12 feet high. How many square yards of wallpaper are needed to cover the wall?

4. A row in a garden is 6 yards long and 2 yards wide. How many tomato plants can be planted in the row if each plant needs 4 square feet?

Set 35 For use after page 268.

1. Phil has 364 books to pack. He packs 30 books in a box. How many boxes does he fill? How many books are left over?

2. There are 50 pennies in a penny roll from a bank. How many penny rolls can be made from 5328 pennies? How many pennies are left over?

Set 36 For use after page 274.

1. 33 students move 450 chairs to a gym. Each student moves the same number of chairs. How many chairs does each student move? How many students move an extra chair?

2. 12 children collect 135 seashells. They want to share them equally. How many shells does each child get? How many shells are left over?

Set 37 For use after page 281.

1. 8640 seats in a theater are divided into 12 sections. There are 30 rows in each section. How many seats are in each row?

2. Carol works after school 4 days each week for 3 weeks. She earns a total of $132. How much does she earn each day?

Set 38 For use after page 292.

1. Jane nails together 2 pieces of wood, each $\frac{3}{8}$ inch thick, to make a block. How thick is the block?

2. Ted buys a piece of ribbon $2\frac{1}{4}$ yards long. He cuts off $\frac{3}{4}$ yard. How much does he have left?

Set 39 For use after page 296.
Copy and complete these magic squares.

1.

2	$5\frac{1}{2}$	
$6\frac{1}{2}$	4	
	$2\frac{1}{2}$	

2.

$\frac{3}{8}$	$2\frac{5}{8}$	
	$1\frac{5}{8}$	
		$2\frac{7}{8}$

3.

$1\frac{1}{4}$	$4\frac{3}{4}$	$3\frac{3}{4}$
		$\frac{3}{4}$

Set 40 For use after page 303.
Add or subtract. Write each answer in simplest form.

1. $\frac{7}{8}$ $-\frac{3}{8}$

2. $\frac{2}{3}$ $+\frac{1}{6}$

3. $\frac{1}{4}$ $+\frac{3}{8}$

4. $\frac{7}{10}$ $-\frac{1}{2}$

5. $\frac{1}{8}$ $+\frac{4}{8}$

6. $\frac{3}{5}$ $+\frac{2}{10}$

Set 41 For use after page 311.
Add or subtract.

1. $3.21 + 4.802$

2. $9.61 - 0.389$

3. $57.6 + 9.867 + 0.28$

4. $301.698 - 4.2$

5. $14.37 + 3.975$

6. $0.201 + 65.3 + 79.001$

7. $0.1002 - 0.013$

8. $8.74 - 1.689$

9. $30.798 + 2.76 + 102.9892$

10. $17.309 - 14.016$

11. $4.2 - 2.44$

12. $6.01 + 0.522 + 30.6201$

Set 42 For use after page 317.

1. Manuel lives 18 kilometers from Oak Grove. Jan lives 1.25 times that far from Oak Grove. How far from Oak Grove does Jan live?

2. Cindy buys 14 notebooks for $1.89 each. Tom buys 12 boxes of pencils for $2.21 each. Who spends more money?

Set 43   For use after page 325.

1. Find out from your teacher how many students there are in four different classrooms. Make a horizontal bar graph to show the number of students in each room.

2. Use a newspaper weather report. Record the highest temperature in your area each day for four days. Make a horizontal bar graph to show the temperatures.

Set 44   For use after page 328.

1. Make a circle graph to show how Mark spends $1.00: $0.25 for bus fare, $0.50 for two apples, $0.10 for a pencil, and $0.15 for a newspaper.

2. Keep a record of how you spend your time in class one day. Make a circle graph to show how much time you spend on each subject.

Set 45   For use after page 329.

Use graph paper. Make a graph like the one on page 329. Mark the ordered pairs. Connect the points in order. What do you find?

1. (5, 2), (7, 1), (15, 1), (13, 3), (12, 3), (10, 7), (12, 7),

   (14, 9), (9, 9), (9, 10), (11, 10), (13, 12), (11, 14), (9, 14),

   (7, 20), (7, 15), (3, 19), (7, 13), (7, 2), (6, 3), (5, 2)

Set 46   For use after page 331.

There are 16 marbles in a jar. 8 are red, 4 are blue, 2 are green, and 2 are yellow.

$\frac{8}{16}$, or $\frac{1}{2}$, of the marbles are red. If you make 30 draws, you can expect about $\frac{1}{2}$ of 30 draws to be red marbles. $\frac{1}{2}$ of 30 = $\frac{1}{2} \times 30$, or 15. About 15 out of 30 draws will be red.

1. About how many draws would you expect to be blue marbles if you made 20 draws?

2. About how many draws would you expect to be yellow marbles if you made 24 draws?

3. About how many draws would you expect to be yellow or green marbles if you made 8 draws?

4. About how many draws would you expect to be red or blue marbles if you made 20 draws?

Measurement Tables

Metric System

Length
10 millimeters (mm) = 1 centimeter (cm)
10 centimeters = 1 decimeter (dm)
$\left.\begin{array}{l} \text{1000 millimeters} \\ \text{100 centimeters} \\ \text{10 decimeters} \end{array}\right\}$ = 1 meter (m)
1000 meters = 1 kilometer (km)

Area
100 square millimeters (mm^2) =
  1 square centimeter (cm^2)
10,000 square centimeters = 1 square meter (m^2)

Volume
1000 cubic millimeters (mm^3) =
  1 cubic centimeter (cm^3)
1,000,000 cubic centimeters = 1 cubic meter (m^3)

Capacity
1000 milliliters (ml) = 1 liter (ℓ)
1000 liters = 1 kiloliter (kl)

Mass
1000 milligrams (mg) = 1 gram (g)
1000 grams = 1 kilogram (kg)
1000 kilograms = 1 metric ton (t)

Customary System

Length
12 inches (in.) = 1 foot (ft)
3 feet = 1 yard (yd)
1760 yards = 1 mile (mi)

Area
144 square inches (in.^{2}) = 1 square foot
9 square feet = 1 square yard (yd^2)

Volume
1728 cubic inches (in.^{3}) = 1 cubic foot (ft^3)
27 cubic feet = 1 cubic yard (yd^3)

Capacity
2 cups = 1 pint (pt)
2 pints = 1 quart (qt)
4 quarts = 1 gallon (gal)

Weight
16 ounces (oz) = 1 pound (lb)
2000 pounds = 1 ton (T)

Time
60 seconds (s) = 1 minute (min)
60 minutes = 1 hour (h)
24 hours = 1 day (d)
7 days = 1 week (wk)
28 to 31 days = 1 month (mo)
12 months = 1 year (yr)

	minus
	times
$or \div$	divided by
$\frac{3}{4}$	three-fourths (fraction) *or* three divided by four (division) *or* three to four (ratio)
$=$	equals *or* is equal to
$\neq$	is not equal to
$>$	is greater than
$<$	is less than
( )	do the operation inside parentheses first
. . .	pattern continues without end
8 r2	eight remainder two
20.7	twenty and seven-tenths (decimal point)
20%	twenty percent
3:5	three to five (ratio)
$^{+}2$	positive two
$^{-}2$	negative two
(2,3)	ordered pair
$\llcorner$	right angle
$\angle ABC$	angle ABC with vertex B
$\overline{AB}$	line segment AB with endpoints A and B
$\overrightarrow{AB}$	ray AB with endpoint A
$\overleftrightarrow{AB}$	line through points A and B
$\triangle ABC$	triangle ABC
$°C$	degree Celsius
$°F$	degree Fahrenheit

Glossary

acute angle   An angle that measures less than a right angle.

addend   A number that is added.
   Example $5+8=13$ The addends are 5 and 8.

addition (+)   An operation on two numbers to find how many in all or how much in all.
   Example $7+9=16$ 7 and 9 are **addends**. 16 is the **sum**.

angle   Two rays that start at the same point. The point where the two rays meet is the **vertex** of the angle.
   Example   Point B is the vertex of $\angle ABC$ or $\angle CBA$.

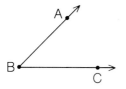

area   The number of units, usually square, needed to cover a surface.
   Example   The area of this rectangle is 6 square units.

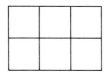

associative property of addition   The way in which addends are grouped does not change the sum.
   Example $(3+2)+4=3+(2+4)$

associative property of multiplication   The way in which factors are grouped does not change the product.
   Example $(5\times3)\times2=5\times(3\times2)$

average (mean)   The quotient found by dividing a sum by the number of addends.
   Example   5 is the average of 7, 6, and 2 because $7+6+2=15$ and $15\div3=5$.

bar graph   A graph with bars of different lengths to show and compare information. A bar graph can be vertical or horizontal.

capacity   The amount a container will hold when filled.

chord   A chord connects two points on a circle.

circle   A closed curve with all points an equal distance from a center point.
   Example   Point D is the center of circle D.

circle graph   A graph that can be used to show parts of a whole.

common denominator   A common multiple of the denominators of two or more fractions.
   Example   12 is a common denominator for $\frac{2}{3}$ and $\frac{1}{4}$ because $\frac{2}{3}$ equals $\frac{8}{12}$ and $\frac{1}{4}$ equals $\frac{3}{12}$.

common multiple   A multiple of two or more numbers.
   Example   15 is a common multiple of 3 and 5.

commutative property of addition   The order in which addends are added does not change the sum.
   Example $7+5=5+7$

commutative property of multiplication   The order in which factors are multiplied does not change the product.
   Example $3\times7=7\times3$

cone   A solid with one circular face and one vertex.

congruent   Having the same size and shape.

coordinate graph   A drawing of numbered lines that cross at right angles and are used to name the positions of points. The names of the positions are written as **ordered pairs**.

cube   A solid with six congruent square faces.

customary measurement system   A measurement system that uses inches, feet, yards, and miles as units of length; cups, pints, quarts, and gallons as units of capacity; ounces, pounds, and tons as units of weight; and degrees Fahrenheit as units of temperature.

cylinder   A solid with two congruent circular faces.

decagon   A polygon with ten sides.

decimal   A number that uses place value and a decimal point to show tenths, hundredths, thousandths, and so on.
   Example   5.75   Read *five and seventy-five hundredths*.

degree Celsius (°C)   A standard unit for measuring temperature in the metric system.
   Example   Water freezes at 0°C and boils at 100°C.

degree Fahrenheit (°F)   A standard unit for measuring temperature in the customary measurement system.
   Example   Water freezes at 32°F and boils at 212°F.

denominator   The numeral below the bar in a fraction.
   Example $\frac{2}{5}$ The denominator is 5.

diagonal   A line segment that joins two vertices of a polygon that are not next to each other.

diameter   A line segment through the center of a circle with endpoints on the circle. Also, the distance across a circle through the center.

difference   The answer to a subtraction problem.
   Example $8-3=5$ The difference is 5.

digit   Any one of the ten symbols 0, 1, 2, 3, 4, 5, 6, 7, 8, or 9.

distributive property of multiplication over addition   The product of a number and the sum of two numbers equals the sum of two products.
   Example $3\times(4+6)=(3\times4)+(3\times6)$

dividend   The number that is divided in a division problem.
   Example $3\overline{)18}$ *or* $18\div3$ The dividend is 18.

division ($\overline{)}$ *or* $\div$**)**   An operation on two numbers that tells the number of equal groups and the number left over, or the number in each group and the number left over.
   Example $5\overline{)37}^{\ 7\,r2}$ 5 is the **divisor**, 37 is the **dividend**, 7 is the **quotient**, and 2 is the **remainder**.

divisor   The number by which the dividend is divided.
   Example $4\overline{)36}$ *or* $36\div4$ The divisor is 4.

edge   The line segment where two faces of a solid meet.

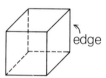

endpoint   A point at the end of a line segment or ray.

equal fractions (equivalent fractions)   Fractions that name the same number.
   Example $\frac{1}{2}$ and $\frac{2}{4}$ are equal fractions.

equation   A number sentence with an equals sign ($=$).
   Examples $6+4=10$
              $8-7=1$

estimate   To guess a likely answer. One way to estimate an answer is to round the numbers before doing the problem.

even number   A whole number that is a multiple of 2. An even number has 0, 2, 4, 6, or 8 in the ones place.
   Examples   6, 78, 112

face A flat surface of a solid.

factor A number that is multiplied.
Example $6 \times 7 = 42$ The factors are 6 and 7.

fraction A number that names part of a whole or group.
Examples $\frac{1}{3}, \frac{3}{4}$

graph A drawing used to show and compare information. Some types of graphs are bar graphs, circle graphs, line graphs, and picture graphs.

heptagon A polygon with seven sides.

hexagon A polygon with six sides.

identity property for addition If one of two addends is 0, the sum is the same as the other addend.
Example $57 + 0 = 57$

identity property for multiplication If one of two factors is 1, the product is the same as the other factor.
Example $17 \times 1 = 17$

intersecting lines (line segments, rays) Lines that meet or cross.

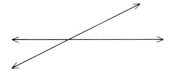

length The measurement of an object from end to end.

like fractions Fractions with the same denominator.
Example $\frac{1}{4}$ and $\frac{3}{4}$ are like fractions.

line graph A graph in which a line is used to show change.

line of symmetry If a shape can be folded along a line so that each half is the same size and shape, the fold line is a line of symmetry.

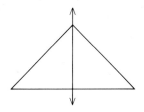

line segment Part of a line with two endpoints.

metric system A measurement system that uses centimeters, meters, and kilometers as units of length; milliliters and liters as units of capacity; grams and kilograms as units of mass; and degrees Celsius as units of temperature.

mixed number The sum of a whole number and a fraction.
Example $2\frac{1}{3} = 2 + \frac{1}{3}$

multiple A number that is the product of a given number and a whole number.
Example 0, 3, 6, 9, and so on are multiples of 3.

multiplication ($\times$) An operation on two numbers, called **factors**. If one factor is the number of groups, the other factor is the number in each group.
Example $7 \times 8 = 56$ 7 and 8 are factors. 56 is the **product**.

negative number A number less than zero. Zero is neither positive nor negative.
Examples $^-1, ^-18, ^-149$

nonagon A polygon with nine sides.

number line A line with equally spaced points named by numbers.

$$\overset{\longleftrightarrow}{\underset{^-4 \quad ^-3 \quad ^-2 \quad ^-1 \quad 0 \quad ^+1 \quad ^+2 \quad ^+3 \quad ^+4}{\bullet \quad \bullet \quad \bullet \quad \bullet \quad \bullet \quad \bullet \quad \bullet \quad \bullet \quad \bullet}}$$

number sequence A group of numbers given in a specific order. Such numbers are usually given according to some rule or pattern.
Example 20, 25, 30, 35, . . .

numeral A name or symbol for a number.
Examples $\frac{1}{3}, 2.3, 5, 15\frac{3}{4}$

numerator The numeral above the bar in a fraction.
Example $\frac{2}{5}$ The numerator is 2.

obtuse angle An angle that measures greater than a right angle.

octagon A polygon with eight sides.

odd number A whole number that is not a multiple of 2. An odd number has 1, 3, 5, 7, or 9 in the ones place.
Examples 9, 21, 243

outcome Each possible result in a probability experiment.

parallel lines (line segments, rays) Lines that do not intersect. Parallel lines are always the same distance apart.

parallelogram A quadrilateral with opposite sides parallel.

Examples Rectangles, rhombuses, and squares are parallelograms.

parentheses ( ) Symbols of grouping. Parentheses tell which part or parts of a problem to do first.

Example $(6-4)+1$ Do $(6-4)$ first.

pentagon A polygon with five sides.

percent (%) A ratio that compares a number to 100.

Example $\frac{4}{100}=4\%$

perimeter The distance around a figure. The perimeter of a polygon is the sum of the lengths of the sides.

period A group of three digits set off by a comma in a numeral.

Example 342,674,408 From right to left, the periods are the ones period, the thousands period, and the millions period.

perpendicular lines (line segments, rays) Lines that intersect at right angles.

place value The value given to the place in which a digit appears in a numeral.

Example 32 The place value of 3 is tens. The place value of 2 is ones.

point An exact location. A dot is often drawn to represent a point.

polygon A closed shape formed by three or more sides.

Examples Triangles, quadrilaterals, and pentagons are polygons.

positive number A number that is greater than zero. Zero is neither positive nor negative.

Examples +3, +64, +125

prism A solid with two parallel faces that are congruent polygons. The other faces are parallelograms.

probability The chance of an event occurring, written as a fraction between 0 (the event cannot occur) and 1 (the event must occur).

Example You toss a coin. The probability of it landing heads up is 1 out of 2, or $\frac{1}{2}$.

product The answer to a multiplication problem.

Example $4\times12=48$ The product is 48.

proportion A statement that two ratios are equal.

Example $\frac{2}{3}=\frac{4}{6}$ Read *two is to three as four is to six*.

pyramid A solid with one face that is a polygon and three or more faces that are triangles with a common vertex.

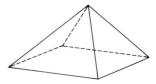

quadrilateral A polygon with four sides.

quotient The answer to a division problem.

Example $16\div8=2$ The quotient is 2.

radius (*pl.* radii) A radius connects the center of a circle with any point on the circle. Also, the distance from the center of a circle to the circle.

ratio A comparison of two numbers.

Example There are 3 squares and 5 triangles. The ratio of squares to triangles can be written as 3 to 5, or $\frac{3}{5}$.

ray Part of a line that has one endpoint and goes on and on in only one direction.

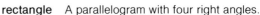

rectangle A parallelogram with four right angles.

rectangular prism   A prism with six faces that are rectangles.

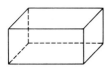

remainder   The number left over in a division problem. The remainder must be less than the divisor.

Example $5\overline{)17}$ The remainder is 2.
(with 3 r2 above)

rhombus   A parallelogram with four equal sides.

right angle   An angle with the same shape as the corner of a square.

Roman numerals   Symbols used by the Romans to name numbers.

Examples
I	V	X	L	C	D
1	5	10	50	100	500

rounding   Expressing a number to the nearest thousandth, hundredth, tenth, one, ten, hundred, thousand.

Example   4825.5 rounded to the nearest hundred is 4800.

scale   One of the number lines used to record the information on a graph. Also, the ratio of the size of a scale drawing to the size of the actual object.

scale drawing   A drawing that shows the correct shape of an object but not its actual size.

side   One of the line segments that forms a polygon or one of the rays that forms an angle.

similar   Having the same shape.

simplest form of a fraction   A fraction or mixed number in which the numerator and denominator cannot be divided exactly by the same number greater than 1.

Examples $\frac{1}{2}$ is the simplest form of $\frac{4}{8}$. $4\frac{1}{2}$ is the simplest form of $\frac{18}{4}$.

sphere   A solid with all points the same distance from a center point.

square   A rectangle with four equal sides.

square number   The product of a number and itself.
Example $4 \times 4 = 16$ The square of 4 is 16.

square root   When a number is written as the product of two equal factors, each factor is the square root.
Example $4 \times 4 = 16$
$\sqrt{16} = 4$ 4 is the square root of 16.

subtraction ($-$)   An operation on two numbers to find how many are left or how much greater one number is than the other.
Example $12 - 7 = 5$ 5 is the **difference**.

sum   The answer to an addition problem.
Example $11 + 7 = 18$ The sum is 18.

trade   In addition, subtraction, and multiplication, to make one group of ten out of ten ones or ten ones out of one group of ten.
Example $14 = 1 \text{ ten} + 4 \text{ ones}$

$$\begin{array}{c} \overset{1}{28} \\ +36 \\ \hline 64 \end{array} \qquad \begin{array}{c} \overset{4\,14}{\cancel{54}} \\ -27 \\ \hline 27 \end{array} \qquad \begin{array}{c} \overset{1}{37} \\ \times\ 2 \\ \hline 74 \end{array}$$

Also, to make one hundred from ten tens, one thousand from ten hundreds, and so on.

trapezoid   A quadrilateral with one pair of parallel sides.

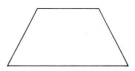

triangle   A polygon with three sides.

triangular prism A prism with two parallel faces that are congruent triangles. The other three faces are parallelograms.

unlike fractions Fractions with different denominators.

Example $\frac{1}{3}$ and $\frac{1}{4}$ are unlike fractions.

vertex (*pl.* vertices) The point at which two rays of an angle, two sides of a polygon, or three or more edges of a solid meet.

volume The number of cubic units needed to fill a solid.

Example The volume of this cube is 8 units.

whole number Any one of the numbers 0, 1, 2, 3, 4, 5, and so on.

zero property for multiplication If 0 is a factor, the product is 0.

Example $17 \times 0 = 0$

Index

2
3
D 4
E 5
F 6
G 7
H 8
I 9
J